HAUNTED OHIO V:

200 Years of Ghosts

CHRIS WOODYARD

Kestrel
Publications

1811 Stonewood Drive
Dayton, OH 45432

ALSO BY CHRIS WOODYARD

Haunted Ohio: Ghostly Tales from the Buckeye State
Haunted Ohio II: More Ghostly Tales from the Buckeye State
Haunted Ohio III: Still More Ghostly Tales from the Buckeye State
Haunted Ohio IV: Restless Spirits
Haunted Ohio V: 200 Years of Ghosts
Spooky Ohio: 13 Traditional Tales
The Wright Stuff: A Guide to Life in the Dayton Area
Ghost Hunters' Guide to Haunted Ohio

First Edition 2003
Printed in the United States of America by C.J. Krehbiel, Cincinnati, OH
Typesetting by Copy Plus, Dayton, OH
Cover Art by Larry Hensel, Hensel Graphics, Xenia, OH
Library of Congress Catalog Card Number: 91-75343

Woodyard, Chris
Haunted Ohio V: 200 Years of Ghosts / Chris Woodyard
SUMMARY: Tales of ghosts and haunted houses from around Ohio
with an emphasis on historic Ohio sites.

ISBN: 0-9628472-8-3
0-9628472-7-5 – Library Binding
1. Ghosts
2. Ghost Stories
3. Ghosts—United States—Ohio
4. Ghosts—Ohio
5. Haunted Houses—United States—Ohio
6. Haunted Houses—Ohio
7. Ohio—History
398.25 W912H
070.593 Wo
Z1033.L73

For Anne, Marsha, Sarah & John

You know who you are....

And you know what you did....

ACKNOWLEDGMENTS

George Adams, Jean Adkins, Massillon PL, Dusty Alvis, Becky Anderson, Staff, Arcanum PL, Dave Avalos, The Chokolate Morel, Jeff B. Barklage, Bill Barlow, Rick Barnes, Mike Barnett, Renaissance Theater, Jacki Barnett, Renaissance Theater, Debbie Benz, Glenna Berres, Barbara Berry, Fulton Co. Historical Museum, Carol Bertone, Fairport Marine Museum & Lighthouse, Randy Braden, Pat Bratton, Chip Brookins, Margaret Brookins, John Carpenter, The Warehouse Restaurant, Joseph A. Citro, Julie A. Clark, Janet Coffman, Angie Copas, Karen Craigo, Richard Crawford, Clermont Co. Historical Society, Curt Dalton, Robert Davis, Town Hall Theater, Sandy Day, Jefferson Co. Library, Charlotte Dennett, John Destatte, Ft. Meigs, Tom Dilley, Jason Dye, Marlene Errett, Gene Evans, Indian Creek Local, Lawrence Everett, Michele Fabbro, Indian Creek Local, Carl Feathers, Sue Fisher, Jefferson County Library, Martha Fort, Renaissance Theater, Eddie Fox, Marjie Gilliam, Melinda Gilpin, The Harding Home, Mary Ellen Given, Roscoe Village Foundation, Ryan Gladwell, Scott Gross, Renaissance Theater, Martha Hardcastle-Guthrie, Barbara Hamilton, Marsha Hamilton, Amanda Harbaugh, The Chokolate Morel, Mike Harden, Carol Higgins, Wallace Higgins, James and Patricia Irvin, The Colonel Taylor Inn, Chuck Jacobs, Wolcott House, Pam Jones, Raymond-Newton Historical Society, Pam Justice, Emmitt House, Angie Justice-Copas, Bianca E.V. Kelley, Logan County District Library Bob Kelley, Pam Kennedy, The Chokolate Morel, Jodi Kerekes, Club Bijou, Todd Kramer, Renaissance Theater, Mary Lou Lardi, Barbara S. Lehmann, Frank-o Levin, Pat Lillie, Shari Lorbach, Humanities, OSU, Mark Lozer, Fulton Co. Historical Museum, Kathleen Madison, Linda Marcas, Irene Martin, Toledo Public Library, Todd McCormick, Logan Co. Hist. Soc., Randalph Meade, Mark Metzger, Town Hall Theatre, Jeff Morehead, Shannon Morris, The Harding Home, Jill Muncie, Logan County District Library, Amy Murray, Media Relations, OSU, Dr. Larry Nelson, Ft. Meigs, Pat Olvey, Joye Opt, Douglas Osborne, Tonee Osborne, Anne Oscard, Dana "Bud" Painter, Julie Perdue, Marysville Public Library, Wayne Pfaff, Portsmouth Public Library, Raymond Branch, Marysville Public Library, Putnam County Library, Kim Ream, Nick Reiter, Mark Rogers, 20th Century Productions Inc. and Habits Café, Helen Ryan, Susan Ryan, Randy Sarvis, Wilmington College, Craig Schermer, Lori Schillig, Melanie Seaman, Juanita Seery, Keisha Skaggs, Emmitt House, Suzanne A. Smailes, Wittenberg University, Tracy Thomas Smith, David Stanton, Snow Hill CC, Shelly Suittor, David Tobias, Richard Wallace, Sandy Wardlaw, Arcanum PL, Beverly Willis, Rootstown High School, Danny Woodley, Helen Woods, The Warehouse Restaurant

I apologize if I have inadvertently left anyone out.

TABLE OF CONTENTS

Introduction

Prelude: The Skull Beneath the Skin

INTRODUCTION

*That's not because there are more ghosts here than in
other places, mind you. It's just that people who live
hereabouts are strangely aware of them.*
-The Uninvited, 1932-

I swore I would not write another *Haunted Ohio* book. So
why am I writing another *Haunted Ohio* book? There are
several reasons. In 2003, we celebrate Ohio's Bicentennial as a
state. I wanted to contribute something in honor of the
occasion. After all, Bicentennials don't come along every day.
Also, I knew I had to find stories from Shelby, Union, and Van
Wert Counties, my previous "dead zones," or die trying....

Perhaps the most overpowering reason is that I have
always been fascinated by history. I am not an historian. Ask
anyone who knows me and they will tell you that I am hopeless
with dates. But I remember the personalities, the stories, the
little details of life — and death — that make up the fabric of
the past.

Just as death is the Great Leveler, so are ghost stories a
common denominator. In these pages you will read ghost
stories nearly 200 years old and yet, in their essentials, they
could have happened yesterday. While every effort has been
made to verify historical facts, there will always be differences
in matters of interpretation. When ghosts are involved, facts
are elusive and interpretation hotly argued. If something is
legend, I've tried to make it clear in my story that this is so.

In the last few years, ghost hunting has blossomed.
Reading the literature and searching websites, it sounds as if

everything is possible, even probable. We are on the edge of a breakthrough! cry the believers. We have proof positive! We are in possession of the One True Protocol!

This optimism reminds me of the Spiritualist researchers like Sir Arthur Conan Doyle, absolutely confident that they were on the right path and would shortly provide to a longing world the irrefutable proof of survival after death.

Yet after having lived with ghosts all my life and having researched them for the past 15 years, I am as ambivalent as ever. I still cannot answer the question, What are ghosts?

Perhaps spirits are our own psyches, thoughts, and emotions, projected externally. Maybe they are archetypes: the lost child, the hanged man of the Tarot deck, the weeping woman, the soul in torment, the stuff of folklore. Perhaps they are what we fear to believe—the spirits of departed souls, battering against the window that separates them from the living pleading, "Remember me. Remember me…"

I have met the wandering, lonely ghost, lost and caught in some private Limbo. I've seen the suicide, horrified by his own actions, afraid to stay and afraid to go. I have encountered the "memory ghost," nothing more than a shadow of a life. But I can prove nothing.

Many people claim to have the answers. I continue to have questions.

When I heard that the state had decided to adopt a new tourism motto, I was devastated. "Ohio the Heart of It All" moved so easily into "Ohio the Haunt of it All." The new motto is the bland "Ohio, So Much to Discover." But times change and so must we all. For the new motto of the state of Haunted Ohio, I propose: "Ohio, So Much to Disinter…."

Bring your shovel along on this unique Bicentennial tour. Let's see what grave dirt we can dig up on Ohio's historical people, places, and ghosts.

NOTE: Names with an * beside them have been changed to protect privacy.

The Skull Beneath The Skin

And I am filled with a pity of beholding skulls.
-Allen Tate-

Most mornings I work out at a local gym. I've gotten to
know most of the regulars by sight: the stumpy, turnip-shaped
guy I privately dubbed "Dilbert;" the distinguished-looking
man with silver hair who blew his nose on his shirt and spit on
the track; the rail-thin woman who relentlessly pounded the
cross-trainer machine while leafing through pictures of food in
women's magazines. But I didn't recognize the man who stood
there one morning staring at trainer Marjie Gilliam, who writes
a popular fitness column, "Road to Fitness," for *The Dayton
Daily News.*

Lots of men stare at Marjie—with good reason: she's
lovely and incredibly fit. But this was different. The man with
the pale skin and dark-rimmed hipster glasses stood there
staring openly at her with a terrible hunger in his eyes. It was a
longing in which there was no desire, except for life.

I studied him, anxiously. And suddenly I realized that I
wasn't seeing his face anymore. I was seeing a death's head
where his face should be. The effect was like segments I had
seen on forensic TV shows where the image of a face is
projected or superimposed over a skull to establish the identity
of the dead.

"Is he a serial killer?" I thought wildly. "Is he stalking her?
What is this—a death aura?"

And he, noticing that I was staring, flushed and walked
away.

Marjie finished her set and I rushed up to her.

"Marjie!" I hissed, jerking my head towards him. "Do you know that guy?" I was still thinking he might be a stalker or something worse.

She followed my glance and nodded sympathetically.

"Oh, he's a really sad case," Marjie sighed. "He's got skin cancer. It's spread all through his body. He's only got a short time to live. Why?"

In an undertone, I told her what I had seen. She was horrified but she believed me.

I watched him furtively until he headed for the locker room. The skull did not reappear. Life went on at the gym.

I never saw the man in the dark-rimmed glasses again. Marjie told me that he died two months later.

DISEASE AND DISASTER:
The ghosts of tragedies past

I can only see death and more death, till
we are black and swollen with death.
-D.H. Lawrence-

FIRE AND ICE
The Ashtabula Bridge Disaster

On the night of December 29th, 1876, in a blinding
snowstorm, the No. 5 Pacific Express plunged into the
Ashtabula River gorge when the railroad bridge collapsed. The
bridge broke in the center, just as the first engine, "Socrates"
reached the western side. The second engine, the "Columbia"
hung in air for a moment as the rest of the train's cars plum-
meted to the bottom of the chasm. Then the engine was pulled
down after them, killing any survivors in the cars on top. Of
those who struggled out of the debris, some fell into the icy
river and drowned. They were the lucky ones.

The varnished wooden passenger cars were heated by coal-
fired stoves and lit by oil lamps. Rescue workers stood by
helplessly as the flames, fanned by the gale-force winds, raced
through the smashed cars. Although firemen reached the scene
with a steamer and hoses, no one gave the order to put out the
fire. Railroad policy was to let any train fire burn, a policy
which assumed that no passengers would be involved. The fire
chief, an alcoholic, seemed in a stupor and was heard to mutter
that there was no use throwing water on the flames. This
inaction led to later rumors that the railroad company had given

orders to let the wreck burn to destroy any evidence of their wrong-doing.

Witnesses never forgot the screams of agony as people trapped inside the wreckage burned to death. Afterwards, bushels of shoes were recovered from the wreck, some with feet still inside, since feet do not contain enough fat to readily burn.

Survivors told of being robbed by the human vultures that descended into the snowy gulf to strip money and jewelry from the living and the dead. Even the trunks from the baggage car were hauled away. Some bodies, charred beyond recognition, could have been identified by their clothes or jewelry. Yet they were denied their rightful identities by the thieves.

The chief engineer of the Lake Shore & Michigan South-ern Railway was Charles Collins. He had refused to approve the fatal Ashtabula Bridge design, as did engineer Joseph Tomlinson, who resigned over the matter. But the president of the railroad, Amasa Stone, ordered it built. Charles Collins was a local man who had worked for the railroad over 30 years. Only days after the tragedy, he was found dead in bed at his Cleveland home, an apparent suicide. He was buried in a gothic crypt, not far from where the monument to the "unrecognized dead" was later to be raised. Three weeks later, some thirty-two bodies and fragments were buried in nineteen coffins.

The "unrecognized dead" covered the famous and the unknown. The most famous was undoubtedly the popular hymn composer P.P. Bliss, who was traveling with his beloved wife Lucy and who, it was said, went back into the inferno to rescue her. No trace of either of them was ever found. It was never established how many people were killed or even how many were on the train. Estimates range from 92 to over 100. It was the worst railroad accident in United States history.

The new book, *Bliss & Tragedy, The Ashtabula Railway-Bridge Accident of 1876 and the Loss of P.P. Bliss* edited by Thomas E. Corts, is a masterful re-assessment of the historical record surrounding the tragedy. Six authors discuss the disaster, the grim task of identifying the victims, the life of hymn-writer P.P. Bliss, Ashtabula's response to the disaster, the investigation into the railroad bridge's construction, recovering artifacts, and, most controversially, the original autopsy report of Charles Collins. This remarkable document concludes that his death was murder and not suicide, but it seems to have been suppressed at the time of Collins's death. Author and historian Barbara Hamilton, who wrote movingly about the identification of the victims, said that members of the Collins family have thanked the authors of *Bliss & Tragedy* for proving what they had already known. After her husband's death, Mrs. Collins was shunned, lost her house, and died penniless in a relative's home. The revelation of the truth came too late for her, but brought some comfort to surviving relations. Amasa Stone, the man who had designed the bridge and pushed for its construction, was unrepentant to the last. Blamed by the coroner for the disaster, he shot himself six years later.[1]

Barbara Hamilton writes about the heartbreaking letters written in desperation by families in distant cities, describing their loved ones and trying to find if they were among the victims. The dead were identified by means we are now familiar with from recent disasters like 9/11. One man was identified by a sock knitted by his mother and a single leg was sent home for burial. As with 9/11, families needed proof of death to collect insurance, but in some cases all traces of the body had vanished. In a few cases persons listed as dead were found alive. Fraudulent claims were made for nonexistent relatives traveling with lavish and equally nonexistent jewelry. The more things change....

It wasn't until 19 years after the event that a monument was raised over the graves of the unknown. It wasn't until a few years ago that any ghost stories began to emerge about the disaster. Perhaps that is because ghost hunting is a relatively modern hobby.

I spoke with David Tobias, who wrote about his excavations of the crash site and the gulf, as the steep-walled chasm where the Ashtabula River flows is called locally. He's collected thousands of artifacts from the crash: buttons, shoes, glassware, and pewter, many articles bubbled from the heat. As someone who has studied the crash and probably spent more time in the area than anyone in Ohio, he had this to say about Ashtabula Bridge Disaster ghost stories:

"I've never really heard any stories other than [Mary Lou's] (see below). I've heard other people say that they've heard people talking. I've heard kids swear that they've heard voices down there. But in the gulf noise carries. Someone can be talking a hundred yards around the bend. The sound will circle around and you don't know where it's coming from." There is a hospital on the bluff overlooking the crash site. Even voices in the parking lot float eerily down into the gulf.

David and I discussed how a disaster of this magnitude *should* have generated a huge number of folktales, ghost tales, and such like. The only thing it seems to have generated is the monumentally dreadful poem "The Ashtabula Bridge Disaster," by Julia A. Moore, "The Sweet Singer of Michigan," revered as America's greatest bad poet. Set to an offensively lilting waltz tune, it begins

> Have you heard of the dreadful fate
> > Of Mr. P. P. Bliss and wife?
> Of their death I will relate,
> > And also others lost their life;
> Ashtabula Bridge disaster,
> > Where so many people died
> Without a thought that destruction
> > Would plunge them 'neath the wheel of tide.[2]

"We did get the usual treasure story out of it," David commented. The tale runs that there were millions of dollars in gold on the train. Either it was stolen and the crash was staged to hide the robbery or the gold was stolen from the wreck. There never was any gold, but that's the kind of story that disasters create. David is as puzzled as I am that no ghost stories began to circulate either at the time or in the years after the crash. Barbara Hamilton agrees. As a native of the area, she says there were no traditions of ghost stories surrounding the crash. So it is only recently, on the Internet, that ghost stories have begun to emerge, each one more elaborate than the last.

David did tell me a strange tale about the dedication of the Monument in 1893. "There was a huge cloth draped over the monument. At the given time, someone was supposed to pull the string to unveil it. When they pulled the string it broke and the cloth just lay there. Then, out of nowhere, a big wind arose and blew the cloth off the Monument...."

It was also David who told me a story of a mysterious photo in a house connected with the disaster. Several phone calls and letters later, I was in touch with Mary Lou of Conneaut who e-mailed me the photo. Unfortunately it will not reproduce well enough to print in this book. The first download showed only fog, a bit of a ceiling lamp, and a corner of a rug. There were two small white wing-like objects in the middle of the photo. A second, sharper version, put under my magnifier made my blood run cold. The wing-like objects were the sleeves of a woman with high-piled hair, large hollow eye-sockets, and high cheekbones. It was startling and terrifying.

Mary Lou told me the story behind the photo. The family had experienced patches of "exhaust" or fog inside their house. Her daughter had seen what seemed to be a man standing by the kitchen sink and called her parents. As Mary Lou tells it,

"We hurried home to a dining room filled with 'fog.' My son was taking a photography class at the time, and I grabbed his camera, which was loaded with black and white film, to take a picture. It was really cold and really foggy (and we weren't in Ireland!). What is really strange is that when the photograph was developed by the high school, what appears in the photo is not what was in my lens. There appears to be a figure standing in front of the dining room chair, but it is not my dining room. We have an oriental rug under the table. The rug in the picture is not my rug. The dining room table is not the same table. The wallpaper and chair rail have also vanished. My brother-in-law, who is an engineer, said that I would have had to have been standing outside to get the chandelier, the fog, and the rug all in one frame.

"Our connection to the Ashtabula Train disaster is C. H. Simonds, the gentleman who lived in this house in the early 1900's and was married here. He was a deputy in the Probate office at Jefferson, the Ashtabula County seat, during the disaster. He was responsible for recording the dead. Most probably he was at the scene as well. His furniture store in Conneaut also sold funeral supplies.

"All I know is we hear doors shutting, as well as pounding and sawing. The lights come on occasionally. We set up a video camera for two hours one night. After four minutes, as soon as we all trooped out and got in the car, the camera moved in and out trying to focus on something in the dining room.

"We do not feel threatened. We have lived in the house for 26 years. What is ironic, though, is things didn't start to happen here until we took a ride through Chestnut Grove cemetery where the train disaster people are buried in a mass grave." Was the lady in the photo one of the unknown dead, trying to make her presence known? Or was she Mrs. Simonds, who died in the house?

I visited Chestnut Grove Cemetery on one of the loveliest summer's days you could picture. It was a beautiful place, very quiet and a bit lonely but a less eerie setting would be hard to imagine. I stood on the hilltop by the monument to the unrecognized dead. Sections of the obelisk are roughly carved in bands that look like they are charred.

The only anomaly was that I felt like I was being watched. There were no other cars, no other people. The feeling was uncanny and I kept spinning around, trying to figure out who it was. Out of the corner of my eye, I caught a glimpse of a man in dark clothes standing by a small stone crypt. Automatically I snapped a picture of the area and forgot about him.

When I got home, I downloaded all my photos, but didn't really go through them closely. Then I read something about Charles Collins being buried close to the Disaster monument in a gothic crypt and of his appearances at the site. I recognized the crypt as the one I had photographed. When I went back to my photos, there were the views of the monument, but not of the crypt. I don't expect to find any "extras" on my photos, but I also don't expect to find photos vanishing from the camera.

Modern tales are told about Charles Collins's spirit heard crying at the vault in the cemetery. Perhaps, now that Collins's name has been cleared of the taint of suicide, he can rest in peace. And what of the unidentified bodies that lie beneath the monument? Do they wander, crying out to be named and reunited at last with their loved ones? I do not know. I heard nothing except the distant whistle of a train.

AN X-RAY VISION
The Cleveland Clinic Fire

One of the most horrific tragedies in Cleveland's history was the Cleveland Clinic Fire. Wednesday, May 15, 1929 was an ordinary busy day at the famous medical Clinic. A steam leak had been reported above the room where old nitrocellulose x-ray films were stored. A workman ripped out the insulation, releasing a jet of steam, then returned to his workshop to turn off the line and wait for it to drain and cool. When he came back to the x-ray storage room, he found a cloud of yellowish smoke. He emptied a fire extinguisher at it, but was overcome by the fumes. As he crawled to safety, an explosion flung him into another room. A second explosion followed.

The fumes from the burning films quickly spread throughout the building through heating ducts. About 250 people were in the building at the time and when the firefighters arrived, the hospital was shrouded in a heavy yellowish-brown cloud. A few minutes later an explosion blew out part of the roof, releasing the gas. Rescuers were hampered by the heavy concentration of gases inside the building, but managed to extinguish the fires and help survivors down ladders. Nobody knew that they were dealing with an extremely deadly gas. They only knew that the brownish fumes caused lung and throat irritation, coughing, and difficulty breathing. Some victims who made their way outside without other injury, later died from inhaling the toxic fumes.

It was all a terrifying mystery until an investigation by the Chemical Warfare Service determined that burning or decomposing nitrocellulose films produced carbon monoxide, instantly fatal in high concentrations. More horribly, it produced nitrogen dioxide which became nitric acid on contact with moisture in the lungs, with corrosive, poison gas-like results. It has never been proven whether the leaking steam line caused the films to decompose or whether they were ignited by an open light bulb or by careless smoking. The Clinic disaster resulted in worldwide adoption of revised safety codes for storing films and led to the use of the more stable acetate safety film that was less likely to spontaneously combust or explode.[3]

The Cleveland Clinic was just blocks from Drury House, haunted by the Lady in Brown. (*Haunted Ohio II*, p. 144). Her appearance was benign—a lady in an old-fashioned brown skirt. The manifestations at the house were about what you'd expect from a mild-mannered ghost: sash windows opening and closing by themselves, creaks and groans, the general feeling of invisible people throughout the maze-like corridors of the old mansion.

The gothic structure was built in 1912 by Francis Drury, who made his fortune in cast-iron stoves. In 1972 the building was taken over by the Ohio Adult Parole Authority for use as a half-way house. In 2002, it was reported that an inmate convicted of arson was awakened by a strange woman's voice far away. Half-crooning, half-speaking, the voice would rise to a terrifying shriek like a steam whistle, then die away. He found himself sweating, but realized that it wasn't just from fear—the room was growing as hot as an oven. He could feel his hair crisping and the blood beginning to bubble in his brain.

Suddenly he found that the screaming woman was in the room with him. She had long dark hair and wore a white gown. Her skin was ash-pale. Her hands were outstretched, imploring. As he watched, a flame burst from around her feet and ate its way upwards, writhing around her like a fiery serpent. Then her skin began to bubble and darken. She burned away, dissolving like a piece of decomposing film, vanishing in a brilliant burst

of white fire. Once again the room grew cool. The scream
lingered inside his head.

The inmate interpreted this vision as a visit from the
Virgin Mary. He underwent a conversion experience and swore
off crime. He lived a changed life but he died never knowing
what he had really seen: the last, tortured moments of one of
the 123 victims of the Cleveland Clinic Fire, a lovely, ivory-
skinned woman with long dark hair. [4]

THE UNQUIET DEAD
Cholera

"Subdivision Built on Cemetery." When I first heard about
the ghosts of Massillon's Black Plague cemetery, it sounded
like a lurid tabloid headline or something out of the movie
Poltergeist—the coffined dead bobbing up in the swimming
pool—or the terrifying book, *The Black Hope Horror* in which
innocent householders move into homes built on a former
cemetery. Not all the bodies were moved and *the dead are not
happy about it….*

The Massillon hauntings are more subtle: a neighbor's
warning not to dig in the yard, another neighbor hitting a corner
of a coffin as he spaded a flowerbed, tombstones used for
foundations.

Cholera, also called the Black Plague, for the darkening of
victims' dehydrated skins, was one of the most dreaded
diseases of the frontier. Its agonies struck so suddenly that a
man could be in good health in the morning and be buried by
nightfall. Today we know that it is spread mainly through
contaminated water, but our ancestors knew only that drinking
cold water in the summer or eating unripe plums could kill.
Victims would be prostrated by chills, vomiting, and diarrhea,
and die of dehydration. I have seen post-mortem photos of the
cholera dead. Their faces are withered to skulls.

Massive cholera epidemics swept across Ohio in 1831,
1833, 1849, and 1852. Survivors were so terrified by its
virulence that contaminated houses and even towns were
sometimes burned to the ground. In the face of such fear, the

dead were hastily buried, flung into mass graves. There have always been rumors that some cholera victims were buried alive in the plague pits.

These are the stories of three families whose houses were built on the Black Plague pits and who live with the unquiet dead.

"Our house is built on the first cemetery in Massillon," Pat Bratton told me. "That might have something to do with our ghosts...."

Pat and her husband Charles moved into the house in 1961, but didn't really notice anything significant until 1967, when her daughter had come home from school one day for lunch. They were at the kitchen table when, "We both heard somebody chasing someone else upstairs!" Mother and daughter stared at each other as the heavy footsteps pounded upstairs, then stopped, and began again in the basement.

"We fell over each other to get out the door. A few minutes later my mother was there, my husband had come home from work and we all had butcher knives! We were certain that someone had broken in. We searched that whole house from top to bottom. Nothing."

Two previous owners of the house were two old maid sisters named Horne, one was a seamstress and milliner and the other had a wooden leg.

"When my first two sons were born, they had the back bedroom upstairs. One of the boys got up and said that he'd been woken by a 'square-headed person' at the foot of the bed. Fifteen years later I was standing in the laundry room talking to the other son in the kitchen when he said, 'Mom! There's a square-headed figure looking around your shoulder!' I saw a picture of one of the Horne sisters in the paper. She looked like she came from a different century and with her hair and the shape of her face she was as square-headed as they come!"

Pat was fortunate in having an elderly neighbor, Mrs. Tipping, who had researched the history of the area. "When we first moved in, I was standing out in the front yard talking to her. She said, 'Do you know you've got a little four-year-old girl buried right where we're standing.' I said, 'Good Lord, no!' She told me she had picked up her little flat tombstone and took it to the local historical society museum. She only knew the child's age and that she had died in the 1800s, but not her name."

The tombstone has since disappeared into the depths of the museum. But the little spirit has apparently remained. Pat's sons Bobby and David have heard her singing in the kitchen, years apart from each other.

"Some of the kids have seen her, but I never have. She's tugged on me—down low, like a 4-year-old would."

She seems to be treated almost like one of the family. Pat's son and daughter-in-law saw her in the laundry room. "Oh, by the way," they casually mentioned to Pat, "the little girl was peeking at us around the edge of the dryer."

Another semi-regular visitor is the woman who walks out of the bathroom off the kitchen, which probably used to be a porch, and up the stairs. She's been seen by Pat's husband and at least one of her sons. Pat hasn't seen the woman, but has felt the cold air as if someone has just walked by and has watched the cats sitting and staring while something walks up the stairs.

An unusual feature of the Bratton's ghosts is that they imitate voices.

"One night my son was in the bathroom when he heard me calling him from the living room. 'What'd you want?' he said 'You were calling me.' I wasn't.

"Later that same night I heard my husband calling me so I went upstairs. He was asleep and I woke him up. The next night Charles came downstairs and said, 'You were calling me, but I see you're asleep....' So all three of us got the treatment in two nights!

"Both my son David and I play the piano. Charles came in one day and thought it was David playing. Then he realized that somebody was playing, but not David. No one was there, but the keys were going up and down.

"I've seen a man standing by the piano, all dressed in black and white. He's short and I've only seen him in profile. I also saw a man upstairs leaning on the hall tree. He wore a big crazy grin and it scared me to death! It was the only time I've seen a full face.

"I've heard the sound of throat clearing, and coughing sounds, just like Charles makes. Once the baby was in the high chair in the kitchen. I heard the door knocker on the back door go BAM BAM BAM. I wasn't imagining it because the cat and the baby looked at the door.

"I was sleeping on the davenport. It was hot and I had my feet uncovered. Something took a finger and thumb and flipped my foot. Now, if it's 900 degrees, the feet stay covered!

"I've felt somebody sit beside me on the davenport—the cushions go down. My daughter felt someone shuffling up behind her in the kitchen. She and I were sitting at the kitchen table one day. She said, 'Do you think anybody's in here?' So I said out loud, 'if you're here, do something!' At that the lazy Susan in the center of the table made one complete revolution. My daughter looked at me and said, 'Don't you ever do that to me again!'

"My husband and I have separate bedrooms, since he's a restless sleeper. I sleep downstairs and he sleeps upstairs. My husband has a ghost woman up there quite a lot!"

One night, he told Pat, "I saw a woman standing on the attic steps. I realized when you vanished, that it wasn't you!" He always sees the same woman. She wears a long dress, but she vanishes before he can see her face.

Pat's daughter Leslie was 18 when she noticed "something" in bed with her. All she could see was an indentation in the pillow. The covers were puffed up as though something was under them. For several hours, this "someone" wiggled constantly. Finally Leslie got so annoyed that she took her fist and hit the covers, shouting, "Go away!" The something vanished and never came back.

Although Pat assured me that "there's nothing bad in any way, shape, or form in the house!" she admits that she doesn't like being up in the attic. Some of her experiences there would have had me out the door in a heartbeat. Like the time she was up in the attic, looking into a garment bag and something went between "me and the light bulb." Or the time she heard a sound like someone pounding violently with their fists on the attic stair landing, a landing she would have to walk through to get out of the attic. "I was afraid to go down the stairs thinking, 'I'm probably going right through somebody!'"

Then there was a run-in with an aggressive carry-on.

"I had a carry-on piece, folded flat up on the shelf beside the attic stairs. It was about 2 feet tall made of soft vinyl that folded flat until you filled it. If it was empty, it lay flat. It didn't have any hard surfaces. One time I opened the attic door and there was this carry-on bag standing there on the attic stairs.

"'You can't even be standing!' I yelled.

"It wasn't touching anything. It had come off the shelf and down the stairs to stand there and scare me. I must have a strong heart. I later threw it away. I hope it isn't haunting anybody else.

"The *Canton Repository* ran an article about the house. Up and down the block our neighbors came and told us that they've had similar things happen, they just didn't want to talk about them."

It's possible that the cemetery underlies more of the neighborhood than believed. The elderly neighbor told Pat that when people died of the Black Plague the bodies were buried deep, too deep to bother digging them up. Some were left behind when families died out or moved away and no one knew where to contact relatives. It sounds like the Brattons have a lot of company.

"We know we're not alone. And they're welcome," said Pat, adding quickly, "just as long as they don't scare me in the attic!"

THE FAMILY PLOT

Chip and Margaret Brookins live in the same subdivision as Pat Bratton. Margaret's family lived in the house from the time it was built in 1904-5. Chip heard that "two or three" bodies had been moved from the house site when it was built. He also heard from Mrs. Tipping, the neighborhood historian, that as they were building the road where the Brookins live, they dug up bodies by the truckload with bulldozers. There were few grave markers and in some cases, there were up to 40 people in mass Black Plague graves.

Chip took up the story, "My wife and I were married in 1970. Nothing went on in the house until the mid-1970s. We had just put carpeting in the house. I was hurrying down the stairs in my socks. I was just above the landing when I slipped. I felt a hand grab me by the upper left arm and set me back up. It was really cold. But the freaky thing was—I could see the imprint of the hand on my arm. After that I didn't touch any of the other steps!

"When our son was born in 1980, we had a cradle in the dining room. One morning I came downstairs to the kitchen. Out of the corner of my eye, I saw what I took for my wife, walking across the doorway to the dining room wearing (I thought) her long dark green robe. I asked her, 'How do you want your eggs cooked?' No response. 'How many eggs do you want?' I asked. No response. I walked into the dining room and found our big black tomcat in the middle of the room. He was all puffed up, facing one corner of the room, hissing. This was a 20-pound cat who usually didn't puff up for anything. Being the kind of person who wants to know what's what, I put my arm into the corner. It was at least 10-15 degrees colder than the rest of the room.

"Eventually we turned the dining room into a TV room. One November, about dusk, my wife and I were watching TV. I sat up and saw what I thought was a person standing in the living room. 'Who's that?' I said. My wife sat up to look and the person disappeared. Looking in the room at us was a short, older lady, wearing dark-colored clothing with some lace around the neck.

"My daughter, who was born in 1984, would wake us up with her giggling after we'd put her in her 'big girl bed.' She explained that she was 'Just talking to the lady, Dad.' We believe that it's my wife's grandmother, Maebelle Geis, who is still here. She died in the house in 1928 and was laid out in her coffin in the living room.

"She likes to play tricks. You can go to the kitchen, open the drawer, and what you're looking for is not there. Then you go to the dishwasher; the thing's not there. But when you go back to the original drawer, there it will be, sitting on top. Sometimes we'll be looking for something and will say, 'This is not funny, Maebelle!' Then you'll find what you're looking for. She had a good sense of humor. I think she's very protective."

Besides the ghost of Grandmother Geis, it seems like Chip and his family have a lot of walk-through traffic.

"I've heard people walking around downstairs. So has my daughter. The back door also opens by itself. I justify it by saying this is an older home, but sometimes the door is locked and should not have been able to open. We live with it."

Chip's wife Margaret also spoke with me.

She said, "I haven't experienced things as extensively as my husband. He's Native American. I'm practical German and Scotch! What I experience is when things disappear or move around. A week ago we were trying to hang a picture on the wall by the stairway. Chip dropped a 2-inch long nail. We searched on hands and knees down the stairs and found absolutely nothing. He went to get another, then there was the old nail in the middle of the landing. I know I searched there. That happens pretty regularly. After awhile you think you're going crazy.

"My grandfather bought this house in 1905. He died when I was three. Last Christmas I visited with my half sister. I never lived with her, but she did live in this house. She even had the same bedroom as our daughter. We mentioned some of our experiences and she said, 'you know, that is really bizarre!' When she was a child, a lady would come into that same bedroom and stand by her bed. She would wake other family members with her crying because it scared her.

"All the visions have been so fleeting. It would be fun to think that we're not alone. I've never felt fearful of anything that happens in this house. Even the mischievous episodes were nothing to be afraid of.

"Our neighbor came over last year, almost hysterical about the stuff going on in her house. 'I don't know what it is!' she said, 'Have you ever had things go on in your house?!'" The Brookins explained about the cemetery.

"It was the original cemetery as far as her house," Chip commented. "And did *her* house have bodies under it!"

THE PLOT NEXT DOOR

"Her" house belongs to Eric and Tracy who also live in the cemetery neighborhood in a house built in 1923. That year some 500 bodies were exhumed from the "abandoned" cemetery. "I've seen a photo of some of those bodies stacked in a truck, ready to be moved," said Tracy.

When Tracy and Eric first moved into the house, nobody told them anything about the history of the land. Tracy bought an old rocking chair with a needlepoint seat and back. To her amazement, she saw an old woman sitting in the chair. "When I told my husband, he thought I'd lost my mind. I thought I was having a nervous breakdown. But I knew in the back of my mind that I wasn't. I did some research and then I found out that a woman who lived in the house next door was named Anna. She was a teacher and she did needlepoint. The problem is that the description her family gave me is slightly different from the woman I've seen in the chair. But I've started doing needlepoint...

"The seat of the rocking chair is broken so I pushed it up into position and put a doll on it to keep people from sitting on it. I'll find the seat broken down and warm; I'll push it up from beneath, then I'll find it broken again. I guess she keeps sitting on it. I also smell old-lady perfume."

Even after Tracy had convinced Eric that she wasn't crazy, he was still a little skeptical. Then he started seeing things, along with Tracy's children. "We've both heard children playing in the attic, balls bouncing, children laughing. We've both heard a man weeping on the stairs. There are presences in some rooms and in the basement. Some days there are so many people you can't even push your way in.

"The only person I've actually seen is the old woman, but I see things almost in my head. I'm not sure how I know what I know, but I can tell you what they look like, how tall they are, what they're wearing, their names, what they did for a living, everything about them. I wrote down a list of about 25 people and was going to compare it with the names of people whose bodies were transferred to the other cemetery. But there aren't any lists. Nobody has any information.

"One day my husband was away. I was busy cleaning the house. I carried the laundry to the basement, which meant going down one flight of stairs and through the family room. I put the basket under my left arm and reached around the door to turn on the light in the laundry room. And I felt a man's hand.

"I dropped the basket, the light came on, and I ran over to Chip's house going, 'I'm losing my mind!'

"I want to say to them, 'please don't show yourselves.' But you always hear things, people crying, people walking up the stairs. We've watched cushions fly off the couch. The main door screen door will open and close, then the front door will open but nobody's there. Some people say they've been pushed and pinched.

"I don't feel like they're here to hurt me. It's almost as if I'm supposed to be a messenger. They all have a story to tell, they're suffering, they're all heartbroken. That man on the stairs, he's crying over his child, he's holding her, weeping.

"I can't see them being angry about their bodies being moved. I believe you just bury a body and the person doesn't care about it anymore. But the thing that bothers me is why they would have built houses over the cemetery.

"I had put in a new pond in the backyard. The woman behind me came over to look at it and asked, 'Do any weird things happen in your house?'

'Don't get me started!' I told her.

When she was younger, the neighbor said, she was digging in the yard and came across some bones. Her mother told her, 'cover them up! And don't you say a word about this!' I've met her mother. She advised me not to do any digging...."

Do the dead really not mind their bodies being left behind? Or did they resent being thrown into deep pits, perhaps still with a spark of consciousness left—just enough to try to scream. Either would encourage an unquiet spirit to wander. And it seems that no matter how many bodies are unearthed, there will always be one more....

THE CHILDREN'S WARD
The Influenza Pandemic of 1918-1919

The Influenza Pandemic of 1918-1919 was the stuff of horror movies. No one really knows where it began, no one really knows the germ that caused it. There was no vaccine against the disease, there was no cure. The disease spread like wildfire among the troops in training camps and on troop ships going to Europe to fight in the trenches of the Great War. Worldwide, the influenza killed 20 to 50 million people—more than were killed in World War I. Hard-hit communities reported running out of coffins, of not having enough live people to bury the dead, or of bodies kept unburied for weeks in sheds, coal bins, and garages.

It wasn't the stomach upset we call flu today, or the exhausting scratchy-throated bug you get in February where you just want to lie in bed and sleep. It was a relentless, drowning pneumonia that cruelly targeted the young and fit, sometimes killing within hours. People who die suddenly or before their time, like so many of these influenza victims, may easily become ghosts.

Jeff Barklage, who experienced technical difficulties while working in the basement of Habits Café, (see p. 109) told me this story from Cleveland.

"I shoot a lot of commercials. I was up in the Cleveland area, shooting for the Visitors' Bureau on the sound stage of a local production company. The building where we were filming was originally built as a kind of businessmen's club. It was once a library, and during Prohibition, it was a speakeasy. There are tunnels running under the street where they brought in the liquor.

"The man who owned the sound stage told me that there was a bowling alley in the basement. We'd shot all day and after we were done wrapping, he said, 'Hey, you want to see the bowling alley? I've also got some old movie lights down in the basement.' I said, 'Sure.' So we went down in the basement and were walking around with a flashlight. It was a really cool bowling alley with the wood inlaid into the floor.

"Well, the owner's pager went off and he left me in the basement to go unlock the loading dock. Up to that point, I hadn't heard anything about the building except that it had been a speakeasy. Suddenly I heard these little girls giggle. The first thing I thought was that they had some kind of editing facility in the basement and they were running an edit. So I started walking around and I found that I was back where I started. Then I heard it again. It sounded like it was in the next room. It was always two little girls giggling. I'd go to the next room and it would be in the next room over. I never could get to it! When the guy came back I said, 'Hey, are we near a daycare center or something?' Then I thought, 'But it's midnight....'

"The owner was very casual about it. 'Oh, yeah, people have been hearing that here for over 60 years....' Then he explained that, during the Influenza Epidemic, the building had been an orphanage for children who had lost their parents. An quarantine ward was set up for infected children. Some of them undoubtedly died in the building." Some still remain today, quarantined by death, playing their happy games in a far off children's ward.

9/11

During the night of September 11th, 2001, I heard the sound of my daughter's bedroom door opening. I heard her footsteps go down the hall, then come back, and her door shutting again. The next morning at breakfast I said, "I heard you get up last night. Couldn't you sleep?"

She shook her head.

"I had the strangest thing happen. I was asleep, but I woke up and thought, 'Oh! There's a strange woman standing by my bed!'"

"What did she look like?"

"She was dressed in a skirt and blouse. She had short, curly hair and wore glasses. She reminded me of the character Jane Fonda played in the movie *9 to 5*—her clothes were kind of outdated. She was all silvery grey, like she was covered in dust. And I got the idea that it was up to me to show her the door, show her the way out. So I walked down the hall, kind of pulling her behind me. I pointed down the stairs so she could see the door. Then I went back to bed."

Hearing this, I was reminded of Joan Grant in *Far Memory* who described, as a girl, "dreaming" of the battlefields of World War I. She wrote,

"I used to find myself on a battlefield, grown-up and usually in the uniform of a Red Cross nurse, although occasionally I was a stretcher-bearer. I knew I had reported for duty and received specific orders; either to explain to a man who had just been killed that he was safely dead, or to encourage him to return to a body that was not due to die yet although it had been severely wounded."[5]

The child Joan would wake exhausted from the horrors that she witnessed in her sleep, the sights, fears, and smells. Yet she soldiered on, believing that it was her duty to help the dying and the newly dead. Was my daughter briefly enlisted in the same cause, to help a lost and nameless woman find her way out, the door to the land beyond?

DINING WITH THE DEAD:
Haunted restaurants and bars

The Spirit of Wine sang in my glass
-William Ernest Henley-

The ancient Greeks used to believe that the dead could be placated with troughs of ox blood. Native Americans had a belief that the dead would eat the smell of food offerings. In Singapore, there is a "Hungry Ghost" festival where the dead are lavishly fed to keep them from harming the living. Why shouldn't our ghosts also go where they can eat and drink, at least vicariously.

REBECCA

As with any dish, presentation is everything. The Chokolate Morel Restaurant in Mason has been painted a mellow golden brown, like cocoa dusted on a truffle. From the quirky shelves of cookbooks in the back hall and wreaths of corks to the elegant gold-framed mirrors and bronzed ceilings to the gilt sign on the glass kitchen door: "Kitchen Cast Only Please," the Chokolate Morel is by turns fresh-spirited, dramatic—and haunted.

It was in the 90s outside, so I shouldn't have been shivering with cold in the building. It may have had something to do with the restaurant review I'd read. It told about a woman being murdered in the house by her husband. That was all that I knew.

When I first visited, Pam Kennedy, one of the owners of the Chokolate Morel and Amanda Harbaugh, the dining room manager, were sitting at one of the copper-topped bistro tables in the front room. Pam, a porcelain-skinned blond with intense blue eyes, explained how the restaurant got its name. "I'm a pastry chef—so the 'chokolate' is for me. And my partner, Dave, really likes morel mushrooms. There's something of both of us. And it's easy to remember."

In August of 2002, Pam and Dave moved into the building and started renovations. "We began running our catering business out of the building while working on the rest of it. Then we opened the restaurant part."

The "restaurant part" is a wildly successful, dinner-only operation, with intimate private dining rooms on the second floor, and more mainstream seating in the formal first floor dining room decorated in rich burgundy and gold, whimsically accented with filled wine crates.

After our introductions, Pam sent me off to tour the building. I was drawn to the upstairs with its beautifully carved stair rail. The room to the left of the stairs was painted the same cocoa-powder color as the outside brick. As I took notes in this room I felt an unexpected pinch on my elbow.

Later I was told that the ghost of a black man had been seen in this room. The staff thinks that it might be his apparition that made three wine glasses fly—one, two, three!—out of their rack there. According to rumor, there is an Underground Railroad tunnel that runs diagonally across Main Street to the bakery. Since another house once stood on this site, it is possible that the man, fleeing to freedom, died and was buried in that house, then had the current building built over him.

I continued to the room to the right of the stairs. It was a bright, sunny room painted white. It seemed a comfortable place with its high ceiling and airy curtains. I got a sense of a man in the room—perhaps this had been the master bedroom? I found myself shivering again.

The series of small dining rooms on the second floor was charming. But the server's pantry at the end of the hall held a memory of misery. Someone was crying. She was a small woman, dark-haired, I think, and I never got a good image of her face. But I could see that she was exhausted with weeping, her face smeared with tears. There was something very young, very immature about her. She sobbed and screwed her fists into her eyes, like a toddler. Over and over I repeated, "It'll be all right. Everything will be fine. It's OK," until she wiped her eyes and smiled a wavery smile. She was looking wan, but brave when I went back downstairs.

I hunted up Amanda, who took me down to the basement. The steps were a treacherous spiral. She showed me around the storage areas. The black man from the second-floor dining room has been seen here also. There is a small hatch cut between two of the basement rooms. Justina, one of the cooks, saw somebody walk past it, once, then a second time. Justina told me, "I thought, 'When did we hire a black guy?' Then I realized that we didn't have *any* black guy on the staff. I came upstairs. That was it!"

I wandered into what seemed to be a dead-end workroom, but found a narrow hall leading into a tiny stone-lined room.

There I saw a man with his back to me holding a woman by the throat. I watched in horror as he methodically bashed her head against the floor. I heard the soft crack of bone. I felt each blow in my teeth. Shuddering, I scurried for the door. Then I turned back.

"I don't want to, but it's my job," I muttered to Amanda. I had to at least try to get a photo. But the figures were gone.

"Brrrrr," I said, shaken.

We rejoined Pam and Jen, the wine rep, who had set out three bottles on the table. I did a double take: the brand was "Cockfighter's Ghost," an Australian wine named for the ghost of a horse drowned in quicksand on a doomed outback expedition. It seemed an omen.

The ghost's name was Rebecca, Pam explained. She had been murdered in the room to the right of the stairs.

"The white room?" I asked.

"It's painted sage green," she said.

I raised my eyebrows. When I dashed back upstairs for a second look, I saw that, although it had white trim, it was in fact, a rich green, not some pale pastel that I might have mistaken for white in the afternoon sunlight. Shaking my head over this, I asked, "How did she die?"

"She was bludgeoned to death with an ash log," Pam said. I winced. Such a thing seemed utterly at odds with the lovely room upstairs.

When I described the horrific vision I had seen in the basement furnace room Pam nodded. "That was where she ended up. The murder was quite brutal."

Pam showed me a clipping about the murder from a local newspaper. I found more details at the Warren County Historical Society in Lebanon. John and Rebecca McClung were an eccentric elderly couple living in Mason. John McClung was an irritable, jealous, moody man, always accusing Rebecca of vile things. He was fourteen years older than his wife, who was still lovely in her sixties. To anyone who knew Rebecca, accusations of immorality were ludicrous. She was an agoraphobic. She had not left the house in over 30 years, but sat in her room with its two walls of windows, watching. She knew all that went on in downtown Mason. Perhaps it was easier for her to retreat to her room rather than face her husband's jealous rages every time she left the house.

The McClungs were rumored to be very rich. They had recently sold their house to Mrs. Baysore, a dressmaker, although they continued to live there in an apartment. Mrs. Baysore was awakened on the morning of April 12, 1901 by screams coming from the McClung apartments. She called out to Rebecca, but there was no answer. Then she heard someone coming downstairs, John McClung by the sound of it. Realizing that something was wrong, she dressed and went into their apartment. Upstairs, she found Mrs. McClung horribly beaten, blood spattered all over the room. She called the marshal and the doctor.

Dr. Van Dyke found Mrs. McClung lying across her bed around 6 a.m. Her skull was shattered. The upper part of her face was terribly crushed, probably by a log of firewood. Rebecca had apparently been in bed when attacked and had pulled the covers over her head after the first few blows to protect herself from the murderous assault.

Dr. Van Dyke noticed blood on the coat of John McClung. Van Dyke also testified that he had frequently seen McClung with bloody hands, wiping them on his clothes. Whether this was from injuries, farm chores, or from routinely hitting his wife, the doctor did not specify. Dr. Van Dyke also claimed he heard footsteps descending the stairs as if someone was groping their way down the dark hallway.

During his trial for manslaughter, rather than murder, John McClung said that the blood spots on his coat were from a cut on his hand. He showed the scars. McClung said that he had risen about 4 a.m. and, after dressing, considerately tiptoed out of the bedroom. He built up the fires and then went to the stables to feed the animals. When he returned and went to call 'Becca, he found her lying dead in a pool of blood. He disclaimed all knowledge of the crime, saying that if he had committed it he did not know it. In a telling bit of testimony, McClung denied that he had one time beaten a horse to death with a rail and when his wife implored him to stop replied to her that "if she didn't shut up he'd give her some of the same."

According to contemporary newspaper accounts, during the trial McClung sat in a rocking chair next to his sister, Mrs. Sarah Jordan, much of the time with his eyes closed, utterly indifferent to the proceedings.

The Defense tried to suggest that it was well known that Old Man McClung kept barrels of money in his house and that some ruffian had broken in and murdered his wife for it. Recent examples of daring daylight robberies and burglaries were cited to suggest that a gang was to blame. Perhaps the defense created a reasonable doubt with this line of testimony. John McClung was acquitted. Lacking a trial transcript, I cannot say why.

The jury may have seen that McClung was not in his right mind. Or he may have been such a prominent citizen that they felt they could not convict him. There were also rumors that he hadn't actually done the deed, but had paid someone else to beat his wife to death. McClung was sent to an insane asylum immediately after the trial. Two years later he was released to the custody of his sister, Mrs. Jordan, at whose house he died October 30, 1904. He is buried by Rebecca under a large McClung family monument at Rosehill Cemetery in Mason.[1]

I've speculated that McClung may have had dementia, which can cause the sufferer to be paranoid and unreasonably jealous or even tertiary syphilis, which can cause violent rages. There may have been insanity in the family. John's brother, W. Elmer McClung, drove his wife and children out of their home one mile north of Mason, set fire to the house, and then committed suicide.

Or was John McClung simply evil? I think Rebecca was beaten and abused many times before her murder. I wondered if the murderer had actually begun his work in the basement or if I was seeing a previous incident from Rebecca's private domestic hell.

I dispatched my daughter to have dinner at the Chokolate Morel, partly because she enjoys really good food and partly because I wanted to see what she would pick up. During her teen years, she lost a lot of her sensitivity to ghosts as her energies went into growing up. We hadn't done much ghost hunting together for several years and I frankly didn't think she would find very much.

I was wrong and I apologize. Here is what my daughter told me:

"One of the ladies took me down in the basement. Nobody told me anything. I looked around and thought, 'There's nothing down here, why did my Mom want me to look at the place?' I didn't really trust myself because, initially, I didn't feel anything. I started exploring. I didn't like the bit beyond the hatch AT ALL. [This was where Justina saw the black man.]

The farther back I went, the worse it got. That dark little corridor, to the left? There was something in the dark but I forced myself to walk past it and go into the little stone room.

The light was on, thank God. And I thought, 'This is bad!' There was definitely a man there; it was very unsettling. Not happy at all. Not a place I wanted to be.

"Afterwards, they told me that my Mom saw somebody beating a woman's head against the floor in that room. And the lady who had taken me downstairs said, 'Now I'll take you upstairs and show you the room where the lady was murdered!'

My daughter told me that she had eaten dinner in the murder room but hadn't really felt anything there. She too thought the room was white until I showed her a photo.

"After dinner the lady who took me downstairs said, 'I want to take you out in the back yard.' She stopped at the fence and said, 'It was in this area.' It didn't matter that she told me. The atmosphere was heavy enough that it was *very* obvious. The first thing I noticed was the hole, covered up by the board. I thought, 'That is scary!!!!'

"As I looked at the stairs coming down from the right back door, I saw a man carrying or dragging a woman. I don't know if she was dead. I saw a white petticoat and black pointy shoes that laced part-way up the ankle. I also saw a purple dress over the petticoat. It was very upsetting. It was like I had crossed over some threshold. He is a horrible man. I felt him so strongly in the back yard! Some dessert….," she finished, looking at me severely.

Several psychics have been through the building. One psychic said that Rebecca kept asking plaintively, "Why did he kill me?" over and over. She wanted to hold a séance and bring back John McClung, to ask him why he murdered his wife. Wisely, Pam decided against it. We know that McClung was violent and perhaps insane. His grasp of reality was not good while he was alive. Would it be any better now? It seems cruel to force a murder victim to confront her killer. Who could say what the consequences would be of unleashing a violent spirit like McClung?

I don't know how much Rebecca ventures downstairs. Dave, the restaurant's co-owner has seen a woman in black several times, usually when he is alone in the building. Does she see her room as a refuge from her husband's tempers and the uncertainty of the outside world? Yet, on at least one occasion, Rebecca seems to have ventured out of the house after her death.

The groundskeeper at beautiful Rose Hill Cemetery just up the street from the restaurant reported that a woman stopped by one day looking for the McClung grave. He gave her directions, noting vaguely that she was dressed in very old-fashioned clothes, then turned his back. When he turned back a second later, she was gone. A few weeks later at the Mason Historical Society, he saw a photo of a woman on the wall.

"That's the woman who came to the cemetery!" he exclaimed.

"That couldn't have been her," the historical society worker said, "That photo is of Rebecca A. McClung—the woman buried in that grave."

It's a strange thing about ghosts: some linger on, embittered or terrifying, poisoning the atmosphere. Others grow and change as if they were living beings, blossoming if they are appreciated or cherished by their hosts. In the case of this charming restaurant, the positive energies of the modern inhabitants and visitors to the building have overlain the horrors, erased the aura of a murder room, soothed a sad ghost, perhaps even coaxed her into a smile. The atmosphere in her old bedroom is happy and convivial. Time is doing its healing work. When Rebecca ran this site as a boarding house at the turn of the century, she was noted for her "fine table." She must be proud to see the many modern-day diners enjoying the noteworthy cuisine and impeccable service. Perhaps it makes up, a little, for all her years of sadness to find that she is loved and remembered.

ARNOLD AND PHOEBE SIT FOR THEIR PORTRAITS

Roscoe Village was once a stop on the Ohio and Erie Canal, the link built between Lake Erie and the Ohio River to carry people and goods the length of the state. In its heyday, the village would have swarmed with mosquitoes and flies. The canal boatmen, a notoriously rough and drunken lot, would have been smoking and quarreling in the streets. Those streets would have been unpaved and possibly contain a hog or two rooting for food or lying in the muck.

Building the "Big Ditch" as the Canal was called was an unbelievable feat of engineering. Ohio's forests were said to be so thick that a squirrel could cross the state without ever touching the ground. The canal diggers had to first hack their way through these forests, then dig a ditch a mere 26 feet wide at the base, 40 feet wide at the water line, four feet deep, and nearly 300 miles long—from Lake Erie to the Ohio River. The ditch was lined with pounded clay to make it watertight. A series of locks were lined with sandstone blocks weighing two to four tons, all moved by manpower. By the time it was finished, the Ohio and Erie Canal featured 153 locks, 14 aqueducts to carry the canal over streams and rivers, 203 culverts to carry streams under the canal, and 14 dams. Workers, mostly Irish immigrants, were paid 30 cents a day, and a ration of whiskey, believed to stave off the effects of malaria or Canal Fever. It was said that one Irishman was buried for every mile of canal.

That was in the 1830s. Today a well-scrubbed, sand-blasted, tuck-pointed, hog-free Roscoe Village throngs with visitors. Children on school field trips, women ducking in and out of the many shops, and men carrying bags of candles, pottery, or potpourri for the women ducking in and out of the shops. But at night, the skin between the present and the past grows thin and the past begins to intrude into our world—or it is we who intrude into the world of the ghosts?

In November, 2002 at a local book fair, I met Mary Ellen Given, the Director of Marketing for Roscoe Village. She and several other local people told me that I needed to investigate The Warehouse. During the heyday of the canal, what is now The Warehouse Restaurant was just that: a warehouse standing next to the canal. It is a three-story brick building, with a row of small double doors on the ground floor. The top floor is lit by two fanlights, slant-eyed, like eyes in a jack-o-lantern with a three-part window in between for a nose, while the eight windows lighting the second floor form the toothy grin.

The Lock 27 Pub in the basement of the Warehouse recalls the barrels of whiskey that were once unloaded here from the canal boats. The building also housed a mill, a marketplace, a post office, and years later, the village hearse. The end of the building still shows the rusty exterior stone.

That March day of my visit, I had spent an exhausting afternoon at Prospect Place near Dresden and I was ready for some hot food. It was late on a cold and blustery Sunday night. The restaurant was nearly empty. I savored my dinner over an old *Fortean Times* magazine. Several times it seemed like someone was standing in the aisle expectantly, waiting for me to look up. But whenever I did, nothing was there.

Idly looking to the end of the room, I saw a ghostly woman at the left window, gazing out intently at something below, where the canal would have been. She wore a full-length dark calico-print dress with long sleeves. Her hair was in a bun. She was slim and, by her posture, still young, perhaps in her mid-20s. There was a no-nonsense, confident air about her, as if the goods would be unloaded properly or she would know the reason why! She was standing impossibly close to the left wall and, if real, would have had to levitate to stand that high in front of the window.

After dinner, I introduced myself to John Carpenter, the soft-spoken manager. Mary Ellen had told him that I'd be visiting and he sent me off to walk around the building undisturbed.

The halls were dimly lit, carrying me back to an era of soft kerosene lighting and candlelight. You could almost hear the sound of canal waters lapping against the stone blocks. But it was only traffic hissing by on the road that replaced the canal.

The banquet rooms were in darkness. In the Walhonding Room, someone stood by the back windows. A man's voice said in a friendly manner, "Well, *hello!*" In the front banquet room, someone looked out the *front* windows. Everywhere I went there were people looking out windows.

The décor, with its antique furniture and warm wood floors was quite soothing. The attic was a different story. The attic was full of shelves of the prosaic: linens, glassware, silverware, Christmas decorations, even a string of plastic skull Halloween lights. The underside of the roof was blackened with years of dusty cobwebs. I hugged myself against the cold. The attic somehow seemed very *busy.* The lighting was dim and the monster furnace throbbed. There was something watchful there and I was too frightened to say whether it was benign or not. It didn't really matter. Could it have been the furnace vibrations? Some scientists say that vibrations can affect the eyes and brain, that they not only create a feeling of unease and being watched, but can even conjure up figures.

I went down to the next floor where John has had most of his experiences. He showed me his office. "I was behind the office door, where the safe is. It was about 11:30 p.m. I was getting money out of the safe. I felt a cold breath on the back of my neck. I immediately locked up and got out of there!

"One festival weekend, about 6:30 a.m. I was outside the men's room on the second floor when I heard a large bang. I thought, 'Great! I've got someone in the building with me!'" Bravely he opened the door, only to find that the paper towel machine had banged open against the wall and the whole roll of towels had flown out.

A server was in the same restroom when the stall door locked and wouldn't unlock. Finally it unlocked itself as he watched and the door was flung open like someone was playing a joke. Everyone else in the building was downstairs. "He came flying downstairs," said John, chuckling.

Next, John introduced me to Helen Woods, who has worked at the restaurant for 30 years. She pointed out table number twelve.

"Two glasses in two days flew off that table. It wasn't a case of sliding off. They flew!"

She also described how she and another server were standing by the table folding silverware into napkins when, out of nowhere something flew across the room, through the doorway and smacked into the switchbox. They were the only two people in the room. Even if a living person had been standing there, the angle was impossible for any human hand. The object would also have had to dip under the low doorway and *up* to hit the switchbox.

An unknown woman who spotted several ghosts while dining at the restaurant called Helen over to her table, "Do you have a ghost here?"

"Umm, why do you ask?"

"She just walked past my table." The diner described a lady who came around the corner of her booth by the door in a *big* hurry. She was dressed in 1920s clothing and her hair was streaming back behind her ears, she was moving so fast.

"And you've had a fire here," continued the customer.

"Well, yes, there was. Why?"

"I can see it out the window." She gestured towards the general store where there was a devastating fire in 1812.

In the strangest incident, several photographers were shooting the façade of The Warehouse Restaurant when something extra showed up in the photos. One of the photographers, Jeff Morehead, methodical and understated, told me the following story.

"It was October 9, 2002. We were asked to come over and shoot some photos for Roscoe Village. At that time we were starting to use more digital equipment. We had recently hired [Dale] a photographer with over 48 years experience. Instead of trusting our digital completely, I had him shoot film as backup. We'd shoot simultaneously.

"We went to the Old Warehouse that night. I had never heard *one word* of any kind of ghost story. It was 8:37 in the evening. We walked across the street and shot from that angle, on the street corner. Dale shot film; I shot digital. We were looking for identical images.

"After we were done, Becky Anderson and I went with the digital images back to the hotel. Dale went off and put his film away. He wouldn't be able to process it until he got back to the darkroom. Every shoot we do, we burn the original images, unretouched, on a CD. The camera has only so much storage space so we put the images into the computer and opened them up. We looked at the warehouse images and stopped. We looked at each other.

"I said, 'Are you seeing that?'

"Becky said, 'I'm seeing that woman in the window with the Victorian hair-do.'

"I said, 'Yep.' I looked at other window. Shivers went down my spine.

"'Do you see that guy in the other window?' Becky said.

"'Yeah, and he creeps me out.'

"We blew the pictures up as much as we could without losing everything. We kept seven or eight images. All have the same thing.

"We went back down the street to the building the next day but we didn't see anything which could have caused those reflections.

"The next day we were talking with Mary Ellen Given and told her about the window photos. 'What's up there?' we asked. 'Nothing,' she said. 'A mannequin or something?' 'No, there can't be,' she said. 'There's no floor there, there are only rafter beams with no angled trusses.'

"'Well that doesn't make any sense,' we thought and we asked to go up and look. There was just not a thing, not even a rafter that comes down vertically. Weird!

"Then, between the manager and the waiters, we began to hear the stories. It was the first we'd heard anything about ghosts."

The film photographer didn't want to acknowledge it. "Ah, you just got a nice reflection," he scoffed. "OK, I'll buy that," Jeff said. "But what I really was wondering was, 'Do we have it on film?'"

"We went back and looked to see what might have caused a reflection. We stood on the same corner; we set up our tripods again in the same exact places. We noticed that there are [fake] owls on the building across the street to keep pigeons off. Maybe it was a reflection from them? But we couldn't see them or anything else. Was it a reflection of the ornamental towers on the building across the street? No, the light all shines away from the Warehouse. Was the window dirty? Did the window have something on it? We never came up with anything."

Later when the film was developed, Jeff and Becky were startled to see the same images in the prints.

"The two tripods were about 3 feet apart, so if this was a reflection, you would have thought that the images would be different. Even a slight shift can take away a reflection."

Jeff says that 70% of viewers say, without being prompted, "Oh, there's a woman there." Some people don't see the man in the other window at all. Others say, "That guy's creepy!"

"We still don't know what we've got. The whole thing's just intriguing. We've never seen anything like it.

"It's important to know that we do lots of retouching, but for every shoot, we burn the original images, unretouched, on a CD. It's easy to add things to digital images. Anyone could say that we just put something in the windows. But we were shooting film too. And the fact that we have them both, eliminates that possibility [for fraud]."

Jeff sent me the digital copy, with the windows cropped and blown up and it was a very creepy, disturbing image. The woman, who is sitting in profile, has clothing and hair like the woman I saw looking out the window. She looks like a charming, primitive portrait of a lady from the 1830s. The man in the next window over, on the other hand, has a wild and haggard look, like Rasputin and looks like a drawing rather than an actual human face.

Mary Ellen says that they call the man Arnold, after Arnold Medberry, a prominent local businessman and Roscoe postmaster, who built the original warehouse. The woman is

Phoebe, after his wife Phoebe Denman. By all accounts
Medberry was a stern but fair man with something of a sense of
humor.

The man in the attic window looks quite angry. That may
explain why a musician who frequently plays in the basement
club says that she senses a woman and also an unhappy man, a
very dissatisfied man, up in the attic. It could explain why I
was so uncomfortable there.

Mary Ellen suggests that the level of belief might have
something to do with what is seen in the photos. "I can see two
figures, the man rather more clearly than the woman. Our very
non-believing maintenance guy doesn't see anything. But it's
fun!"

Roscoe Village *is* a fun place to visit on any bustling day.
But it is also a place to stroll in the twilight, listening for distant
voices, seeking the multiple layers of existence in this historic
town. I was studying the Roscoe Village website when something caught my eye. The village motto is, "Look closely,
there's something special here."

Be sure to take your camera.

A DRINK THEY CALL LONELINESS

It's 8 a.m. on a Thursday.... I tried, unsuccessfully, to fit
the words of Billy Joel's "Piano Man" to the grey morning. The
exterior of Toledo's Club Bijou was grey too, with a sign
advertising a wet t-shirt contest and gates chained across the
entrance doors. I drove around the block a couple of times,
watched the man in the cherrypicker truck changing bulbs on
the signs and idly noted a shadowy face peering through a slit-
like glass window on the second floor. It meant nothing to me
at the time.

Jodi, the club's secretary and bookkeeper for the past nine
years, unlocked the gate. Reed-slim and wearing stylish dark-
rimmed glasses, she was immaculately turned out for 8 a.m. in
matching jeans and jacket, black platform heels, and a sleek
swing of dark hair framing her ivory skin. We walked from the
daylight world into darkness. Even with all the lights on, the

club was wrapped in that timeless twilight of bars. Faded paisley carpet, faux marble-stucco walls, vintage European posters advertising cigarettes and liqueurs. Even with all the lights on, it was dark.

Jodi bustled about, switching on lights, providing flashlights, and then, without a word, let me wander.

I looked down on the deco linoleum dance floor from above. It was filled with perhaps half a dozen ghostly couples—the women in evening dress of the late 1930s, the men in tails. They moved with stylized, impersonal correctness, suggesting a dance competition or exhibition. As I stood there, looking down, I thought, "I'm being watched."

Turning, I went up a few steps to one of a series of terraces. I made a note or two at a small table, then looked up towards a bar running the length of the top terrace. The bar stools were upended on the bar, rows of legs upraised like the June Taylor dancers. I smelled smoke. Not surprising, I thought, considering the used ashtrays and a pack of cigarettes on one of the tables.

At the end of the bar I saw a ghostly man leaning back in a kind of boneless slouch. He had shaggy, sandy hair and a mustache. He was a lean, leathery young man and had a cigarette in his mouth. When he saw me looking at him, he smiled crookedly, and nodded his head upward, tipping his cigarette at me as if to say, "Hey, how ya doin'?" Then he put his head back and blew smoke at the ceiling.

He looked laid back and burned out at the same time. He lived to party and at Club Bijou every night was party night—for eternity. I wondered if, like the bartender of "Piano Man," there was some place he'd rather be. As I walked up towards the stairs to the projection booth, he moved back a fraction. I brushed by him. "Excuse me," I murmured automatically.

Then I forgot about him as I looked up the stairs and felt the punch to my stomach. I heard a crash from somewhere overhead. Gulping, I clunked up the metal stairs past the mold-mottled walls to what had been a projection booth. I saw the cherrypicker outside the tiny windows and realized with relief that the man changing the bulbs had made the crash. Only later did I remember that the shadowy face I had seen as I first drove up had looked from the left of these windows. The booth was a small room, made smaller by the old projection equipment and control panels. The heavy metal fire doors on either end of the room were as heavy and sinister as the doors of a meat locker or a crematorium furnace.

A ghostly man with a cigarette hanging from his lip, wearing a white shirt and an open vest, eyed me with irritation as he bustled by. I tried to ignore him, but he was obviously very busy and very annoyed to find me there. "Get the hell out of my way!" he grumbled. I snapped a few pictures and stumped back down the stairs, holding the handrail carefully.

It turned out I was right to do so. The wife of the previous owner of the club had been pushed down the stairs by some ghostly hand, Jodi told me later. The incident frightened her badly although she wasn't hurt.

I wandered down onto the dance floor and then up onto the stage. On the stairs to the right of the stage slumped a young blond woman, the picture of misery. She raised a pair of tear-stained eyes to look at me without interest, without hope, then put her head back down on her fists. To judge by her long straight hair and her dark eye makeup it was still the 1960s or 70s in the twilight world she inhabited.

Crossing the stage, I stared down the steps to the basement club. "There ought to be a sign," I thought: "This way to a sublevel of hell."

I descended into the downstairs club, aptly named The Underground with its oppressively low ceiling. Harsh spot-lights lit the room. The walls were hung with posters picturing black cats, serpents, and a dark silhouette of a cloaked man against a dull blood red background. The atmosphere was jagged, shrill, like the dissonant sound of too-loud music in a confined space. I put up my hands to shield my eyes from the glaring lights.

Walking by the bar I was seized by an obsession: I needed a drink and I needed it *now*! I normally don't drink at all; a sip of wine makes me woozy. But at that moment I would have killed for a bottle. I had only one thought: to drink myself into oblivion.

I once read about an Ohio doctor, Carl A. Wickland, who believed that dead drug addicts and alcoholics could "obsess" the living, trying to slake their cravings for drugs and alcohol through the body of another. He claimed to have successfully dislodged these possessing entities by giving insulin and shock treatments to the obsessed victims.

I shuddered as I hurried on. I didn't need the spirit of any thirsty drunkard climbing onto my back like some foul parasite.

Something beyond the bar made me spin around. There was a chair in the corner, a yellow-green cut velvet chair, a 1970s Dream Chair, with a dead man sitting in it. He was very young, slumped over, mouth agape, as if merely asleep. An overdose? I wondered.

I walked through storage rooms with boxes of New Year's noisemakers, plastic leis, and Mardi Gras beads. Behind the furnace was the image of a body coiled in a fetal position. Some transient, no doubt, who had found his way in through the secret passages that Jodi told me about later. But this poor soul never found his way out.

I climbed back to the first floor to interview Jodi.

"Everybody has a story," Jodi began. "the cleaning crew, the light people—anyone who spends time here alone. *I* spend a lot of time here alone and of all that has gone on, two things stand out."

One evening Jodi was running the totals from the register in the front office. "I put the key in, the receipt comes out. I'm standing by the register. What light is on the register slowly fades out. It was a like a shadow came over me and the register. I looked in the mirror; there was nothing but me. Out of the corner of my eye I saw this tall, grayish brown form standing over me. I said to it, 'Would you knock it off!' It faded away slowly and gradually, the same way it came over me. It was almost like it was saying, 'OK, I just wanted to let you know

I'm here.' I don't know if it was just that I let it get so close the first time, but I was out on the dance floor, running the totals on the register there, when the same thing happened. That time I said, 'OK, now you're scaring me....' And it faded again."

When I told Jodi about the laid-back ghost leaning on the bar, she nodded. "That's just where the other people saw him. His name is Billy."

In 1997 several parapsychologists came through the building. They told Jodi that the ghost said his name was Billy. He knows you, they told Jodi, so don't be afraid to say "hello." So the next time Jodi came into the theatre by herself she called out, "Hi, Bill! It's just me!" He answered with a muffled screech, like the sound of a human crying out underwater. The sound went up the ramp from the floor, fading as it went.

Now Jodi is used to "Billy" and always greets him when she walks into the theatre. "It's just like he's saying, 'I'm here.' I'm not scared of him anymore. But," she added, "he does have this dirty trick thing.... If I'm down under the bar, something pulls my hair from above. This happens on a regular basis. He's just playing little tricks."

The cleaning crew has seen a figure which ducks behind a pillar at the bar. "These are people in their 40s, not nervous young kids," Jodi observed. One saw a man's face looking down at him from the bar. It stared, then moved away to duck down and hide.

When Jodi prints out cash register receipts, they normally come out 6 to 8 inches long. Once when she started a printout on the dance floor register, she left that machine to print and went on to the next one. When she returned, the first register was still spitting out tape. She waited and waited. Finally it finished. It was three feet long.

"I looked closely. It was nothing but a column of 666s. You can't program the machine to do that." She ran into the office. "I thought of keeping the tape to prove the story someday. But it was too creepy! I threw it away. Something was here that was very angry! I didn't know what I was dealing with."

Jodi also told me about the building owner's wife being pushed down the projection room stairs. The psychics also said that the man in the projector room doesn't approve of anything. "It shouldn't be a night club!" he grumbles. When I told her about the sad young blond woman on the stairs, she nodded again. "The psychics said her name was 'Maureen*.'"

Jodi came to work one day to find the cleaning lady locked in the office. "There's someone out there!" she told Jodi, hysterically. "I'm not going back out there!"

Jodi soothed her and said they'd walk out to the dance floor together.

"*She* stopped at a certain point. I kept going onto the dance floor. I got up to the storage area on the right of the stage when I heard a beer cap fall and spin on the floor of the room. I walked right back to the dance floor without going in."

Perhaps the sad Maureen had popped a cool one.

Jodi put me in touch with Frank-o, who does maintenance at the club. He told me about his experience with "Billy."

"I was working there one night on the upper level of the bar, putting tile down. I was using a work light set up so it would throw a 10-foot circle of light. I had my tools around me and I was down on my hands and knees. I thought I saw a figure just outside the glow of the light. I figured it was just my imagination, so I ignored it. I worked a few more minutes; I saw it again. I could tell it was a male. I thought, 'Boy, I'm flipping out! This is crazy!' I didn't believe in stuff like that.

"I moved the light. It came closer. When I tried to look at it directly, it wouldn't be there. So I worked some more. Then I turned around and saw the male figure, half in and half out of the light. I saw it all that evening. I couldn't see a face. It wasn't exactly a shadow, but it would break the light beam, just to get my attention. I didn't tell anybody about this because they would have thought I was a loony.

"Another night, I was doing some plumbing in the same area. There was definitely this solid-looking figure. He was just outside the glow of the light. This time I could tell he was wearing a cut-off sweatshirt or t-shirt. It kept getting more and more into the light, almost like it wanted to get my attention or like he was teasing me. He was a younger person with a slight build. I could only see the whole figure when I wasn't looking right at it. I didn't say anything to anybody until Jodi was telling me about how many times she's seen him."

Jodi filled me in on some of the club's history. It was built in the heyday of Toledo nightlife. "Mobsters used to stop over here," Jodi said. "They kept families, girlfriends in town. Before this was a nightclub, there were escape tunnels, secret passages, hides. There was a lot of liquor smuggling. We finally blocked off all the tunnels. We think.

"This started out as a burlesque house. Pretty much anything they could put on as an act was here including boxing and dancing contests."

Several months after my visit to Club Bijou I spoke to Nita Seery, who used to strip there billed as "Tahiti Niti" and other stage names when the theatre was The Esquire in the late 1970s. "They still had top-name girls—Blaze Star, Tempest Storm—but the girls were in decline by then. Their heyday was in the late 1950s and early 1960s. A nicer bunch of women you'd never want to meet. They'd give you the shirt off their back!"

Nita says it was a little spooky in the dressing rooms under the stage, but "I was more afraid of rats!"

When I asked about the projectionist, she told me about a lighting tech named Ted*. But her description of Ted didn't fit the man in the projection booth. I had a feeling that man had worked at the theatre much earlier.

Next I mentioned the sandy-haired young man slouching by the bar. "Oh, I know him!" she said. "His name was Carl*. He was from Lima. He was gay. His friend died of AIDs, so he may have died too."

Last, I told Nita about the blond woman sitting on the stage steps.

"The woman who was the manager when I first started at The Esquire as a ticket girl, killed herself," she said thought-fully. 'Her name was Suzette*. "She was really nice," Nita said. "She lost her daughter in a child-custody dispute. I always felt terrible because she told me, 'be sure and call me after the hearing.' All night I kept thinking, there's something I have to do. It wasn't until the next day that I remembered and called her. Then it was no answer, no answer no answer. Another girl called me and said, 'Suzette's dead.'"

She had taken an overdose of barbiturates. Nita heard rumors that someone had had Suzette killed. But Nita believed the distraught woman had gotten drunk and took too many sleeping pills, maybe by accident, maybe on purpose. Nita described her. She was blond, really good looking, always wore lots of eye makeup. She was only 27 when she died. But, Nita said, she had curly hair. I saw a woman with long blond hair, like Peggy Lipton's straight blond hair on *Mod Squad*. "She wore wigs," said Nita.

But when I mentioned Peggy Lipton, Nita remembered another girl. "Her name was Marlene*. She looked like Peggy Lipton. I trained her. She started stripping in a sexy Santa suit right before Christmas as 'Donna Blitzen.'" Then Nita told me some personal details of Marlene's life, incidents that would have given her reason to sit on a stairs and cry.

Suzette or Marlene? Both had been sad young women. One was dead; the other had been traumatized in life. I was no closer to finding the identity of any of the ghosts of Club Bijou.

The sun was just beginning to break through the grey when I emerged from the twilight of the club. I felt as if I had been there for an eternity. Once again, I began to toy with the lyrics to "Piano Man," thinking about the Bijou's lonely souls who just can't go home when the party's over.

"Well, I'm sure that I could go to the Light
   If I could get out of this place…"

THE DEVIL DRINKS BUD LITE™

I wasn't sure what to expect from a place named "Hawk's Taverne at the Mill." Perhaps something cozy n' colonial with saucy serving wenches in low-cut costumes. I didn't expect the stark brick building by the railroad tracks, its front windows blinded by green plastic paneling, much of its brick overgrown by vines.

"Ookie," I thought.

Kim who invited me to the Taverne was a tall woman with sleeked back dark hair and large dark eyes. She's been at the Taverne for six years. She turned on the lights, unlocked doors, and gave me free rein to roam around. I headed for the basement through a door marked, "DANGER NO ADMITTANCE."

As short as I am, I felt I had to stoop in the basement, narrowly missing a very effective roll of hanging flypaper. It was like being in a Hammer horror film crypt, with its scabby stone walls, sealant foaming out between cracks like oozing adipocere, and the sound of dripping water far away. And there was a smell—something I couldn't identify.

I stopped to photograph a whimsical Halloween mask: a jolly skull smoking a real cigarette. I felt like I was being watched and turned around to find a woman in a long white gown staring at me with a kind of dull insanity in her hooded eyes. She had long tangled dark hair, was very pale, and I felt, rather than saw, that there were spatters and smears of blood on her face and shoulders. Her gown could have dated from the 1890s to the 1920s. The bloodied woman did nothing, just stood there looking at me, her shoulders tensed, waiting. Deliberately, perhaps to test my nerve, I turned my back. To her left there was a large flash of light and when I looked back, she had disappeared.

I walked past a grouping of broken toilets and into a sinister little corridor. I slid through it quickly, afraid that something was going to slither out of a small side tunnel. Standing beside a collection of damaged bar stools, I saw a mist move in front of a crack of light in the coal chute door. I blinked and squinted, then shrugged. I figured it was just dust sifting in from the outside.

The basement had an apprehensive feel about it, like something hiding, holding its breath in fear of being discovered. I wondered if anyone was buried under the building. Just then, I found a grave-shaped patch of earth framed in cement, sprouting clumps of pallid toadstools like a grave planting.

I just barely missed the flypaper strip on my flight upstairs.

The fancy new pool room on the second floor didn't have much to say to me so I opened a door to a huge unfinished room just off the stairwell. Closing the door to the room shut out most sounds except the rustling and cooing of birds fidgeting in the attic. Clumps of feathers and droppings on the floor and the scrabble of claws overhead hinted at a long occupation. I stood there some time, walking about quietly. There were noises that were surprisingly un-birdlike: sounds of doors shutting and heavy footsteps among the bird-whispers. I went in and out of the room three times, only to find that they were not sounds from the rest of the building.

The windows at the far end of the room were covered in sea-green ribbed plastic panels. There was a mist moving in front of these windows. I closed my eyes, then cleaned my glasses. Even with them off, I could see the shifting curtain of mist.

Next I headed to the ladies room, pausing outside to grope in the dark for the light switch. I had the irrational idea that if I went into the room in the dark, someone would lay a hand on my bare arm. When I later laughed about this with Kim, she smiled uneasily. "When I came in this morning, I turned that light on."

My last stop was the dry storage area and the office. Kim opened the vault, an arched brick crypt-like structure in the manager's office, with a six-inch thick, metal-strapped door and then left the room.

I looked around the small office then stepped into the vault. Standing there I heard the rustle of clothing and breathing behind me. Then someone walked through the dry storage area up to the door of the office. "I thought Kim was going to stay out at the bar," I thought, annoyed at being disturbed. Again, I heard the noise of clothing and a few breaths. I made sure my skirts weren't rubbing on anything and held my breath. The noises came again, intermittently. The picture I was getting was of a fussy little clerk. Who did he remind me of? I knew! It was "Woodcock," the character in *Butch Cassidy and the Sundance Kid* who gets blown up in his boxcar defending the payroll for Mr. E. H. Herriman of the Union Pacific Railroad.

Chuckling, I went back to the bar. There Kim told me that the basement, dry storage, office, and vault are the most active areas of the building. Nobody likes being down in the basement. People have seen patches of mist and often report feeling like they are being watched there. When Nick Reiter and Lori Schillig of The Avalon Foundation visited the Taverne, Lori felt an angry "female energy" in the basement.

As for the office, Kim told me, "You'll be in the office and often you'll hear footsteps come right up to the door. And there's nothing there." Her boyfriend Dusty, who is one of the managers, has also been in the back office and heard what sounded like someone opening and slamming shut the ice machine doors. He has also heard footsteps which seemed to stop right at the office door, even though he and another employee were the only two there. He swears the jukebox turned on and played for a few moments, although he had unplugged the jukebox himself. Dusty believes that ghostly activity seems to increase after lightning storms. He also has forbidden Kim to use the Ouija Board because he said the strange activity tripled after using the board.

Kim sketched the Taverne's history. The building began life in the late 1880s as an oil well supply company during the oil boom at Bremen. It's been a wholesale grocery (you can see the ghost of the words "Wholesale" on the back of the building.), a grain mill, and a farmer's market. It became Hawk's Taverne at the Mill in the early 1990s.

Kim told me about a helpful spirit she and her mother encountered. Both of the women were up on ladders painting window trim in the pool table area.

"I heard someone say, 'Be careful!' It turned out that my Mom heard someone say it too. I know she didn't say it to me and I know I didn't say it to her! A young roofer fell to his death from the roof at that corner of the building."

What about Woodcock? Kim knew about a previous owner. He was a fussy, particular, tight-fisted man, who wanted everything done his way. At one point there was a break-in. The thieves blew the vault door off with dynamite. The door flew, intact, through the window and part of the wall and out into the parking lot. Unlike Woodcock, the owner had only gotten his vault blown up, not himself.

As Kim and I were trading stories at the bar, Jason, another staff member, came in. As we chatted, I noticed what a busy place the Taverne is. There is a constant chuffle of ceiling fans, the intermittent crash of ice machines. Close-captioned TVs and neon signs flicker silently. Banners flutter in the breeze. With so much ambient noise and movement, it is hard to tell what are normal everyday noises and easy to see things from the corner of your eye. But that doesn't explain everything.

In late spring of 2003 Jason was telling a new server about the strange things that sometimes happen at the Taverne. Dusty had already briefed her about the ghosts. But, Jason reassured her, "If I'm here, you won't have any problem. They don't like me and ghosts never do anything cool around me!"

All the oil candles on the tables had been extinguished. As Jason walked by, to his surprise, he found a candle relit. He pointed to it and asked the server, "Hey, those stories Dusty was telling you, were they anything like that?" She got pale and said that she was ready to go home!"

Then Jason told me a weird story:

"The bar had just opened. I was having a bad day for various personal reasons. I was sitting behind the bar listening to some songs on the Direct TV setup, all of which sort of spoke to me. I noted the artists' names because I wanted to check out more of their music. This guy comes up and sits down and says, 'I can tell you're upset.' He started talking and he got into my personal life. And he shouldn't be able to know this stuff! It's very personal, very intimate. I poured him a pitcher of Bud Lite™. He was an older man in a brown jacket, not anything unusual.

"He told me his name was—well, I've forgotten the name he gave me, but I began to get freaked out because it was the name of one of the musical artists I had just listened to. That's when I realized that something was not right. Without a word from me he looked into my eyes and said, 'That's right.' I got very ill at ease, almost frightened.

"He started giving me advice, and made disparaging comments about my friends that were obviously lies. When he saw me getting upset, he said, 'So this is the way it's going to be. So be it. I'll walk away and not speak to you again.' He told me very forcefully that I wasn't to tell another person what he'd told me, like 'Out of respect, you won't say anything!' His tone became quite menacing at this and insistent. It escalated to threats. He wasn't really threatening me, but implying what could happen. Finally he took his pitcher and walked upstairs. I was now confused and terrified and told Dusty I was going to have to leave, that I was too freaked out by the old guy I was talking to. He stated that I was white as a sheet upon turning around and that he had not seen me talking to anyone. I talked to some of the regular customers and to my friends. They all said, 'Dude, you weren't talking to *anybody*.'

"I've forgotten a lot of the details because it is *not* one of my fonder memories. He was not a nice figure, entity, or whatnot…."

Jason's story has many parallels to the classic Men in Black experience: a stranger who knows intimate details, the threats to enforce silence, the disappearance. It is this off-balance quality I noticed about the Taverne. A nice, well-run bar with all the amenities: a crypt-like basement, a bloodied Woman in White, footsteps in the office, a Man in Brown at the bar raising a glass of beer to his lips. It was cold in the bottle; it steams in the glass. Hell is a place with no ice….

But Hawk's Taverne has plenty of ice, plenty of good food, plenty of good company. Just stay out of the basement. And avoid that guy in the brown jacket. He's got a hell of an attitude.

THE FINAL STATION:
Ghost of the Underground Railroad

And before I'll be a slave, I'll be buried in my grave!
And go home to my Lord and be free.
-Spiritual-

THE UNSEALED ROOM

The history of the Underground Railroad seems full of potential for ghostly activity: clandestine comings and goings, secret tunnels, sealed rooms, mysterious lights and rappings. Yet surprisingly few of the sites known to be associated with the Underground Railroad actually have ghost stories. I have shared a few stories from Ohio's abolitionist history about Xenia's Eden Hall (*Haunted Ohio II*, p. 76), a house in Old Washington (*Haunted Ohio IV*, p. 85.), and Prospect Place in this chapter.

I also wrote about the ghost of a gentle-spirited innkeeper at a Lake County inn, known as a stop on the Underground Railroad. But I believe there is a darker side to this charming hostelry. On a lovely, sunny spring day, my daughter and I impulsively stopped by the inn on our way back from a trip to Vermont. The owner wasn't there, but I introduced myself to an employee and asked if we could look around. We enjoyed the hand-hewn beams in the pub and the displays of antiques.

Then she kindly took us upstairs and showed us the guestrooms. We admired the beautiful Bridal Suite and the charming, well-lit rooms. The Inn is built in several sections, each tacked onto the one in front, like a series of boxes. It was at one of these joins that we passed a tiny door, scarcely more than a sliver of darkness. My daughter and I looked at each other and groaned dismally in unison, "uggggg."

Pretending to be cool and rational, we strolled on to the end of the hall, puzzling. Standing at the end of the hall, I was so distracted that I decided I needed to find out just what the problem was.

I walked boldly back to the room. It was a perfectly ordinary looking guest room, although scarcely bigger than a walk-in closet. Its flowered wallpaper included a sample of the original pattern preserved behind a pane of plastic and it was furnished cozily with a bed and a desk. There was a rag doll and other stuffed toys on the bed and a Noah's Ark lamp on the desk—all adorable and about as much use as a recliner in a torture chamber.

There was a film over it all, a touch of the darkness that was not dispelled when I turned on the lights. I walked to the center of the room. I could practically touch both walls with my outstretched arms. The room was foul. I felt like it should have been bricked up, walled up, and never entered again.

Suddenly I was assailed by what I thought of as "death rays." Some kind of energy bombarded me painfully, like knife thrusts. I ducked this way and that, trying to escape like someone dodging arrows hissing narrowly by. In a panic, I rushed out of the room.

All I could think was, "I *have* to have a witness before this disappears!" Then I did something that even now makes me flinch with shame. I grabbed my daughter and thrust her into the room.

She stood there blinking in surprise. Then her forehead puckered with distress. Later she said that she felt the same awful energy, a feeling of compression or walled-up-ed-ness, and she began to have pains in her head.

She came rushing into the hall.

"*Mom!*" she said. "That wasn't very *nice!*"

I don't know what it was. It did not seem like an entity, but an atmosphere. It was unusually strong. We turned the light off and then on. It was almost worse with the light. I was twisting and weaving and trying to get away from it, but it just wouldn't quit.

Back in the hall I turned to our hostess.

"What *was* that room?" I asked in a daze.

She told me that all the rooms in the inn had originally been that size. When the other rooms were enlarged, this room had been left a linen closet. Now it mostly housed children when their parents were staying in the room next door.

Children?!? It seemed like the ultimate horror to make a child stay in that abomination of a room. And I had just pushed my own child into it....

We wondered if it could have been an Underground Railroad hiding place. It had a hemmed in, smothering feeling. My daughter wondered outright if someone had suffocated there. Sadly, there were cases of slaves dying in the sealed rooms that were supposed to be their salvation or of babies being smothered when their cries were stifled for fear of discovery.

We were still shaking our head as we drove away. The day seemed a little darker as I contemplated the malevolent, chaotic energy in that tiny room.

"It should be sealed up again, bricked up, boarded up."

My daughter nodded solemnly.

How lucky we were to be able to drive away from that room with its century-old echoes of terror. I cannot imagine slaves having come this far, almost within sight of Canada and freedom, waiting in anguish for a deliverance that never came. Perhaps some are waiting still.

DARK PROSPECTS

That March day as I drove through the town of Dresden, full of basket shops and Disney-esque village charm, there was no hint of what lay ahead. Snow still lay in dirty heaps beside the road.

Just outside Dresden, Prospect Place sits on a rise across a small rivulet. At first glance, it is horrifying: the county poorhouse, the local lunatic asylum, a particularly stark orphanage. It is an angular building, topped with a glassed-in square cupola. Yet at a second glance, you can see the comfortable country home it once was, like a Currier & Ives engraving or a plate out of a county history illustrating a country gentleman's estate.

I eased the van up the long muddy drive. The first thing that struck me was the immensity of the house. There were massive crockets beneath the rotten eaves, carved with what looked like monstrous beaks and claws. Crenellated chimneys raked the sky. Salts leeching out of the bricks formed patterns in which anyone could find ghosts.

I sat there, the van shivering as the wind buffeted it, listening to the dogs bark and eyeing the sea of mud in the yard. The back door opened and George Adams came out in his rubber boots. He was younger than I had expected from the formal tone of his letters.

"I think you can get across there," he said, helpfully pointing out a high place in the drive that was still mostly solid. "We put gravel down last winter, but with all the snow and then the thaw, it hasn't done much good.

We chatted briefly in the room next to the gift shop about the history of Prospect Place. George is the great-great grandson of the builder, George Willison Adams, a wealthy mill owner and passionate abolitionist. After his first wife's death, he decided to leave that house of sad memories and build a lavish home north of Dresden. The new house was to be called Prospect Place and was an extravagant structure, full of marble fireplaces, carved wood, and the finest wallpaper. Begun in 1855, it took three years to complete. Just hours before Adams was to move in, the first Prospect Place was torched by a bricklayer who wanted to make more work for himself.

Work was begun again and the present structure was completed in 1858. George Adams hated slavery and, according to family tradition, had been running an Underground Railroad route through one of his mills. In 1850 a new Fugitive Slave Act was passed that made it a federal crime to aid an escaped slave, even in free states like Ohio. The act made it legal and profitable to hire slave catchers to find and arrest runaways. This was a nightmare for the free black communities of the North. Slave catchers often kidnapped legally-free blacks as well as fugitives. But these seizures and kidnappings brought the brutality of slavery into the North and persuaded many more people to assist fugitives. The Fugitive Slave Act also allowed property used in aiding fugitives to be confiscated. Adams didn't want to risk losing his mill, so he designed his house with hidden tunnels so that it could be used as a station on the Underground Railroad. Oral tradition says that a slave catcher was hanged in the barn.

It was one of the first houses in the area with indoor plumbing and water closets. The indoor plumbing was more than a mere convenience. Slave catchers would watch to see if unusual amounts of water were being drawn from outdoor wells. If so, they could deduce that runaway slaves were being harbored in the house. With indoor plumbing, no one could tell how much water was being used.

By all accounts life was busy at Prospect Place. Adams had seven children, many of them educated at home. Brilliant parties were held in the house. One brought 150 guests from Coshocton, Zanesville, and Columbus on special trains. There was a caterer in the observatory and an orchestra in the ball-room. Turkey and ice cream snowballs were served.

George W. Adams died in 1879. He is buried out in front of the house. After Adams' death, the house went to his daughter Anna. Her playboy husband quickly ran through much of her money and then abandoned her. The house began to deteriorate. Anna, who died in the house in the 1920s, left it to her son George Cox. It is possible that she is also buried on the property. George Cox sold the house in the late 1960s. It stood vacant and crumbling for thirty years. Now it has come back to the family.

George sent me off on my tour. The doors are all spring-loaded, "to keep the dogs out," George told me. I walked through the first door. It shut behind me. I was in a different world. The sun spotlighted the widening cracks above the dining room door. I could have put a fist through the holes and seized handfuls of horse-hair plaster. Something whispered, far off. The ceilings were stripped to their skeletal lathes.. A lady's tinted portrait hung high on the wall. George later told me that she had been a poor relation who had come back to work at Prospect Place as a servant. The dining room was warmer, but there was a smell like mold. I opened one of two side-by-side doors. The inside of the closet door showed what the original woodwork must have been like: it had a painted, combed, faux-wood-grain finish. The sun filtered weakly through the wavy glass. The freezing wind was whipping across the fields, making the windows rattle. What a cold house this must have been, in spite of fireplaces in nearly every room. Distorted by the glass, I saw a family walking up to the front door for a tour. They knocked and then walked around to the back.

I emerged from the dining room into the main hall and stared up the dizzying stairwell, coiled tightly as a shell, soaring into the distant upper reaches of the house.

Something moved at the other end of the hall by the original front door. It was a little girl, perhaps 4 or 5 years old. She seemed small for her age. She danced and giggled and cavorted the way young children do.

At this point the tour guide Ruth came into the hall with a family of four. Their two children, a boy and a girl, were both well over the age of the child in the hall. I ducked into the master bedroom to avoid getting distracted. I heard Ruth take them down the hall. Then they walked past the master bed-room door. As they did so, a child began to cry bitterly. It wasn't an infant, it was an older child. I assumed it was one of the children with the party. I found out later from Ruth that it wasn't. The child cried on and on, bitterly sobbing like one scolded unjustly or frightened or hurt. I tried to screen it out. I can't stand to hear a child cry.

As I prowled around the master bedroom with its dressing room with built-in drawers, its sophisticated bathroom, I became aware of a substantial man, wearing dark clothes, with dark hair, parted in the middle and a mustache. He seemed irritable, impatient. I got the impression that he didn't like his wife, couldn't stand her, in fact.

I tried to ignore him as I went from room to room. Usually I don't have any trouble seeing a building the way it was or imagining how it can be again after restoration. But this house troubled me. Either it was too far gone or my vision had deserted me. I could imagine being the last mistress of this house before the birds, the snow, and the rain took over, worming their way through small cracks, enlarging them patiently, steadily, until the ruin was complete.

Everything I saw was so unfinished, so barely started, so hopeless. Heating ducts punched through holes in the floors. Fireplaces ripped from walls, like teeth from their sockets. Gouged plaster like once-beautiful, scarred skin. Each room with its high ceilings, plaster friezes, chandeliers, mantelpieces, paint, and wallpaper would cost more than a small house to restore.

The further I looked, the more I despaired. "This house is a lifetime of work to restore," I thought. "It's almost beyond repair…"

"Poppycock!" the man in dark clothes said crisply.

Having been properly told off, I tentatively felt my way down the stairs to the basement, clinging to the rough wood railing as something in the darkness below watched. I sensed someone begging for help.

The floor was covered in sand. It was like walking through some Egyptian tomb. The first room to the left had a "well" of stone in the floor, choked with sand. There is believed to be an escape tunnel for slaves running out of the well. A rough plywood door led from this room to the outside. There was someone massive standing just outside. I could feel, rather than see, his threatening shadow beneath the door. He was very tall and wore a broad-brimmed black hat.

At this point, my camera began to malfunction. Whenever I hit the button, the camera would turn off instead of shooting. I had put in new batteries, but they seemed to be completely drained. I fiddled and fiddled with the camera and finally, after much to-do, managed to get a few photos of the basement rooms.

Each room had its own fireplace. Some were clogged with sand. Others were flayed of their brick halo of molding. I was fascinated by them, wondering if any of them hid an escape route or hidden room.

I wandered further down the dark hall. In one corner of the end room on the left stood an exhausted black woman. She was achingly thin, her bony shoulders sagging, belly thrust forward. Her head was tied up in a bandana and she had some kind of head injury on her temple. She couldn't see me; she just stood there, caught between hope, despair, and resignation in that dark basement. I wonder if she had died there and was still waiting for the conductor to take her on to freedom.

Hurrying back along the dark central hall, I passed a dead-end tunnel, like a crypt.

"EEEK," was my only thought, as I scurried by.

"You think you're a match for me?" called a gruff male voice out of the darkness. Never one to turn down a challenge, I stopped just beyond the tunnel, stuck the camera out and shot several photos at random. But my bravado stopped far short of walking into that dark place. The camera worked; the photos showed nothing except the dressed foundation stones at the end of the tunnel.

I stood in the lighted area at the foot of the stairs and again tinkered with the camera, shooting a couple of random shots in the crawl space behind the stairs. Suddenly I realized that, standing in the light at the end of the dark hall, I was too much of a target....

I went back up to the lobby area off the kitchen to change batteries. George unlocked the door at the bottom of the steep stairs to the servants' quarters. It was very, very cold up there. I looked across the field to the blackened stone gateposts, like those of a cemetery. The room labeled "servants' bedroom" was painted a powdery blue—"haint blue" according to the sign, which was meant to keep away ghosts. I had heard of the

Greeks painting their doors blue to ward off the Evil Eye, but this tradition, which I've since seen described as common in Appalachia, was new to me. In the servant's bedroom I heard music, old-time fiddle/guitar music. I assumed it came from the lobby below, but George said that he hadn't been playing any. Others had heard music in that room also, he assured me. The servant's quarters were remarkably well-equipped with running water in a smooth slate sink.

A door led from the servants' quarters into the main hall behind the staircase, it was warmer, yet I shivered. Part of the stair's railing was patched with two by fours.

"Don't go near the railing!" someone scolded. I flattened myself against the wall.

Looking out the window of the front left room, a sitting room with an elaborate plaster cornice and tattered remnants of wallpaper, I saw a slash of a trench, like an open mass grave, the intended sewer tiles lined up like bodies ready to be buried. Next to the trench, an abandoned glove lay, beseeching, palm up to the sky.

The front upstairs door opens on emptiness. There had once been a porch; it was gone now. I looked out and shuddered. "Plunge to stone steps," I scribbled on my notepad.

As I walked by the stairs, I glanced down through the stairwell at the door to the dining room. A black clad figure suddenly materialized in front of the dining room door and walked briskly around the corner. The door had not opened, but he was there abruptly, like he owned the place.

I climbed all the way up to the cupola, then down to the attic. The windows rattled ominously, letting in gusts of cold air. I wandered around in the huge unfinished space, frankly puzzled. "What in the world did they *do* up here?" I wondered. There was a single plastic folding chair sitting rather forlornly in a corner. I saw an equally forlorn elderly black man sitting superimposed *over* it, slumped, his hands folded, arms resting on his knees, a picture of quiet resignation.

Once again I was struck by the massive crockets under the eaves, carved in sharp curves like the beaks and claws of some monstrous bird. Through the back windows I could see crenellated chimneys, a dismal barn. By those windows I smelled a sweet perfume and saw tiny wet footprints on the floor. There was a giggle, but I didn't see the little girl I'd seen in the downstairs hall.

As I walked down the stairs from the attic, I put my hand on the bare plaster wall. "Up and down! Up and down!" I heard a female voice complain. Later, when I heard that the attic had been the ballroom, I wondered if it was one of the maids who had to climb those stairs laden with food, silver, and punchbowls.

On my way back to the kitchen, I passed by the master bedroom. It had a tight spring on its door like all the other rooms, but it swung open a few inches. "Could that door have come open by itself?" I asked George. He smiled and nodded. "I've heard that before."

Adams also nodded when I mentioned the little girl. "The little girl," he mused, "there is *huge* folklore about her. She lived here in the late 19th century. She was not an Adams, but a servant's child." The story goes that she was sickly. One winter's evening, when she was in a fever, she wandered out onto the roof of the portico. It had rotted away and she fell to her death on the steps below. The child's body was put into the root cellar with ice around her. The mother went down there every single day to visit her dead child. "We just know her as 'The Girl,'" said George. Her real name is not known. She has been seen by the woman who ran the florist shop formerly in the house and by several tour guides.

On Thanksgiving Day, 2002, George was alone in the house cooking dinner. The dogs were tied up outside. "I heard steps in the room above the kitchen. They were coming from a room in the servant's quarters that had been locked up. The key had been lost so no intruder could get in."

Randy Braden, who works with George guiding tours at Prospect Place, has been involved with the unseen world for a long time. He told me a frightening story of his involvement with the forces, human and inhuman, that are tied to Prospect

Place. Since his religious conversion, he has worked at clearing houses of negative entities and counseling people about the dangers of the paranormal. He came to the house on a tour in 2002; he's stayed on to help investigate and contain the mysteries these walls hold.

The first time he took a tour with his daughter Lindsay. It was a quiet Saturday night and while the group waited outside the south entrance, where the balcony had been, a stone came flying off from out of nowhere and hit one of the women in the group, right in the chest. The stone seemed to do a perfect arc, then dropped straight down, bouncing off the woman to the ground. "It was the kind of thing a child would do," Randy said.

Randy didn't feel much activity that night in the building until they got up to the attic. "Something was going on up there!" He watched as a strange rash crawled up the arm of the woman who had been hit by the rock. He recognized the feeling, the bad atmosphere, from other afflicted homes he'd visited in the last 17 years. After that evening, he asked if he could volunteer at Prospect Place. So he became part of the team.

"I've really experienced a lot of stuff over time. I became familiar with the different spirits in the home. The first thing that struck me, right off the bat were the 'elementals,' 'non-human spirits,' whatever people want to call them. Some had been there for a very long time. Some had been conjured there more recently. There were also earthbounds as well," he said, meaning what I would normally call a ghost.

Randy told of one such experience. "Somebody had reported that they had seen green eyes in the basement. I walked around the basement perimeter by myself in the evening. I looked in the far left door which was partially open. There were two green eyes with round black pupils, illuminated with a light of their own, staring at me. I couldn't see the head or the face. I kind of blinked, stopped and looked. I thought, 'Well, I'm not going to run.' I looked again, and then walked on. The symbols painted in that room made it obvious that somebody had been playing around with forces they didn't understand. And they had released something.

Randy feels that the negative energy in the basement arrived between about 1970-80. During that period the Sheriff's Department had to come up to the house to evict and arrest various unsavory squatters.

Randy continued, "In October, George and Felix were going to be gone, so I was going to open the place by myself. I got there just before dusk and came in the main entrance and walked towards the well room. I went to the back reception area and set my bag down. I clearly heard someone walking on the second floor, humming. I thought Felix was up there. Felix is 84 years old and I thought he must have changed his mind and stayed behind.

"'Felix!' I yelled. I headed up the old servants' staircase and pounded on the door to his office. Of course he wasn't there.

"I've seen the spirit of a man with lamb chop sideburns and a rather intense look on his face. I don't know if it's the original Mr. Adams. Whoever he is, I have not seen a happy man. I kind of believe it was him up there, walking around."

Randy and some people in the tour groups have seen a woman in Victorian clothing at the top of the first floor landing. She is a solid black silhouette who makes repeated appearances at the same place.

"One night we thought we would wait on the stairs at about 3:30 in the morning. Instead of getting [the black silhouette] there was a terrible commotion in the building. It came from the well room, while we were at the landing. It sounded like someone throwing large rolls of plastic sheeting all over the place. Everybody was very quiet. I had a large group so I counted heads. Everybody was there and accounted for. And then we heard lumber or boards being thrown, crashing and banging.

"That evening I had another man volunteering with me. I signaled to him, he signaled to another woman. He was going to circle around to make sure nobody had broken in. We found nothing out of place even though it had sounded like two by fours being thrown.

"I think it was that same night, as we were camping out just listening quietly, we heard the sound of a violin playing from the third floor ballroom. We heard it far away like it was playing on a bad AM radio. There were five of us and we just sat there and looked at each other. Suddenly you could hear a man singing with the violin. It went on for maybe 45 to 90 seconds, then it stopped. That was all."

"Something that really struck me, that haint blue. It's an Irish/Scottish tradition, brought to Appalachia. People would paint their doors blue to keep evil spirits away. I found it curious. What could be visiting these people that they felt it necessary to paint the entire room this color!

"One night I had a couple on the tour in the basement area. We were talking. A male African American voice said, 'Look!' Like a warning, like something was coming.

"There have been two times over the past 17 years when I have actually run from a place in a hurry. This was on another night. I was sitting in the basement by myself. I wasn't being *too* stupid, I was sitting on the bottom of the basement steps with the lights on, looking over the basement. Something started coming together, you could actually see it. It felt so— *evil* is the only word you can say, that something inside of me said, 'Leave, get out of here now!' Whatever it was was starting to materialize. I didn't want to see what it looked like.

"The others were smoking on the back porch. I flew up those stairs and backed out the doors, my eyes big as saucers. These folks know me. And they know that not much shakes me. 'What is wrong with you? They asked. I told them, 'I don't know and I don't care to know!'

Randy has seen the little girl only recently. "I am always very skeptical when people report seeing lights. They could be reflected headlight beams from the road or maybe a flashlight beam from another floor, so I try to rule out everything. But there was a light, the size of a small apparition that appeared on the second floor landing. The group I was with spotted this strange light first, and as I looked, it slowly dimmed and then got brighter. There was a break in the middle of the light as if there was a sash tied around the middle. I knew it to be a child. We sat and watched this apparition apparently observe us for a good 5 to 10 minutes. In the meantime, three or four of our group who were seated along the wall could see a dark figure pacing in the original little girl's room on the second floor, the room to the left of the staircase to the ballroom."

Randy wonders about the reports of nonhuman things that wander the property. There have been reports of grotesque figures on the roof and peering in the windows of the ballroom, a fire-eyed apparition materializing in a photograph of the basement.

"There's something missing. How did things so evil get in? Some of this got in long before kids broke in, playing with things they shouldn't. The house was occupied for about 50 years, then nobody lived in it for 30 years. When did these arrive?"

Randy also tries to discourage people from getting too caught up in things paranormal. He knows from his own personal experience that it is easy to get sucked into some vortex of unhealthy curiosity and obsession. With considerable understatement, Randy added, "The whole place is an interesting study, both in human and inhuman spirits."

It was getting dark as I got back into my car. The wind was blowing more fiercely than ever beneath a lowering sky. I eased the car out onto the road beyond the crooked iron gates. I had still to drive to Roscoe Village and then onto Steubenville. Miles to go before I sleep....

I thought of the many souls who had dragged themselves miles over the fields to reach this Underground Railroad station and of the many weary miles they still had to go before they could sleep as free men and women. I thought of George Adams, the builder, staring out of the windows over the winter-desolate fields at a world he never envisioned. The world has moved on while he stands still, always frozen in time.

How many more miles, how many more years before he and the other restless ghosts of Prospect Place can sleep?

PHANTOMS OF THE FURNITURE:
And other eerie objects

I think we are in rats' alley
Where the dead men lost their bones.
-T.S. Eliot-

Just as ghosts can get attached to a house, they can be drawn to a beloved object, a piece of clothing, or furniture. Rocking chairs are a particular favorite. I've suggested that the motion of a rocking chair "records" a ghostly image in the chair, but it may just be that the ghosts find the chairs as comfortable as the living.

LETHAL WEAPON

This story was written by Mike Harden and printed in *The Columbus Dispatch*, 14 July 2002. Used by permission of *The Columbus Dispatch.*

A revolver stored at the Morgan County Historical Society packs plenty of history for such a small weapon.

The saga is entwined with the murder of a town marshal, the suicide of a young prosecutor — and a ghost tale that lingers like cigar smoke in a closed room.

"I don't believe in ghosts, but something happened," said Barb Nichols of McConnelsville. The incident occurred, she said, in the genealogy room of the Morgan County Courthouse — the room in which the gun claimed its last life.

"My daughter and I were doing genealogy work," Nichols recalled of a few years ago, when a 4H project sent the pair sifting through the county archives. "The door kept swinging shut," she said of the small second-floor room where she and her teen-age daughter, Kelly, pored over musty files in search of a family will. "We finally found something to block the door open."

After finishing the day's research, Nichols mentioned the curious problem with the door to an acquaintance.

"Haven't you ever heard of the ghost in the courthouse?" the friend inquired. Nichols hadn't. Some people claim to hear footfalls along with opening and closing doors.

"I don't know about that," said Robert Richmond, trustee of the Morgan County Historical Society. "I've never been in there late at night."

The believers blame the odd occurrences on the wraith of Francis "Frank" Parsons, whose unquiet grave has occupied a Mountville Cemetery plot since the fall of 1909.

Late in the afternoon on a Sunday in October, Parsons, the 34-year-old county prosecutor, walked from the home he shared with his widowed mother to his office — where he shot himself. Parsons had reportedly battled ill health for years. Several months before his death, according to his obituary in the *Morgan County Herald*, he had suffered "a spell" while conducting a trial. Friends tried to persuade him to resign, to no avail.

Four years before the suicide, the gun first became known as the chief exhibit in the murder trial of Wood Stuard. The McConnelsville resident, who suffered paranoid schizophrenia, was beset by the delusion that village Marshal Horace Porter was conspiring against him. In 1905, Stuard ambushed Porter in an alley near the livery stable and fired three shots into the back of his head. The killer, judged mentally imbalanced at his trial, was sent to the state hospital for the criminally insane at Lima.

When he became prosecutor, Parsons "inherited" the weapon upon discovering it in an office safe.

Mrs. Nichols knew little of the story until she was briefed about "the ghost."

The next day, she returned with her daughter to do more research in what once was the prosecutor's office.

"Mr. Parsons," she said aloud, "I want you to leave the door alone today. I'm claustrophobic."

The door stayed open, she said.

The old will that the mother and daughter were seeking turned up in a drawer they had scoured the day before. This time, however, a corner of the document was sticking out above other archives stuffed in the file.

At the rear of the Common Pleas courtroom, a small photograph of Frank Parsons offers the only reminder of his brief tenure — before he fell victim to what the newspaper described as "a fit of melancholy."

Unless, of course, one believes in ghosts.[1]

THE HERO IN THE MIRROR

I first wrote about the ghosts at Johnson's Island in *Haunted Ohio III* (p. 152).

During its years of operation as a prisoner-of-war camp, Johnson's Island was home to over 12,000 Confederate officers. Like so many Civil War prisoner-of-war camps, Johnson's Island quickly became a hell on earth. Union and Confederate authorities routinely exchanged prisoners. But in 1863 General Grant, realizing that he was only releasing Confederate prisoners to fight again, ended the prison exchanges.[2]

The population of Johnson's Island swelled to over 3,000 souls sheltered in cheaply built barracks meant for 1,000 men. The bitter cold of Sandusky Bay, disease, and starvation did their work. In the spring of 1864, food rations were abruptly cut back to retaliate against the Confederate prisoners for stories of tortured and starved Union prisoners. Hearing of the conditions at Johnson's Island, some Confederates decided to attempt a daring rescue of their comrades by capturing the Federal gun-boat *Michigan* standing on guard in Sandusky Bay.

Two men emerged to lead the plan: John Yates Beall, known as "The Pirate of Lake Erie" and Captain Charles H. Cole, who claimed that he was an officer in the Confederate Navy, but who had been discharged from the Tennessee Infantry for "chronic lying."

In a labyrinthine plot, Cole posed as a rich oilman from Pennsylvania living at the posh West House in Sandusky. He spent money lavishly, entertaining the officers of the gun-boat *Michigan* and the Union officers of Johnson's Island. When he discovered that the Union officers couldn't be bribed, Cole decided to drug their drinks at dinner. After Cole gave notice that the Union officers were out of the way, Beall would seize the local steamer, *Philo Parsons,* pretend to collide with the *Michigan*, as if by accident, then board her and use her to free the inmates of Johnson's Island.

Captain Carter, commander of the *Michigan*, heard rumors of the plot and hired a man to infiltrate the conspirators' circle. In a comic-opera twist, on the morning of September 19, 1864, Beall and his men captured the steamer *Philo Parsons* right on schedule, but Beall found that there was not enough fuel aboard to carry out the plot. The *Parsons* returned to Middle Bass Island. At this point the side wheeler *Island Queen* steamed by carrying about 100 passengers, including some soldiers who were on their way to Toledo to be mustered out. Apparently fearing that the *Island Queen* would compromise the operation, the conspirators boarded her.

Engineer Henry Haines of the *Island Queen* was ordered out of the engine room, but instead fought with the boarders. The engineer was shot point-blank, leaving him a face full of powder marks, which he carried with him to the grave 13 months later. Although obviously wounded, Haines was put back at his post since he was essential to the operation of the ship. The conspirators scuttled the *Island Queen*, then realized that the signal for the attack on the *Michigan* was not coming. They put the passengers ashore, set the *Parsons* adrift, and ran for Canada.

Beall was arrested at Toronto and shot as a spy in New York, He was only 22 years old. John Wilkes Booth was a good friend of Beall and he was enraged by Lincoln's refusal to commute the death sentence. Cole was never tried. It has been suggested that he was a Federal spy.

Wayne Pfaff, originally a native of Sandusky, found the following unusual tale in the course of researching his family's history. Capt. Henry Haines was his great-great Grandfather.

"A curious story told by a number of well-known and respected people here has revived much interest in Spiritualism. This story, as told by those mentioned to the correspondent of *The New York Times*, is as follows:

"Mrs. Haines was the wife of Capt. Henry Haines, who gained historical distinction for his part in the repulse of the Confederate raiders who attempted to release the prisoners of war from the United States prison on Johnson's Island, in Sandusky Bay, during the rebellion. Mr. Haines was chief engineer of the steamer *Island Queen*, a passenger vessel, which the confederates attempted to seize to transport the prisoners to Canada. Mr. Haines fought those who boarded the boat, and was shot in the face with a pistol bullet, a portion of the flesh being torn away and the skin about the wound filled with particles of powder. For his bravery he received a personal letter of commendation from the War Department.

"He died a few years ago [He actually died in October, 1895, only 6 months before this strange incident.] Mrs. Haines and her daughter, Mrs. John Ohlemacher, also a widow, have since occupied the homestead, in the north wing of which Capt. Haines died. His room has never been used since his death, and has been entered but seldom. The furnishings today are as they were when the Captain died. Mrs. Ohlemacher entered the room Thursday to dust the furniture, and upon glancing at the pier glass which stands near the bed, she says she saw outlined upon it the features of her father, as perfectly and distinctly as in a photograph. The picture was true to life in every detail, even the pits made by the removal of the burnt powder showing plainly on the face. Mrs. Ohlemacher says she stood for a moment in amazement before the picture, and then summoned a servant and sent for Mrs. Haines, who entered, looked at the picture, and burst into tears. Mother and daughter stood for a time and gazed in astonishment at the likeness, and then called in some of the neighbors, among whom were ex-Councilman Henry Harris and his wife, Major Thomas White, Mrs. White [Mrs. Haines' niece] and several others who had known Capt. Haines intimately in life, and all of whom pronounced the picture perfect in every respect.

"Mrs. Haines touched the picture with her finger and found she could not erase it. An hour later, however, it began to fade, and soon completely disappeared, a mist seeming to rise from the glass as the picture dissolved, and as the last faint lines faded from view there came upon the glass seven clear and distinct taps, four in succession, then a pause, and three more taps, which were interpreted to mean 'good-bye.'

"The Haines family are not Spiritualists, but claim to be satisfied that no human agency had anything to do with the picture. Their only regret now is that they did not at once have the strange likeness reproduced by a photographer, which would have been done had there been suspicion of its temporary character."[3]

Mr. Pfaff tells me that most of the family furniture has been scattered. The strange mirror has now vanished.

THE GHOST-CHILD OF CENTRAL AVENUE

This touching story was written by W.W. Higgins of Circleville.

An old friend of mine told me this story several years ago. I'll just call her Dorothy. When she was a very small child, sometime before the First World War, her family moved into a charming little house on Central Avenue in Athens, Ohio. Many odds and ends had been left in the cellar and her father busied himself clearing them out and making necessary repairs and improvements.

Dorothy's bedroom was a small garret room on the second floor, which her mother had decorated especially for her. The first night she slept in that room, Dorothy had a frightening experience. She was just beginning to drowse off to sleep when a small child-like voice whispered pathetically, "Give back the ball." Dorothy was wide awake in an instant and began to cry. Her mother came up and soothed her, Dorothy told her about the voice. "Just a dream," her mother said. She stayed with Dorothy until she finally fell asleep.

The next night the same thing happened. Dorothy heard the plaintive little voice crying, "Give back the ball." Again she cried out and again her mother came and soothed her until she went to sleep. When it happened again on the third night, her father and mother both appeared. Her father was very concerned. Dorothy insisted that it was not a dream — she really had heard a voice. Worried and perplexed, her father went back downstairs.

The next morning he saw the elderly man next door pottering about in his garden and engaged him in conversation. He asked the neighbor what the family had been like who had formerly lived in the house. The old man shook his head. It was a sad story! A young woman and her little boy had lived there. The husband had been killed in the mines. The little boy was very thin and pale — almost otherworldly, as the old man described him. "He sometimes played under that tree over there in your side yard," the old fellow said.

"One night." he continued, "the little boy took sick. The doctor came but could do nothing for him. Toward morning the poor child died. Shortly afterward, the mother moved away. Very sad."

Dorothy's father listened, appalled at this strange little tragedy. "Did the child ever play with a ball?" he asked the elderly neighbor. "Yes, he did," the old man replied, "a large ball of red India-rubber."

Suddenly Dorothy's father remembered that, among the odds and ends in one corner of the cellar, there was a large red rubber ball. He carried it up from the cellar and placed it in the fork of the tree in the side yard. The next morning the ball was gone and Dorothy never heard the pathetic little voice again.

Was it a ghost-child who had returned to claim his ball? What happened to the ball in the tree? Dorothy couldn't say, but she remembered the strange occurrence vividly and she recounted it often for the rest of her long life. As she has since passed away, perhaps she now knows the answers.

PRESIDENT HARDING AND THE FINCH OF DOOM

At the Harding Home in Marion, the gardens are filled with Mrs. Harding's favorite flowers, exquisite two-tone pink roses. The house itself is painted a cool green and white. A lattice-work porch shades the side door. Inside, it is as if the Hardings had just stepped out to the offices of *The Marion Star*.

The Hardings lived in the house for over 20 years until Mr. Harding was elected to the Senate. It was here that he conducted his famous Front Porch Campaign. Since the Hardings put most of the furnishings into storage when they went to Washington and did not live in the house again, Site Manager Melinda Gilpin estimates that 98% of the furnishings are original. Here is the waffle iron to make the waffles Mr. Harding loved with chipped beef and gravy, Mr. Harding's Sears catalog bicycle, a fragile octagonal lace food cover painted with bluebirds of happiness, meant to keep flies off food, and Mrs. Harding's ermine cape.

Several pieces in the house suggest Mrs. Harding's mystical interests. One is an unusual chair carved with a cut-out crescent moon and cataloged by the original curator as a "medium's chair." Another is Mrs. Harding's most precious jewel: a four-leaf clover in a glass case given to her as a good-luck charm by a disabled veteran.

Mrs. Harding was deeply superstitious. The daughter of an overbearing bully, she looked to the occult for power, for the illusion that she could control her life. She came to believe that there was some sort of magical symbol on her forehead: the Star of Destiny, a sign of her mystical fortune. She visited Camp Chesterfield, a spiritualist center in Indiana. As an Ohio's senator's wife, she consulted astrologers in Columbus and Cleveland. She startled her niece by declaring, "You cannot count on anything in this world, but you can always count on the stars. The stars never fail you." She had little enough she could count on in this world, except that Warren would be unfaithful to her.

In Washington, she was introduced (by a Mrs. Woodyard!) to astrologer and clairvoyant Madame Marcia, who would become the lodestar of her life. It is possible that the medium's chair was used by Madame Marcia in her White House sessions with the First Lady.

In the same bedroom as the medium's chair is one of the more unusual artifacts at the Harding House—Petey, the Finch of Doom, a small brownish bird, stuffed and wired to a perch under a glass bell. He was just a plain finch when he was given to Mrs. Harding after she became First Lady. The irony was, Mrs. Harding, who loved most animals, *hated* birds. However, Petey was a gift from a political ally of Harding and could not be refused. Mrs. Harding saw one bright spot. She called the bird "Petey" for her wastrel first husband whom everyone had called Pete, naming "one birdbrain after another," as she told a friend.

The night before President and Mrs. Harding were to leave on a tour of Alaska, Mrs. Harding covered Petey's cage as she always did. After the cage was covered, Petey began to sing. The superstitious Mrs. Harding saw the bird's song as a Death Omen.

Petey was right.

President Harding, anxious and morose about the soon-to-break Teapot Dome scandal, showed signs of severe heart disease during the Alaskan trip. On the return trip, his doctor thought he'd eaten some bad crabs, but privately two of the other doctors aboard wired for a heart specialist to meet the train at San Francisco. The President was put to bed at a San Francisco hotel where he suddenly collapsed and died on August 2nd, 1923, fulfilling Madame Marcia's prediction of "sudden death" if he was elected President.

When the President's doctors pleaded with Mrs. Harding for an autopsy, she refused, which gave rise to the ugly rumors that she had poisoned her husband to avert the brewing scandal. Given Harding's history of high blood pressure, the doctors gave the cause of death as "Apoplexy" or stroke. Today, most doctors think that Harding died of a series of heart attacks.

Bizarre events shadowed the President's death. As the train bearing Harding's casket rolled across the country, it was haunted by strange weather. In Cheyenne there were huge dust and lightning storms; in Nebraska, an unexpected shower of huge hailstones, near cyclone-force winds, and a rainbow.[4] Back in Marion, the famous "haunted clock" that still hangs on the stairs landing stopped at 10:32 p.m., at the precise time President Harding breathed his last in California.

While President Harding's body reposed in a holding vault until his now-famous tomb could be built, the military honor guards were troubled by a series of annoyances such as stones thrown at the vault, a bugle blowing at midnight, and ghostly noises by "prowlers." Soldiers caught glimpses of a running man and several times chased and shot at him, but no one was ever caught or charged. The Commander suggested that the disturbances might be intended to break the morale of the guards or that they were a cover for flower thefts in the cemetery. Oddly enough, the events above could be typical ghost or poltergeist activity. It is difficult to believe that anyone living, no matter how malicious, would expose themselves to gunfire in the dark.[5]

Mrs. Harding probably gave the bird away after she left the White House. For a bird of ill-omen, Petey had *some* good luck. Petey outlived Mrs. Harding who died just 16 months after her husband. For a Finch of Doom, he looks surprisingly fresh and unruffled.

The Harding Home is a remarkable step back in time and tribute to the Hardings. President Harding has been termed "the worst American president." But this may be more the result of muckraking books and article that appeared after his death, blaming him for the disgraceful actions of some of his Cabinet members, the so-called "Ohio Gang." He was widely respected and extremely popular in his lifetime. Harding's administration slashed taxes, established the Federal Budget Bureau, and was responsible for developing the Veterans Bureau, to reform the system of care given to disabled veterans. His administration dedicated the Tomb of the Unknown Soldier and saw the postwar depression give way to a new surge of prosperity. Harding openly advocated civil rights, at a time when it was certainly not fashionable. Harding was also the first president elected with women's suffrage.

Harding himself always stressed the influence his wife had on his career and his deep respect for her intelligence and judgment. Mrs. Harding was the first First Lady to fly in an airplane, hold a substantive press conference, make a movie, and vote for her husband. She fully supported the independence of women. She worked for veterans' rights and animal rights.

It seems fitting that Petey shares the room with the medium's chair since they are both symbols of Mrs. Harding's sad determination to wrench power from the stars. Scientists tell us the songbird dreams of singing. Perhaps in some alternate universe, Petey, the Finch of Doom, still trills his liquid song.

GHOSTS ALONG THE MAUMEE:
Phantoms at Ft. Meigs

We're all dead men on leave.
-Eugene Levine-

Thanks to Dr. Larry Nelson, Site Manager of the Fort Meigs
State Memorial. The views expressed in this story do not reflect the
views of the Ohio Historical Society.

Imagine an Ohio February in 1813. The United States is at
war once again with England. The war is going badly. There is
every indication that the British are planning an invasion of
Ohio from Canada and that they will come by way of the
Rapids of the Maumee. On the hills overlooking the Maumee
River, soldiers under William Henry Harrison's command hack
holes in the frozen ground to build a fort. It is a matter of life
and death for these men and for the young country. In a few
months these soldiers will be looking across the river into the
mouths of the British cannons.

In late April, after 10 acres overlooking the river had been
enclosed with a wooden stockade, after the seven blockhouses
had been built, and the guns hauled into place, Harrison's
scouts reported that Tecumseh's warriors and British troops
under Col. Henry Proctor were massing at Fort Miami, only a
few miles away. Harrison immediately sent for reinforcements
and ordered Captain Wood, a young West Point graduate, to
prepare for a heavy British bombardment.

Wood gave orders to dig. Behind a screen of tents,
working in filthy weather and a sea of mud, the men burrowed

out holes and piled up dirt to form the "Grand Traverse." This was a 12-foot high redoubt running 300 yards across the length of the fort—an earthen fort-within-a-fort—to shield the American troops, supplies, and animals. A paroled British officer later reported to his superior that the Americans were "dug in like ground hogs."

The siege began on the morning of May 1st as Proctor's guns roared across the river. Before the smoke cleared, the tent screen was pulled down, revealing the Grand Traverse—to the baffled rage of Col. Proctor who had anticipated a quick surrender after pounding the Americans into submission with his artillery.

For 12 hours, the British guns thundered and the British mortars lobbed bombs that burst in midair. The mud inside Fort Meigs was pockmarked with craters. When at last the guns fell silent that first day, two men were dead and four were wounded, one of them Major Amos Stoddard, who died of his injuries nine days later.

On May 2nd and 3rd, over 1,000 British rounds rained down on Fort Meigs. The fort's well wasn't finished and since the men couldn't get to the river, they were reduced to drinking from puddles. Ammunition was also in short supply. Harrison offered a reward of a gill of whiskey for each 6-pound enemy cannonball. The thirsty troops recovered over one thousand useable rounds.

On May 3rd, there was a new threat, the British artillery got the range of Fort Meigs' ammunition magazine. Captain Wood rallied the men to heap dirt on the magazine, passing the whiskey around to fortify their courage. They needed every ounce of it, for just as they were finishing, the British gunners started lobbing red-hot cannon balls at the magazine in a last attempt to blow up the American's gunpowder.

On May 4th, Col. Proctor sent a messenger with a surrender demand. Harrison refused....

Fort Meigs is not a place to visit on a misty unsettled day of cold and wind. Or perhaps it is, to try to feel something of what the soldiers went through back in 1813. Walking past the immense barred gate, I felt if I closed my eyes, I could walk into the past. Clouds hung low and dark over the gravel path around the perimeter of the Fort.

Fort Meigs had three batteries for some 75 cannon. The Grand Battery was the largest, a platform of huge timbers pegged together, overlooking the river. I mounted the battery and walked boldly up to an edge that I couldn't see from above. Something spooked me and I backed away abruptly.

The gap in the wall triggered a panic. They can get in! I thought frantically. I had to remind myself that the guns were hauled away long ago; the enemy was long dead. The present was right in front of me: the river filled with walleye fishermen bobbing like duck decoys in their inner tubes, the swishing of the traffic on River Road, and a stream of cars crossing the modern bridge into Maumee. But all I could hear was the wind in my ears and the honking geese. All I could see was the flood plain, the willows with their ghostly traces of green against the winter-bare forest. This must have been a desolate place in winter with shivering sentries stamping their feet, staring across the river at the British batteries. We know that at least one sentry froze to death after only two hours on picket duty.

The wind was bitter. I watched the birds wheeling against the wind. I kept glancing around, feeling like I was being followed. At the next battery I was startled by the shock of an explosion. And suddenly the atmosphere, which had an earthly chill and quiet, shifted. I hurried on, thinking, "This frightens me. It shouldn't, but it does…"

Just past the Maumee rapids sign was a series of curved traverses. I saw a young man, a ghost, coming along the path between the traverses. He was amusing himself by alternately going up one slope, across the path, and up the next slope, picking his way back and forth, as if sent somewhere on an errand and taking his time about it. He wore a white shirt, open at the neck and breeches. He was a fresh-faced young man, as brash and confident as the adolescent American nation.

At the blockhouse overlooking the parking lot, I saw the shutters in the windows open and felt heads popping out of them. This was the most active area with the feeling of lots of men, lots of bustling. I heard the words "consairn" and "'s a gal," like some bad Leatherstocking dialect.

Walking farther, I saw blockhouses originally used for storage and for a jail. The gun emplacement in the back wall, facing the entrance road and parking lot made me even more anxious that "they" will get in. As I walked along, snapping photos of the large obelisk in the middle of the fort, I saw the same ghostly young man to the left of the obelisk on one of the redoubts beneath a large willow tree. He looked like he was waving his arms at me playfully and I tried to get a photo, but nothing showed up except a shroud of mist caught in the branches.

"How lonely it must be," I thought, feeling sorry for this young man. He seemed so solitary. I had felt a stirring of men in the corner blockhouse, but he was the only one I saw clearly, wandering by himself through the mists.

Immediately I caught the words, "They's good fellows." And I understood that there were others.

As I walked briskly around to the gateway leading back to the Interpretive Center, two fishermen came up from the river carrying their nets and a large walleye. It was back to the 21st century with a jolt.

After my visit, I spoke to Bob Kelly, who had some strange experiences with one of the blockhouses.

"I belong to a Civil War unit: the 9th Virginia, Company F. We always use Fort Meigs for our "School of Soldier," which is where we spend a weekend going over drills, marching, and getting ready for the upcoming year.

"This year [2003], we went out April 4-6. There were probably eleven of us out for the whole weekend. We got there Friday night. Now, whenever we go to a re-enactment, it rains! This time it was not only raining, but sleeting so we were allowed to stay in the blockhouse that overlooks the parking lot by the river.

"We've all heard some strange stories from Fort Meigs in the past, people seeing things. I don't know if things were disturbed with the construction [of the museum.] But this year, it seemed we were hearing more stories than before.

"We arrived about 6 or 7 p.m. By the time everybody got there, it was 9 or 9:30. We started settling down. We tried to build a fire outside. Then we built a fire inside and, of course, once we had it going, it got very smoky. We told one of the younger soldiers to go upstairs and open a top floor window. He went upstairs. As soon as he got to the top of the stairs, he let out a yell, and came running down. I've never seen a guy so white. He wasn't known to get scared. But he was shaking.

"He said he had looked over to the windows and one of the windows was already open. There was a figure standing in the window, holding a rifle. The figure was hazy and was wearing a War of 1812 uniform, a blue shell jacket, a coonskin cap.

"He said he wouldn't go back up there, so three of us went back up. I knew all of the windows were closed when we got there that evening. And the window was closed by the time we got back upstairs the second time.

"None of us slept well. We were also awakened by footsteps above us and the sounds of taps on the back of the blockhouse. Saturday night we sent other people upstairs to make sure the windows were open while the fire was burning. When we went to settle down for the night, the tapping on the walls started again. We also heard the footsteps above us and two gentlemen were awakened by sound of drums beating off in the distance, out in the fields. It sounded like a 'call to order' or 'formation' beat. A buddy of mine went out about a month ago to a History Channel filming and one of the British units had a drum beat just like it. It was used for roll call.

"That same night I had to get to go to the bathroom. So I walked to the restroom which is very far away, especially at 2:30 in the morning. As I was walking, I heard a voice call out, 'Get over here, we need you. We need you now!' I knew everybody else was sleeping. I turned around and started heading back to the blockhouse. I saw that the top window was open again. I asked the guys who called out to me. I thought something was wrong. But everybody was sleeping. I woke everybody up since I thought they were calling me. But it wasn't them—it was somebody else....

"After that everybody all decided to go to the bathroom in a group. When we got back, the window was closed again. Yes, this year really seemed to be more active...."

Several months after my visit, I spoke with John Destatte. John is one of the big guns at Fort Meigs. He interprets a military artillerist, demonstrating the loading and firing of cannons and is also a recruiter for the Fort Meigs Volunteer Association. Altogether he has worked at Fort Meigs for some 13 years.

John told me, "Listen, I'm one of the resident skeptics. I just like to go up there and sit sometimes. I would like to sit out at the Fort one night and meet one of these guys. I would like to shake hands, have them tell me their stories. But to this point they haven't decided to reveal themselves."

Despite his own skepticism, he has heard numerous stories, some from experienced volunteers, some from re-enactors, and some from first-time visitors.

"One fascinating thing about Fort Meigs is we have lots of information on specific individuals who were at the Fort and on the people who perished.

"I like to take one particular individual's information, try to find out what unit he was with, and weave him into a story. Like Amos Stoddard. He was in charge of the artillery. He was injured on the first day of battle by a British shell and died of lockjaw nine days later. You can see his monument inside the Fort today. Some people think he was moved from Fort Meigs back home to Kentucky. There's a question about that. I personally like the idea that the family brought him home and that is why his soul still haunts the fort today.

"That place is polluted with graves. The interior is nothing but a mass grave to begin with. Of course, this is a prehistoric Indian site as well and Captain Daniel Cushing, in 1813, made reference to huge amounts of human remains found there when they were building the fort. They thought it was the site of an Indian battle."

In a macabre passage Cushing recorded unearthing over two dozen skulls under a huge stump near blockhouse #3. He wrote, "In walking around this garrison on the earth that has been thrown up it was like walking on the sea shore upon the old mussel shells, only in this case, human bones."[1]

John added, "Oddly enough, where that stump was dug up, a lot of people get some really strange feelings." He says that various visitors have reported an "Indian presence" in the area of blockhouse #3, which would tie in with the skulls under the tree stump.

Then there's a spirit who has been often seen at the west end of the fort. Sometimes when re-enactors are sitting in camp, visiting at night, they'll see the soldier walking on top of the traverses, usually out of the corner of their eye.

"Wow! That guy's got some really good kit!" they say, meaning, his uniform is beautifully accurate: everything looks worn in all the right places, like he really could have been at the Fort during the battle. But if they crawl up on the traverse to see him more closely, there's nobody around.

"We don't know what this is about," John said. "We do know about soldiers who used to stand on traverses, watching the British guns, trying to figure out where the shells will land, and call out a warning.

"One individual [Alfred M. Lorrain] wrote a memoir and talks about a militiaman on top of the traverses. He calls him the Shot & Shell Guy. He tells of how he could stand on a traverse and, by watching the smoke exiting the barrel of a British gun, could tell where the ball or shell would land. He'd call out, 'Blockhouse number one!' Or 'Look out, main battery!' He got quite proficient. But, Lorrain wrote, 'one shot came which defied all his calculations. Silent, motionless, perplexed, he stood for a moment, and then he was swept into eternity...the fatal messenger was traveling in the direct line of his vision.'[2]

I asked John about uniforms at Fort Meigs. The ghostly young man had been wearing only a shirt and breeches or pants rolled up below the knee. The militia all wore regular War of 1812 uniforms and there was a military tradition that men would not be seen outside without at least some kind of vest and a hat or forage cap. But, he added, when the troops first arrived in February, they had been walking through icy swamps, often breaking through the ice and losing their kit. Some of them had very little clothing. Many more men died of disease and exposure than from enemy action.

John painted a vivid picture of life at Fort Meigs. Much of the interior would have been filled with six-by-six floorless A-frame tents. No one slept in the blockhouses, not even General Harrison. One soldier who was with George Washington at Valley Forge came to serve at Fort Meigs. He reported that Valley Forge was not so bad, in comparison.

"There were supposed to be six men to each tent, but not all six would be there at once. They would rotate shifts. Two would be sleeping, two would be on guard duty and two would be working, drilling with muskets, practicing gunnery, constructing batteries, shoveling and digging the traverses. Drill, drill, and more drill. Maybe 20-25% of the men would be down with dysentery or fever. We see the Fort today with grass on the inside. In 1813 the men were up to their knees in mud. This is clay soil and it is terrible. It was like a swamp. When the museum was being excavated we found a British bomb that had sunk into clay and exploded, but the fragments were held together by the mud. In those kinds of conditions, people just stayed in their tents. All the open sinks [latrines] were outside the walls, but with that many sick men inside, unable to move.... I can't imagine what this place smelled like."

John often finds visitors who don't know the history of the site who experience remarkably accurate visions.

"If you stand at the Woods Battery, the furthest one away from the Museum and look down the hill, you'll see a ravine off to the south end of the fort. That hill is called Kentucky Hill and it's where the Kentucky militia buried their dead. If you know where to look, there are still earthworks from the British gun batteries in the side of that ravine. A major battle was fought in that area when a group of American soldiers under Col. Miller were sent out to silence those guns. They were almost overtaken by a group of British soldiers and their Indian allies. Reinforcements were sent out from the Fort and the Indians were driven off. Many people were killed there.

"About five or six years ago a kid was sitting out there one night by himself. He went home and told his father, 'There's something happening up there at the Fort down in the trees.' He heard drums, horses, fifes, shooting. His father checked with us, but there were no events going on at all. [Historically] there were no other engagements outside of the Fort. If somebody was going to hear drums and horses or if there were going to be restless people outside the Fort, that would be where you'd find them…"

Having spoken with John for nearly an hour, I decided to take a chance. I explained the various things that I had seen, finishing with the young man waving his arms beneath the willows. What he told me chilled my blood:

At dawn on May 5th, Colonel Dudley and a detachment of raw Kentucky recruits were ordered to go across the river and spike the British guns, then return. They accomplished this mission, then, flush with victory, instead of returning to Fort Meigs, the soldiers were lured towards Fort Miami. They fought a desperate battle with Indian warriors and Col. Proctor's troops by what is now the Maumee Library. Dudley's men were almost all captured and either killed or marched to Ft. Miami where they were put into a stockade. There the Indians began to slaughter them until Tecumseh intervened and stopped the massacre.

The men still in the Fort watched in horror as Dudley's men were lured into the trees. They could see, although Dudley could not, that they were being drawn into a trap. Some men stood on top of the traverses, shouting and waving their arms, crying, 'Dudley! Return!' Some of Dudley's troops saw the men waving and shouting and, thinking they were being cheered in triumph, went forward to their deaths.

Of the 846 men that Colonel Dudley started out with, fewer than 170 made it back across the Maumee to Fort Meigs.

Was I wrong in thinking that the young man waving on the traverse was a playful spirit? Could he have been a spotter, a shot-and-shell man? Was he waving to warn his fellows of incoming shells?

Or in helpless terror, for Dudley's doomed brigade?

The traverses at Fort Meigs' walls did their work well, baffling Proctor's troops into a stalemate. Spring planting season was coming. His militiamen wanted to go home to their families. Tecumseh's warriors began to drift away. Proctor lifted the siege.

Several months later Fort Meigs was stripped and dismantled, leaving only a small supply base as Harrison marched into Canada to the fateful Battle of the Thames where Proctor abandoned his own men and Tecumseh was killed. The threat of British invasion was ended.

Today Fort Meigs has been re-created as it was during the pivotal siege of May 1813. It is the largest log fort in the United States. The site includes an amazing museum full of uniforms, artifacts, and quotes from the long-dead soldiers who once manned walls very like these in a life-and-death struggle against the British.

History is filled with epic battles and sweeping political events. Individual participants often vanish, submerged by the tide of time. At Fort Meigs you can come face to face with the terrifying reality of warfare and of siege. Yet, at a site where so many lives were lost, where so much was at stake, it all comes down to the remnant of a single human individual.

I sometimes think about the young man beneath the willow trees and wonder if his body lies in a grave within the fort or if he was one of Dudley's unfortunates buried at "Kentucky Knoll." Is it perpetually 1813 where he exists? What is it like for him and his "fellows"? Do they sit around a spectral campfire and swap yarns? Is he hungry? Is he cold? It worries me.

6

DEAD ZONES:
They live again...

Yes, there's something the dead are keeping back.
-Robert Frost-

Shelby, Union, Van Wert Counties. I call them "Dead Zones." These are the segments of the state where I've had trouble finding stories until some fateful visit where I make a connection with a helpful librarian or the local keeper of ghost stories. Here are the stories that waited to be resurrected....

THE SPECTRES OF SHELBY

The architecture of Sidney has always intrigued me: the flamboyant flaring blue mosaic sunburst of the People's Federal Savings and Loan Association building, the last major commission of the great architect Louis H. Sullivan, the narrow brownstones trimmed with fanciful gothic gargoyles, and a stone castle complete with turrets and statues. It is a great deal of architecture packed into one medium-sized city.

The Shelby County Historical Society is no mere embalmer of the past; it is a living, vital entity. Which makes it all the more ironic that its offices and museum are housed in a former funeral home, The William A. Ross Jr. Historical Center. In the fall of 2001, Rich Wallace, then President of the Shelby County Historical Society and author of the outstanding county history, *Voices from the Past*, took me on a whirlwind tour of three haunted spots around Sidney, starting with the Monumental Building. The Gothic-style building was dedicated in 1876 to commemorate the veterans of the Civil War.

The building has been so beautifully remodeled and sees so much traffic in the course of its daily life that it would be difficult for spirits of the past to linger. Yet a spirit may have been responsible for the building's continued existence.

In 1993, the GAR building was in a precarious state. It was the oldest Veteran's building in Ohio and, while the downstairs had served the veterans, the upstairs had been a Masonic hall and a theatre. The roof was decayed and the entire fabric of the building was in danger.

The Sidney City Manager Bill Barlow, inspected the building. He didn't think much could be done. Discouraged, he went home and brooded, thinking, "What are we going to do?" He went to bed and then—he swears it was not a dream—he was awakened by a Civil War soldier, "Sgt. Fair." The soldier said to him, "Something must be done. Do not dishonor the Civil War dead by letting this shrine fall into further decline."

Inspired by the dream, he recommended the use of Community Development Block Grant funds to save the building. It took $350,000 to seal the windows and repair the roof. Mr. Barlow convinced City Council that it would be a good investment since the city needed a new, more secure courtroom.

The courtroom was originally the Opera Hall. The layout of the room has been retained, including the flying balcony where at least one ghostly spectator still sits. The stage has been replaced by the Judge's Bench, flanked by the dramatic proscenium pillars, giving justice the air of a Greek Tragedy. The dramatic paintings on the domes have been freed from under three layers of wallpaper.

A life-like painted bronze statue of a Union soldier stands, ever vigilant, in a niche high under the point of the roof of the Monumental Building. He was placed there in 1900 and was dubbed "Sgt. Baker" by some. No one knows why. There never was a real Sergeant Baker from Shelby County who served in the Union Army.

309 Shelby County men marched off to serve their country and never came back. It is fitting that the spirit of one of them returned to save this building.

Our next stop was the Ross Historical Center. Rich stood back and I prowled quietly around the house, feeling that I ought to not make a lot of noise. In the dining room, I thought, "He heard footsteps." I was about to say something then thought, "It's like hanged ghosts, there are *always* footsteps..." So I kept my mouth shut, not wanting to sound like a cliché. While the rooms were full of photographs and exhibits on local history, there was very little in the way of a haunting.

That changed when we went down the stairs to the basement. I asked Rich to leave the lights off. An exit sign glowing over the door was the only light, other than the last daylight shining dimly through the dusty windows at the front of the house. My head felt heavy and the familiar exhaustion began to creep over me.

"Who got in at the door?" I muttered, nodding at the door leading outside from the basement office.

"I was hoping you could tell *me*," he replied.

Walking into the other, darker side of the basement, there was an abrupt shift. I saw a thing like a galvanized tin watering trough full of ice. And there was a wicker casket, used to transport bodies to the funeral home.

I heard a voice crying, "Help me! I'm not dead!" I began to go under, to be submerged in the world of the dead, but not quite dead. The world of the ones who desperately wanted to go on living.

At that I was too exhausted to go on. We went back upstairs and out into the still-light evening. We got in the car and Rich told me about how he was working in his basement office one Sunday night. He had locked the door; the security system was on. He heard footsteps on the floor above his head. He started getting nervous. Then they stopped and he decided to go upstairs to check. As he started up the stairs, there was a huge crash from above. In the middle of the floor he found a large poster-size calendar which had somehow unhooked itself from the wall and sailed into the middle of the dining room. The basement area where I had heard the voice, he mentioned, had been the embalming area.

Our last stop was a brownstone house. I've always felt that brownstone exteriors were a bit sinister, like something out of the horror movie *Rosemary's Baby*. This particular former house, while embellished with macabre carvings of gargoyles and ferocious creatures with beaks and claws, housed a charmingly feminine gift shop.

I climbed the stairs to the upper floors. A makeshift plywood door closed off the second and third floors. There was nothing particularly frightening about the rooms. They were mostly empty and my footsteps echoed faintly throughout the floor. Then I heard a baby crying and I froze.

"Why does it always have to be a baby?" I thought wearily. At the back of the house was a tiny room, with windows overlooking the backyard. A woman cradling an infant was standing in the window, her back to me. As I watched, she began to pace back and forth.

I can scarcely bear the sound of a living crying baby, let alone a ghostly one. I began to pick my way down the steep and twisting staircase. Suddenly I found myself wrapped in a woman of the early 1900s. She was being forcibly marched down the stairs by someone, sent somewhere she didn't want to go. I came hurtling down the stairs and she swept out of me and out of the front door. She was not carrying the baby. It has haunted me since. What happened to the child?

THE WRAITHS OF RAYMOND

Union County seemed an impossible place to find stories until the Marysville and Raymond Public librarians told me about Pam Jones. She is the President of the Raymond-Newton Historical Society and she graciously shared the following tales:

There was a house that sat in the middle of Newton—now the town of Raymond in Union County. This was a one and a half-story house built in the late 1800s in the horse and buggy days. In the early 1900s, the family who lived there (I'll call them the Brown* family) would see a gentleman sitting on their front porch whenever they drove up to the house. Just as they got to wondering who he was and what he wanted and as soon as they walked up the front walk, he disappeared. It was maddening!

Some of their friends said, "Why don't you just go really slow, then follow him?" So they walked up the walk very slowly, so as not to frighten the ghost. They saw the ghostly man go into the front door and through the house. But for all that they were too scared to follow him.

"Listen," said the helpful friends (who didn't seem inclined to investigate for themselves), "next time just take two or three of you, and follow him in the door. Follow him until he isn't there anymore!" The Browns took this advice and they followed the ghost through the house, pacing nervously behind the apparition, step by step down into the cellar (although it took all the nerve they had!) and they stood there, dumb-founded, as he walked through the basement's stone wall.

Sometimes a shock like that will dissolve your fears. And after the incident in the basement, the Browns kind of got used to seeing the ghost on the porch. They knew he wasn't hostile. Several years later, when they were adding a back porch to the house, they dug up the foundation. And they found bones—human bones—behind the rock foundation wall where the ghost had walked through.

Pam is also the librarian at the elementary school.

"I used to have play practices for the fifth grade. I was there one evening after everyone had left—I thought!

"I was shutting down the lights when I heard a toilet flush in the old part of the building, built in 1914. 'Darn kids!' I thought, thinking that somebody was hiding in the restroom. But I couldn't find anybody anywhere!

"I shouted, 'Is there anyone there?' Silence.

"Boy, I was really shaken! Until I remembered that other people have heard the sounds of children through the wall. It's like they're talking, but you can't distinguish what they're saying. Now whenever I come into school after hours I always say, 'Hi, guys! I have just come to do some work.'

"This school was built in 1914 although there has been a school on the site for 150 years. Additions were made to the 1914 building in the 1940s and 1990s. No telling what era these things come from!

"My library, which was really just an oversized classroom, was in the oldest part of the building. Occasionally I would miss things. Once I had put a book I needed on my desk. Later when I went to get the book, it had disappeared. I started searching for it. I knew I had put it on my desk. As soon as I said, 'I can't understand where that book went!' I heard a loud BANG and the book I was looking for landed on a shelf. Now I am in a new library addition and it doesn't feel the same without the warmth of the lingering kids.

"I know people say, 'That's just an old building. You're hearing pipes clanking.' In a few years they're going to tear the oldest building down and I'm actually afraid about that. I don't know what's going to happen to whatever or whoever's there when it's torn down. As long as they behave, they will always be welcomed to the new library"

"We have a house in the little town of Peoria that has been continually haunted for the last 30 years and perhaps many years before that. The people who live there have seen a little girl very distinctly. She just stands beside the bed and looks at you. She is about 6-8 years old, has long dark hair, and wears a long pinafore like a child from the early 1900s.

"There is also an old man who continually walks *across* the owners' bed. When they first moved there, he was just a dark shadow that went across the ceiling, from right to left, and then disappeared. After that he got more distinct. He actually makes footprints in the bed as he travels across.

"'Doesn't that wake you up?' I've asked the owners. 'Oh, yes, every time!' they said. One evening the man of the house was putting on his shoes when something flew across the room and grabbed his leg. On another occasion their daughter said someone tried to push her down the stairs. But mostly the ghosts just come and go. They've just got a lot of traffic in their bedroom but they just kind of live with the ghosts."

RETURN TO ELGIN
Van Wert

This rare Van Wert County ghost story was very kindly shared by an anonymous reader.**

Seventeen years ago, my father passed away. I was 10 years old at the time. My father had had diabetes and as the years went by he'd have blackouts and he'd shuffle when he walked. Sometimes he'd misjudge a doorway and end up bumping into the wall.

In August 1978, my mom started talking about hearing voices at night. She said it was two people having a conversation. She heard it every night for about 2 weeks. It was around that time my dad had a stroke. He died one week later in the hospital.

Immediately, things started to happen. The first night, my niece and I were sleeping on the floor and we both heard the sound of shuffling. We talked about it amongst ourselves, but let it go.

About two weeks after Dad died, while I was lying on the couch watching TV, I heard what sounded like a mouse digging in the wall. I got up and got a flashlight and started flashing it into corners. Above the couch was one of those registers that opens from the upstairs bedroom. For some reason, I flashed the light up the register. What I saw scared the hell out of me. I sat there staring into the face of my dad. I can

**Please contact me at the publisher's address so I can get you a free copy of this book.

remember those blue eyes. I dropped the flashlight and ran to wake my mom up. She thought I was having delusions.

It soon got to the point where I would often hear the bed squeak as if somebody turned over in it. My mom thought I was going crazy until one day Mom called to me. I came out of the bathroom and her mouth dropped open. While sitting at the kitchen table, she heard somebody turn over several times in bed (the bedroom was straight across from the kitchen) she thought I had lain down on the bed. Finally my mom was starting to see and hear stuff.

As time went on, both my Mom and I would *feel* the pressure of somebody's hand on our shoulder, as if somebody was trying to comfort us. I felt that every so often until the day I moved out (six years after Dad died.)

Things began to get more strange. We got a mixed breed pup in 1981. The dog followed me everywhere. He always slept on my bed. One night while doing homework, Rocky jumped off the bed and started growling. He just stood there looking at a blank wall. His hair stood on end and he was so agitated! This dog was snarling at *something*. At that point I don't remember what happened. I opened my eyes and the room was black. I could hear a fan running but somebody was lying next to me. I was about ready to scream when I realized that I was downstairs in bed with my Mom. I have no idea of how I got there. My brother, who was visiting at the time, found himself on the living room couch. He had been sleeping in his old room upstairs.

It got to the point that I hated to be alone in the house. The dog would go off at bare walls, at the couch, etc. I heard somebody say my name (it wasn't my dad's voice) several times.

We finally moved out in 1984. Once we moved, it all stopped. It was only after we moved that Mom told me that Dad always used to joke that he wanted to be buried in Goodwin Cemetery in Elgin so he wouldn't have far to walk back (we lived a very short ways from the cemetery.) I guess Dad kept his word.

7

STAGE FRIGHTS:
Theatre ghosts and film phantoms

The curtain, a funeral pall,
Comes down with the rush of a storm,
-Edgar Allan Poe

REVIVALS AT THE RENAISSANCE

There were strange vibes in the air when I arrived at the Renaissance Theatre that morning, but not from the ghosts. Someone was practicing rollicking Sousa marches and show tunes on the Mighty Kearns Wurlitzer organ. As an organist myself, I love theatre organ, but for a ghost hunter, it's a trifle distracting. Perhaps, I thought, I should request something from *Phantom of the Opera*, just to set the mood....

I found the office of Director of Marketing, Martha Fort. She had made the appointment for this particular day since a staff member with a story to tell would be available then. But I hadn't expected the organist, a team of men washing the windows, a whole group of staff members waiting to tell me their ghostly experiences, and the wholly unexpected but pleasant surprise of seeing my second cousin and his wife, whom I hadn't seen in 15 years, who just happened to be at the theatre that morning.

For good measure, a newspaper reporter and photographer and TV crew with lights and cameras were there to interview the staff and follow me through the theatre. Readers of my books know that I don't allow anyone else to walk with me through a site since it's difficult or nearly impossible to feel any ghosts with other people tagging along. Things were hopping at the Renaissance! And the attention rattled me considerably. I began to feel like one of the people stuffed into Groucho Marx's cabin in *A Night at the Opera.*

While the camera crew started interviewing staff members, I began my tour of the site in the balcony. With its striking coral and turquoise color scheme, the original brocade wall panels, and a multitude of gilt detailing, the Renaissance is a tribute to the many volunteers who have worked hard to keep the grand baroque-style building alive.

The Renaissance was born as the Ohio Theatre in Mansfield in1928. Built at a cost of $500,000, the theatre was brilliant with marble staircases, lead crystal chandeliers, and a Kimball theatre organ that went up and down on a lift. Despite near blizzard-like conditions, the *Mansfield News* reported that thousands thronged to the theatre for the initial performance on January 19, 1928 when the audience was treated to an organ recital, a newsreel, a two-reel comedy and three vaudeville acts. The theatre occupied center stage in Mansfield for over two decades, showing such films as *The Wizard of Oz*, and *Casablanca* and hosting headliner acts including Will Rogers, Fanny Brice, and magician Harry Blackstone, Sr.

When television accelerated the demise of the great movie palaces, the once-grand theatre slid into a seedy existence by 1979 as an X-rated movie house and was eventually shut down by public demand. The revival came when the Miss Ohio Scholarship Pageant was staged at the Ohio. Mansfield saw what the Ohio Theatre had been and could be again. A group that had been trying to save the old Madison Theater, just down the street, formed the non-profit Renaissance Theatre, Inc. A generous anonymous benefactor made the property available to this non-profit group and restoration began.

A $2.25 million capital improvements campaign refurbished the original seats, installed new lighting, sound, and stage equipment, purchased and restored the Kearns Wurlitzer theatre organ, and made other repairs and improvements. In December, 1991, the Board of Directors of the Renaissance

Theatre was presented with a memorable and generous Christmas gift—the deed to the theatre from their anonymous benefactor: The Fran and Warren Rupp Foundation.

Walking through the building, it was obvious that the theatre has had a lot of energy put into it. Even in the balcony there was a kind of swirling unrest, as if a ghostly audience were streaming in and out of the theatre. I caught glimpses of figures: a woman usher slumped, asleep, on a gilt-legged stool at the top of the balcony, a woman in a toque hat with a little plume, sitting bolt-upright near the front of the balcony, her attention focused on the empty stage.

One of the technicians had unlocked the projectionist booth and turned on the light for me. I heard whispering in the booth and I stumbled on the first step up. Then I heard a man say cheerily, "Mind your head!" I climbed into the booth and put my notebook on the rewinding table. Turning, I saw a ghostly man standing there, smiling.

"How ya doing?" I said, reflexively, smiling back.

The friendly ghost was an older man, with no special physical characteristics except his easy, affable manner. I got the name "Pete" or "Petey." He pottered around while I snapped some photos. As I headed back downstairs, I turned and waved to him.

"Bye bye!" he said brightly.

I made a tour down to the basement, up on the stage and beneath it, up the stairs to the dressing rooms, and back down into the basement, all the while dodging the TV crew interviewing staff members. I didn't want to accidentally overhear anything that would give me names or clues. I was soon to wish I *had* a clue!

In the basement, I wandered back into a dark area labeled "King Tut's Tomb." The only light shone through the doorway. By this time I had begun to feel agitated since I felt I had to rush through the theatre and not delay any of the many people who were waiting for me to complete my search.

"OK," I said into the darkness. "Don't keep me waiting!" A man's shadow loomed up on the wall behind my own.

Feeling a bit crowded, I decided to go back out into another room. "So show yourself," I grumbled.

"How's this, sweetie?" he said, leaning up against the door I'd just come through. I'm not sure if he actually said "sweetie." It was something slangy and he spoke with an arch familiarity. He was tall and thin and had a kind of misshapen or exaggerated jaw, what some people would call a lantern jaw. His cheeks were sunken beneath jutting cheekbones. It was a very old-fashioned face. I was so rattled that I didn't catch the rest of what he said and didn't write it down. Whatever it was, it was vulgar. I remember saying something to him in disgust and stalking away. I caught the name "Edward" or "Teddy."

As I moved on, I snapped more photos and poked my head into the darkness of the men's restroom. There was a ghostly man stretched full length, face down on the floor.

I went back to the main lobby. I got my photo taken for the newspaper, gave the reporter my contact numbers, and did an interview with the TV crew, including another foray into the projection booth, explaining about Pete.

The ghostly projectionist said, "Back again already?" and patted his projectors affectionately, as if they had been prize horses. He seemed very proud of the equipment.

Then I apologized to everyone for being such a crab and keeping them waiting. We all went up to the ballroom upstairs to tell and hear stories. There was Martha Fort, the Marketing Director and two of her administrative assistants, Scott Gross, Technical Director and Todd Kramer, Assistant Technical Director. To round out the group we had Mike Barnett, Facility Supervisor and his wife Jacki, who was Assistant Manager of the Ohio Theatre when it was a regular movie house.

I started out with the lady in the balcony, whom Martha recognized immediately. Then I mentioned the man in the projection booth, proudly showing off the projection equipment.

"That wasn't here originally," Scott said quickly. "It came from the Madison, a block away."

"Maybe he came along with it," I suggested. Everyone looked skeptical. Nobody knew who Pete was.

Edward or Teddy might have been Edward Rafter, the 48-year-old theatre manager who had come to Mansfield only six weeks before he became one of Richland County's unsolved murders.

The story had all the makings of a *film noir* thriller. As patrons watched *The Green Murder Case* on the big screen on the night of October 30, 1929, shots rang out. By some eerie coincidence, the scene on the screen was a shoot-out; most people thought the gunshots were part of the movie. Harry Delaney, the projectionist, knew better. He rushed downstairs to find Rafter lying in the office doorway. "They got me, Cap!" Rafter gasped, using his nickname for Delaney, then passed out. The telephone had been ripped from the wall and there were other signs of a struggle. Police believed that the gunman had been after the $700 in the safe. Rafter may have reached for his wallet for the safe combination or he may have lunged at the "yegg" as the murderer was called in the newspapers.[1]

The few witnesses produced conflicting descriptions. A salesman from Canton said the man wore a suit with the collar turned up and a slouch hat pulled down well over his face. A woman told officers that she saw a man at the theatre's entrance dressed in women's clothing: a dress of "light washable material with a fox fur piece about his neck. He wore a slouch hat and had a black mask over his face." Another woman saw a man with a fur piece around his neck fleeing the scene. Rafter lived long enough to state that he believed his killer was a black man, wearing men's clothing and a mask that covered his face, but not his neck. Perhaps there were two men: the lookout and the killer. The police were baffled. 75 years later, they still are.

Edward Rafter was shot in his office, which is now part of an open hall. I felt nothing there. This didn't particularly surprise me. Well-traveled areas often have been "overlain" by all the new traffic, so that nothing remains of the original event.

But I sensed that some in the group were disappointed, believing that I should have picked up the trauma where it occurred. Martha showed me a scrapbook with an article about Edward Rafter's murder. There was a photo of a man with a twisted jaw. My heart skipped a beat, but the photo was of Harry Delaney, the projectionist, pointing to the place Rafter was shot. Then Jacki, Mike, Scott. and Todd began to tell their stories and my heart sank further. I hadn't picked up on a single thing they had to say.

Jacki and Mike Barnett have worked at the Theatre in some capacity since 1974. Mike is Facilities Supervisor and Jacki is a volunteer. I explained about the few spots that made me uneasy like the orchestra pit, which just seemed full of tension.

Scott laughed, "Oh, there's lots of bad vibes there!" He explained that they'd been wrestling with the installation of a new lift for the theatre's organ and that it wasn't going smoothly.

When I mentioned a very angry man who told me to "get out!" Mike got excited.

"Did he tell you to 'leave' or 'get out'?"

I thought a minute. "He said, 'get out.'"

Mike told me about his first encounter with one of the ghosts in the theatre.

"This was before I was hired fulltime. I was building sets for summer shows. It was 3 a.m. I was all alone. I was down in that same area below the stage. I heard a man's voice, in an ordinary tone, say, 'Leave.' It was not threatening, but I packed up my stuff and went home. I didn't stay late by myself again."

Naturally, with a theatre that has seen so many musical performances, ghostly music has sometimes been heard.

Jacki told me her story.

"I worked here as Assistant Manager in 1974-5, when this was the Ohio Theatre, a movie house. John, the manager and I were in the office, which, incidentally, was where Edward Rafter was shot. We both heard a piano playing and young women giggling. It sounded like women in their twenties, not teenagers. The piano sounded like an old-time, tinny, ragtime piano. We went to the doors at the back of the theatre, thinking somebody had stayed after the last show and was screwing around. There was nothing and the noises stopped. We came back into the office and were working again when the music began to play again and we heard the giggling. We were scared witless! We crept over to the doors. It sounded like it was coming from the stage where there was an old grand piano. We took our flashlights and crept up on the stage, expecting to be engulfed at any moment. The movie screen was still down. We walked behind it only to find one small work light on and the piano still covered. We stood there for what seemed like an hour, looking at each other with the 'deer in the headlights' look.

"Then we heard a 'thud,' the sound a firm pillow would make hitting a wood floor. It came from the stairwell leading up to the dressing rooms. 'Should we call the police,' I asked John. 'I don't think the police are what we need,' he replied.

"John peeked around the door into the stairwell and clicked on the light. We would have stopped there but we heard a faint shuffling sound up the stairwell. We took deep breaths and started up the stairs. On the second floor we walked through a very cold spot. It was like walking through a cold tube of air. 'Oh my God, did you feel that?' I asked John. 'Is that weird or *what*?' he exclaimed. By this time I had goosebumps the size of chicken eggs.

"'This place gives me the creeps,' John muttered. I certainly was in agreement! We checked all the rooms and found no one. We were feeling creepier by the second. I said, 'I don't know about you...'

"'but we're out of here!' John finished.

"We raced back to the 'safety' of our office, not knowing at the time that a man had been murdered at that very spot. We were uneasy, but went back to work completing our nightly cash-out and reports. Within 10 minutes we heard a bang like a chunk of metal hitting the floor. We looked at each other and said in unison, 'Let's finish this tomorrow.'

"It was very rare after that, that either one of us worked alone to close up the theatre. When I was the last person out, it so creeped me out that I would turn off the lights and literally run out the door. The manager and I never had heard about any ghost sightings in the theatre, so we didn't weren't influenced by someone telling us what we might hear."

Jacki's husband Mike had a strange experience with a lighting fixture in the lower lobby. In August 2001, Mike was hired as Facility Supervisor. A pair of wall sconces hangs on either side of the arch that leads back to the ladies room and to the "Tomb."

Said Mike, "The right sconce was turned sideways at a 45-degree angle. Now these are solid brick walls, not plaster or wallboard where something could slide around. I straightened it, went back into my office, looked around, it's at a 45-degree angle again. I turned it back, went upstairs, came back, 45-degree angle again. I said out loud, 'OK, we can play this game.' So every day for two weeks, we played this game...."

"After the two weeks, I was the last person out of the building. I started saying 'Good night' as I walked through the auditorium with no lights except the 'Ghost Light.' The sconce has not turned since. I think they were testing me to see if I would take care of the building. Now I think that I have convinced them that I have the best interests of the Theatre at heart."

Scott Gross, an energetic and thoughtful young man, is the Technical Director, seeing to the details of lighting, sets and rigging and stage safety. He told a chilling story.

"It was one in the afternoon in December of 2002. Everybody was around. I was in the light booth working on cues for *The Nutcracker*. I was looking down at the light board when I thought I saw Todd walking across the stage. I looked up, thinking it was Todd." It wasn't.

Scott saw a woman in black walking across the stage. "My wife, who sews and does costuming, has trained me to notice details of clothing," he told me, explaining why he was able to describe the clothing in such detail. The woman in black wore what sounded like an early 1920s dress: black, with a raised waist with lace on the bodice, the lace forming a "V" in the front and the back. The dress was almost ankle length and he could see her high-heeled black lace-up boots. That was from the neck down. From the neck up, she had only a misty, smoky fog forming a suggestion of a head, wearing the suggestion of a hat with a suggestion of a veil. He saw both the front and back of her as she walked across the stage. She made no sound.

"She took about three or four steps, got to the 'ghost light' in the center of the stage and disappeared."

He described her disappearance in cinematic terms: "a half-second fade, a wipe. Like you'd film the stage with me standing there, then film it without me and put them together. I'd disappear in the same way."

Amazingly, Scott took the apparition in stride. "'OK,' I thought. And went back to my lights." He shrugs off the ghostly occurrences. "Things happen here, mostly late at night. There are cold spots. I've heard footsteps. I would like to see her again to find out why she is here. She doesn't scare me in the least. Maybe she was just walking down a path she used to walk before the theatre was here."

In talking with the group I got a few minor hits. The lady in the toque in the balcony was a long-time member of the Mansfield Orchestra and patroness of the theatre for most of her 90+ years, noted for her hats. Scott told me that he thought he remembered a man found in the men's room downstairs who had had a heart attack.

I felt like a complete fraud. It's no use second-guessing, although I can see how the theatre would be a completely different place after dark. If I had realized how busy things were, I would have scheduled a night visit. Most of the sightings were reported late at night, when things are quiet. Todd and Scott kindly offered to take me through the theatre late at night, but I was due in Cleveland later that day and since I had already heard their stories, anything I saw wouldn't be evidence.

I was still fretting about the ghostly projectionist. He was so vivid! Scott and Todd went upstairs with me and pulled out some old pay records from the 1950s and 60s. No Pete. Guy Tinkey was one name that stood out.

Scott gave me the number of Mr. S., the Projectionist Union steward, and I phoned him. Not knowing his opinion of the supernatural, I only said that I was doing research on the Madison and some other theatres and wondered if he knew any of the projectionists at the Madison. He told me that the projectors in the Renaissance *were* the original equipment at the Madison. They were made in the 1920s, and according to Mr. S., so well-constructed that they could still be used today.

Mr. S. ran through some names. He thought I would want to interview living persons so he tried to think of projectionists who were still around.

"Was there anyone named Pete or Peters?" I asked.

"He's dead," he said quickly.

I hate to rejoice over the death of any fellow creature, but I felt much better. I wasn't a complete failure. Pete *had* been there. Pete was a motion picture operator, as projectionists were called, at the Madison Theatre with Guy Tinkey, whose name I had seen in the pay records. Unfortunately Mr. S. racked his brain, but couldn't remember Pete's last name. I couldn't find anything in the yellowed clippings in the Mansfield library theatre files either. So that part of the mystery will have to wait.

Regardless of what I saw or did not see, Mansfield's Renaissance Theatre is a gorgeous example of what can be accomplished when a dedicated band of volunteers comes together to save a city landmark. The Renaissance hosts a vibrant series of cultural events and, incidentally, provides a home for the historic spirits of Edward Rafter and Pete the phantom projectionist. It would be interesting to visit after dark or in the quiet hours of the early morning. Maybe Pete would tell me his last name or chat about the latest picture. And maybe the Woman in Black would come back for an encore and tell us who she is and why she walks.

GHOSTS IN THE ROUND

Special thanks to Mr. and Mrs. Wallace Higgins of Roundtown Players

Circleville is a town with a good aura. All the children are good-looking, the downtown is busy and prosperous, there is a thriving library, many beautiful houses, and an air of energy and intellectual curiosity. The town just *feels* good. Some of that feel-good spirit seems to have rubbed off on the ghost at the Roundtown Theater.

The castle-like stone building that houses the Roundtown Theater has been through many incarnations. Its past can be seen at its doors. "Armory" is carved over one arch and "Library" over another smaller arch. "Memorial Hall" crowns the main arch on the front of the building. The main purpose of the building, built by the Monumental Society, was to honor the Veterans of the Grand Army of the Republic. By the 1930s, the last GAR soldier was gone and the Hall saw new uses. It was until recently the home of the Pickaway County Public Library before they moved to their new building. A Veteran's Museum is housed on the second floor. The Roundtown Players took over the third floor and part of the second floor in 1971.

I visited the Memorial Building in the fall of 2002, giving a talk in the main library reading room to a delightfully enthusiastic crowd. I got there early so I could check out the reputed ghost.

Up and down the worn wooden floors of the book stacks I prowled, through the 300s, 400s, and 500s Dewey-classed books on the shelves. I knew that the new library was being built and I noted the water damage to the ceiling, the dingy paint, and the make-do spirit. I was just about ready to go back to the circulation desk when I caught a glimpse of a white shirt in a darkened doorway.

A young man was leaning against the door frame with an air of studied carelessness, as if best to display his youthful figure. He wore knee-high boots, darkish pants and a white shirt, open at the neck. I noted his description, then went back to the desk.

"The ghost was just there," I said to my librarian hostess, indicating the doorway. I later saw him smiling at me out of the dark of the basement offices.

I returned in the summer of 2003 with my friend Alexis* to meet Wallace Higgins, director, playwright, artist, and historian: a local Renaissance man, and his wife Carol, a writer, dancer, and local historian. We slogged up the stairs to the theater on the second floor. The Theater is not air conditioned and it was hot and humid. Climbing even higher to the storage areas, I felt a shove on my chest at the top of the stairs, playful, yet not pleasant. Mr. Higgins explained what the different rooms were used for.

He unhooked a hook-and-ring on the outside of the door to the attic. "I don't know what that's supposed to keep in...."

He left me to climb up to the attic alone. There were no lights and it was hotter and much more humid. The first board I stepped onto gave alarmingly. "I don't want to be here," I said to myself. Plastic sheeting and insulation lay bunched up like rows of corpses in body bags. It was an uncanny effect. I was startled to see something hanging from a high-up beam. This time, thank goodness, it wasn't the ghost of a hanged man, but a dummy, perhaps hung for a prank or Halloween décor. And then it wasn't there.

I tottered back down the steps to the Green Room. A ghostly woman sat smoking in a chair in front of a window, her legs crossed with pin-up girl elegance. In the prop room, I smiled at the cupboard labeled "Body Parts." I don't know if the floors were uneven enough to cause a chain and padlock on one of the cabinets to rattle, but rattle they did, even though I couldn't duplicate the effect by bouncing on the floor.

Most of the upstairs was crammed to bursting with furniture, props, costumes, and scenery. As I gazed towards the exit door in the balcony storage area, a shadow slipped to one side into what seemed to be a wall. My depth perception is poor in the dark so I picked my way to the exit door, past what seemed to be an Amazon rain forest set, and found a stairway leading down to the stage. "Ah, so *that's* where you went!"

I followed the shadow but he was too quick for me. As I stood on the stage below, I could see light coming in behind the mounted spotlights. Behind the left spotlight opening, the dark silhouette of the young man was ducking in and out of the light. I shook my head indulgently. He certainly was a tease.

According to Wallace Higgins, the ghost made his first appearance, if that is the correct term, in the 1970s in the newly installed restrooms off the auditorium. Mr. Higgins wrote: "Two teenage girls opened the theater one Friday night to get ready for a rehearsal. The Library was closed, everyone else had gone home, and the building was presumably deserted. When they unlocked the theater door, the girls heard one of the commodes in the restrooms flush. My daughter bravely, and somewhat foolishly, grabbed up a length of two-by-four, the other flipped on the lights, and they both charged the doors of the restrooms, which are side by side. There was nobody in either room, but in the 'Ladies' the water was still flowing from the tank.

"The ghost with a penchant for plumbing became a standing joke among RTP members. Several persons experienced the same phenomenon. We all assumed that it was some obscure plumbing problem and began calling the erstwhile spirit 'the ghost of John Flushing.' A haunted restroom was too bizarre to be taken seriously.

"But there was more. The people working in the library sometimes heard footsteps overhead at odd hours. It was usually early in the morning when no self-respecting RTP thespian was even out of bed. Yet at those early hours, feet would be heard treading the boards. The librarians hesitated to mention this, but, when they did, it was dismissed as an intruder who had somehow managed to sneak in. As this had actually happened two or three times, it was a possible explanation...Locks were changed over and over again but the footsteps persisted. There was an old tombstone in the cellar with the name Charles on it. The librarians, therefore, began talking about 'Charlie, the Ghost.' They laughed about it—but with a rather uneasy laughter. Very few really believed that it was a ghost—but it *was* strange.

"On another occasion, a young woman was painting scenery on the stage. The upstairs area was totally dark and there hadn't been a sound for 45 minutes. Suddenly she heard a noise in the old balcony area. She stood absolutely still. Heavy footsteps crossed the balcony area from west to east and then from east to west. She called out, 'Who's there?' and 'Is anybody there?' several times but there was no answer. She spent the next twenty minutes sitting in the middle of the brightly lit stage watching as the footsteps continued pacing to and fro in the balcony. Then two men arrived and made a thorough search. It wasn't possible that the prowler could have escaped. The girl had the fire escapes in full view and the two men had the other two exits covered. They even checked the attic. The prowler had vanished.

"Once a young woman saw a reflection in a mirror of a figure in blue. She turned immediately but there was nobody. Some believe it's the ghost of one of the Civil War veterans who built the Hall. Most people shrug it off 'It's some homeless intruder,' they say, 'some kid playing tricks. Imagination! Nerves! Faulty plumbing! Coincidence!'

"I've worked there at all hours of the night and day—often alone. I've performed in some twenty productions over the past thirty years, yet I've seen nor heard neither a wisp nor a whisper, but once, more of a bang.

"The Hall was being renovated and the windows were being replaced. I was leading a tour of seventh graders, about 25 of them. We got everyone seated in the auditorium and I was talking about the Hall and its history. Someone asked about the ghost and I mentioned a few incidents. Suddenly a pile of old windows leaning against the stage wall fell over with a thunderous crash of splintering glass. Two or three girls screamed. I passed it off lightly. 'It's just the ghost,' I said. Was it? Was it mere coincidence? Maybe!

"Strangely enough, one other encounter has even some of the skeptics wondering. Players was preparing for a children's production and the husband of one of the directors (we'll call him Joe) had gotten roped into building part of the set. Joe arrived with his tool kit and the large, friendly family dog. He started laying out his tools on the stage and the dog, happily wagging his tail, lay down on the floor in front of the stage. Everything seemed quite normal and Joe went cheerfully to work.

"The next time he thought about the dog, Joe looked over and was stunned. The poor creature was crouched down, trembling all over, with its eyes rolled back in abject terror. Joe stopped and listened. The quiet was uncanny. There weren't any street noises. In nothing flat, Joe packed his tools, locked the place up, dragged the dog downstairs and into his van. By the time they got home, the dog was his cheerful self again. Why people deny the experiences of human beings but are convinced by the curious behavior of a dog I'm not sure, but such is human nature."

Most of the witnesses are perfectly reliable people. Perhaps there *is* someone or something stalking around the balcony, skulking in dark corners, or investigating the rest rooms. Is it John Flushing? Is it Charlie of the tombstone? Or is it just an atmospheric blast from the past?" Whoever he is, he seems to be a friendly spirit, flitting and flirting behind the scenes of life.

PHANTOM OF THE BELLVILLE OPERA

I was in the Genealogy Room of the Mansfield library, looking for a photo of Edward Rafter, who had been shot at what is now the Renaissance Theatre. When I mentioned my quest for ghost stories to the librarian, he said, "Oh, you have to talk to Melanie! She's over in the children's section."

Melanie Seaman, who works with a group called Highlands of Ohio Folk and Celtic Music Society to bring concerts to the Bellville Opera House, seemed embarrassed by the attention. "Oh, it really wasn't much of anything," she demurred. "I don't even *believe* in ghosts. But this happened two years ago. It was in the summer and it was really hot. I was arranging card tables and setting up for a coffeehouse concert on the third floor of the Opera House. It hadn't been used for years and years."

The Opera House is a plain brick building with a theatre on the third floor. Built in 1879, the building was part jail and part meeting room. The Masons held their meetings upstairs in the early 1900s. Later a stage was added and used for plays and graduations. The upper floor was used as a school during World War II.

"I kept looking back towards the door. There was a sign there on a easel and I kept thinking I saw a man standing there. I kept telling myself, *It's just the easel, just the easel....* After all, I was locked in.

"A friend came to help and I let her in the back door. The front door was still locked. We were hauling tables. She kept looking back at the door and said, "Oh! For a minute I thought that somebody was standing there!" Right after that we were hit by a chill.

"So I asked a local man if he knew anything about a ghost in the third floor of the Opera House. He told me that a long time ago the furnace man came in to work on a project at the building that turned out to require further thought. The furnace man said to him, 'When you three get this figured out, give me a call.' The only people there were the man and his wife."

Oral tradition has it that a local man objected to building the stage and that it is his ghost who haunts the Opera House.

The Highlands of Ohio hosted a concert at the Opera House this summer, but the ghostly man missed the date.

"I kept hoping that he would come during a concert, but he only shows up when it's quiet," Melanie said. "Maybe he's afraid of people."

SIX DEGREES OF APPARITION

It's funny how often one ghost story leads, not just to one, but to a *host* of other hauntings. I pulled up to the dramatic Art Moderne façade of the 20TH Century Theater in Oakley to find a parking lot full of roadies and a wedding rehearsal. In the theatre a band was practicing for an evening concert and I prowled around for a half hour to a pair of dueling flutes shrilling what sounded like a score to an Alfred Hitchcock thriller. I could see that this was not going to be one of those restful chats with the dead.

Beneath the canopies of lights I bobbed around to get a view of the darkened balcony. One door stood open to a lighted room, high up by the ceiling. I briefly saw the black silhouette of a man, looking around the door.

Dark balconies draw me like mice to cheese. I climbed the cement steps to the balcony. My eyes adjusted to the dark and I could see stacks of the original green metal theatre seats, duct work, and piles of lumber. Behind me was the lighted, open door I had seen from below.

I felt edgy and agitated in the balcony. I caught a glimpse of a man with a stubbly growth of black beard and a smudge of a mustache. His eyes were red-rimmed and teary. He was going berserk, throwing things, smashing things. It seemed like a good time to go in search of Mark Rogers, of 20TH Century Productions, Inc.

With his salt-and-pepper beard, wire-rimmed glasses, and slow, deep DJ's voice, Mark looks like a healthier, trimmer version of Jerry Garcia. He told me how the theatre, which was the first air-conditioned theatre in Cincinnati, opened in 1941 with the local premier of 20th Century Fox's *Blood and Sand*, starring Cincinnati-born actor Tyrone Power. The building was designed to be completely fireproof and was noted for its fine acoustics. It operated as a movie theatre until 1983.

Mark said that no one really knows when an older projectionist dropped dead in the projection booth. The return engagement of the projectionist's ghost was easier to date.

Somewhere around 1970, an usher and a young projectionist were misbehaving in the booth. They were smoking and drinking and generally fooling around when the film reel locks popped off. The reels flew off and unspooled themselves, leaving the film a tangled mess. They attributed it to the phantom projectionist.

Mark didn't know about my berserk smasher, but the building stood vacant for seven years. "Kids came in and were huffing and who knows what else," he said. That explained some of my discomfort.

Mark told how, when the building was vacant, a neighbor used to bring his two Dobermans on walks and let them run through the building. The door was open to the balcony; there was nobody else in the building. Usually the dogs ran all over the place. This time they started yelping. They tore down the stairs to the lobby and squatted behind their owner. After that they wouldn't come back into the theatre building.

Mark plans to turn the projection booth into a lounge. He's still got the original projection equipment stored in the basement of Habits Café, Mark's restaurant across the street from the 20TH Century.

"And is there ever a story *there!*" Mark said, smiling.

And indeed there was. Habits Café was supposedly the site of a murder that caused a Cincinnati scandal. The owner of the restaurant and an ex-cop with a long criminal record were in cahoots in a deal to sell stolen property. The cop double-crossed the bar owner, who shot him dead in a basement room. Two weeks later, the bar owner was mysteriously shot dead in a local alley. Nobody was ever charged. I've read newspaper articles about the ex-police officer. He had a twisted history of possession of burglary tools, burglary, and attempted burglary. He was no sooner cleared on one charge than he would be arrested on a new one. Eventually he was sent to jail. Paroled, he went back to his old ways and is said to have died at the hands of the bar owner.

Mark had the room where the ex-officer was shot fixed up to use as an office. "Although we set up offices in the basement, we never used them. It just felt bad and nobody would work there." Employees even refused to go downstairs.

Apparently the basement office was perfect for the site scouts for the movie, *April's Fool*, a darkly comic story of a gambler who ends up in trouble.

Rick Barnes was the sound man for *April's Fool*. He told me, "I've never been a big believer [in ghosts.] If it *is* real, I don't think it's what we think it is.... But really weird stuff started happening when we were shooting in the room where the guy was killed.

"My equipment was on batteries because I don't trust wall current. But I started having trouble. These batteries normally run for 6 to 8 hours. I'd put them in and they'd be gone within 5 minutes. I put another one in; it was gone within 5 minutes. Jeff, the cameraman, got mad about the delay and went with house current. Then the house current went crazy. Then Jeff went to batteries and *he* started having trouble and the camera battery went dead. What drains a battery designed to go 6-8 hours? And not just one, but three separate ones... When I took them upstairs and shot, they ran fine.

"When we were shooting this one scene, without sound, Jeff said, 'Did you see that?' I didn't say anything but I thought I saw something go flying across the room. 'What the hell was that?' Jeff asked. There was this SOMETHING, this light flashed across the room. The whole take was ruined. But the film didn't show what we saw, which was a blue round or oval object flying through the air. When we were in post-production, there was just a flash. 11 frames, half a second, which is really a long time, were ruined completely. Jeff and I were the only two who saw it. Maybe everyone else blinked. We couldn't explain why we were the only ones to see it."

Jeff Barklage was the cameraman on that occasion. He said, "I've always heard it said that if you take photos, sometimes you can find things.... I never believed it. We had a really intense scene set up in the basement, actually in the room adjacent to the one where the guy was killed. The scene was one of the Guido characters yelling at the shyster/gangster guy in his office. We were setting it up and were joking about the ghosts since we had just heard that employees of the restaurant wouldn't go down into the basement by themselves. We were shooting film, using a video assist camera, a little video camera that shows the director what's on film.

"In the midst of the joking, all the actors were in place, ready to go, when all of a sudden not only did the video assist and the other monitor instantly go down, but the batteries died on the audio recorder.

"Now both systems are entirely separate. They are on their own set of batteries; they're not plugged in. They *completely* shut down *exactly* as we were joking. We started freaking. We swapped cables and changed batteries on monitors. We changed the *whole* thing. Nothing worked. Everybody was ready to go, emotions were high and the actors were waiting to pour those emotions out in the scene. It took someone on the set saying, 'Hey, we're sorry!' to get things back under control.

"After the apologies, it was like a switch clicked. The video monitor came back up, the batteries came back up, and we rolled. After that we were very polite."

Jeff and Rick both told me about another ghostly incident while filming a horror movie called *The Factory* at the Peters Cartridge Company building at Kings Mills. Built in the 1860s, the company made munitions for the Union Army and was targeted by Morgan's Raiders in 1863. Legend says that the Raiders took a wrong turn and missed the factory altogether.

Bullets and explosives were manufactured at the site until 1944. Given the nature of the business, it's no wonder that there were numerous worker deaths from fire, accidents, and explosions. The building is huge and creepy. Although some parts are occupied, much of it is derelict and extremely dangerous. (Ghost hunters, take note: the police keep a sharp eye on the place and have orders from the owners to prosecute trespassers.) Some of the ghostly manifestations in the site include footsteps crossing the upper floors and on the roof late at night and ghosts appearing in the upper windows.

During the filming of *The Factory* in December of 2002, an associate director was upstairs scouting for a location. She came down to the staging area, "as white as a ghost," said Jeff. She told the others that a ghostly *someone* spoke to her. She wasn't a fanciful person, but she refused to go back in that area. The whole crew was accounted for. Nobody was playing a prank. The director was impressed by the incident and actually worked it into the film.

It's a long way from the elegant coral stucco waves sculpted into the walls of the 20TH Century Theater to shooting film on location in the tainted office in the basement of Habits Café to making a movie in the shadow of the grim shot tower of the Peters Cartridge Company. But then, that's how it works in the ghost business: six degrees of apparition.

8

POLT-POURRI:
Assorted apparitions and brief encounters

*Don't ask me to give a name to something
which hasn't got a name.*
-The Haunting 1963-

THE CASE OF THE AMATEUR EXORCIST

When I visited the Roundtown Theater (p. 101), I met
Wallace Higgins and his lovely wife Carol, who admitted, with
a charming blush, to having performed an exorcism in their
home. The red-painted doll house of a home was built in the
1830s by Col. Valentine Keffer.

Carol stood in the narrow hall now hung with coats and
hats on pegs and showed me the spot.

She said, "When we first moved in here, I was afraid of
this little hall. It had originally been a side porch, the main
entrance of the house. I would go through and be *very* uneasy.

"'This is really dumb!' I thought. But I felt something
there. It didn't seem to have a human form, but it was *male*. I
was pregnant and I thought, 'We can't have *this*.'

"I went and got a bell, a Bible, and a candle. I lit the
candle, opened the Bible and rang the bell. Then I said, 'I'm
very sorry, but we are about to have a baby and you're going to
have to leave in the name of the Father, Son and Holy Spirit,
Amen.'

"And it was *gone*!

"It left and I was sorry I had to ask it to leave. But it was very accommodating."

GO TO THE LIGHT

I like to tease my friend and Clermont County Historian Richard Crawford about being willing to spend the night *anywhere* in search of ghosts. He usually takes along a pack of friends, some sensitive to the spirits, others unseeing but curious. Most often he's accompanied by his "clairvoyant sidekick," a young man named Eddie Fox, whose brilliant blue eyes seem to look at a world beyond.

It was one such expedition that gathered at the Clermont County Infirmary one chilly October night in 2001. There was a bright moon rising in the cloudless sky behind the dark gothic structure, a perfect night for ghost hunting. The group included Rick, Eddie, and friends Danny Woodley, Robyn Holman, Karen Long, and Greg Gough. Ryan Gladwell had college basketball practice and planned to arrive later in the evening.

The County Infirmary was all things to all sad people. Built in 1883, it was at once an old-folks' home, a lunatic asylum, a nursing home for the disabled and the incurable, and a nursery for babies born on the wrong side of the blanket. Its time of usefulness had passed and the building was scheduled for demolition within a week. This was the group's last chance to visit whatever ghosts lingered there. Rick had been given permission by the county commissioners, who cautioned him to take flashlights, even showing him that the electric lines to the building had been cut or disconnected.

Rick Crawford told me, "I went up alone to room 222 on the second floor in the corner of the building facing the driveway." This room was particularly cold, with that bone-chilling cold that feels so personal, so deliberate. "This had been the embalming room for the morgue of the Infirmary. Most inmates didn't have any relatives who would claim their bodies for burial. These unclaimed souls were buried in the potter's field. I took a step over the door step and I heard, very quietly, 'huh-uh.' It was just a quiet warning, like don't come in here. I stepped back into the hall.

"I moved forward again and I heard, 'huh-uh.' It was almost imperceptible. 'All right,' I started to say, 'Who's playing tricks?' Then I yelled for everyone to get over here, quick! When they showed up, it was apparent that no one had been *near* me. I don't know any ventriloquist who could throw their voice that far and that low."

For Eddie, walking up that first flight of stairs was like entering a different dimension. Eddie later told me, "When I first walked in, I didn't feel anything. But on the second floor, I started getting really bad feelings. When I came to this one room [the embalming room] it was like there was a wall put up. I walked through the cold to get inside. I felt the presence of dead bodies in that room. I felt hatred there. Then I hit cold spots in the hall."

At the end of the hall was a big room. As Eddie walked in, he saw a pale woman, aged 40-50, with long frizzy brunette hair. She wore a white dress and was staring out the window in grief. "She was very depressed," Eddie said, "It was like she was waiting for someone to get her out. It overwhelmed me."

The ghost hunting group gathered in the men's restroom on the second floor when Ryan Gladwell walked in, his 6'4" frame looming up in the dark. "We had forgotten he was coming and he scared us to death!" Rick said.

Ryan said, "I started up the stairs in the dark. I didn't really know what room they were going to be in, but I saw their flashlights. I walked into the room and flipped on the switch. I said, 'Why is it so dark in here?' The lights came on."

Rick said, "We were all looking at each other going, 'Uh-*huh...*' Somebody forgot to tell Ryan the lights weren't working."

"What's the big deal?" Ryan asked.

They explained about the wires being cut. He laughed and thought his friends were lying to him. Then he turned off the lights and tried to turn them back on. "They wouldn't go." He still shakes his head about it today.

Danny Woodley decided to go off on his own.

"I went down this one section of corridor and there was an overwhelming sense of sadness in the air. It was like an ice cold wall in the air. I would not go any further. I went back and got the others. This time we came in from the other end of the corridor. It was the same thing: intense sadness plus a creepy feeling of someone evil watching us. It was a pocket about 30 feet in diameter right at the stairwell. It turned out that a deranged man threw a woman down the stairs. I was standing in the spot where the murder happened."

Eddie had another vision as he and Ryan were walking past the stairs to the third floor. "I saw a bluish-green ball like an oversized orb bouncing up the stairs. It turned into the figure of a boy in old-fashioned clothes. He was about 7-9 years old, had silky hair down to his ears, and a mischievous face. He walked up the stairs, turned around and looked at me. He kind of waved, like, 'C'mon! Come up here!' then he dissolved.

Ryan and Eddie next went to the infirmary room. "It had a chill when we first walked into the room. In the room across the hall from us, lights started flashing, like strobe lights. Then the flashing lights went to the next room, to the next room, then to the room where the depressed woman was, and stopped. They weren't car lights because the windows were on the back of the building, not in front of us.

"Then me and Ryan both got this real eerie feeling: 'We need to go! This is about to get real ugly.' About that time, all the wall lights on that side of the hall flashed. I thought, 'But there's no electricity!!!' It was very cold and the breeze was starting to pick up in the hallway. Like any normal human being, we got *out*. Then it was like something had passed. It was calm and clear after we got outside. You could see the stars and the moon."

Eddie and Ryan found the others outside. Eddie told Rick about the flashing lights. "Did you see any cars? Were you messing with flashlights?"

"No," said Rick. "We thought you were already out here. Those lights were from whatever was inside."

The group stayed at the building past midnight. "An eternity it was," said Rick.

The Clermont County Infirmary was torn down shortly after. Rick and his friends were the last living people to spend the night there.

Rick found out later that the women's jail is built over the Potter's Field. "That part of the jail is haunted too," he said. "And when the Clermont County Municipal Court Building is built, there are plans to dig a tunnel through the Potter's Field to the jail. I wonder what the dead will have to say about *that*?"

SCARE-LET & GREY

I graduated from OSU and later ran a haunted vintage clothing store across from campus (*Haunted Ohio*, p. 4). I have to confess that I never heard a single ghost story about OSU the entire time I attended school there.

The only personal experience I had on campus occurred in Kuhn Honors House on W. 12th, formerly the residence of the President of OSU. Two places struck me while I was touring this beautiful house: the hall directly in front of the elevator and a small office on the upper floor where a ghostly maid was crying.

Two of the most famous spirits on campus are the Lady of the Lake and the Pink Lady. They may be one and the same ghost. According to Bill Wahl, a former director of the University campus tour program, there was a Professor Clark who induced fellow faculty members to invest in an oil exploration scheme. When it failed, Professor Clark put a gun to his head. His embittered wife, who had asked the University to help her despondent husband, vowed that she would never let the University rest. After her death in the 1920s, students reported seeing a woman in a pink dress gliding across Mirror Lake, as if skating. She may be the same ghost whose mysterious footsteps are heard in Pomerene Hall, the site of Professor Clark's suicide.

My favorite OSU story is about Hayes Hall, named, not for Coach Woody Hayes, but for President Rutherford B. Hayes. The hall was finished in 1893, the same year Hayes died.

"The story goes that around 1915 to 1920, the building was used as a residence hall," Wahl says. Two residents were chronically late. One autumn evening, they stayed out late "studying," and didn't roll home until about 10 p.m. The doors were locked. The students tried tossing gravel at the windows and called as loudly as they dared. Nobody came down to open the door.

Just as they were about to give up, an old gentleman with a beard opened the door to them. When they asked who he was, he said, "I'm the curator of the building."

The next day the students mentioned that an old man had let them in the night before. Nobody knew who this might be. But a few days later they saw a portrait of the "curator" hanging in the hallway of the building. It was the late President Rutherford B. Hayes.

The statue of William Oxley Thompson has always scared me. I assumed that he got off his pedestal and prowled stiffly around campus at night. Oxley Hall, now used as office space but originally the first women's residence hall, has its share of ghost stories. The attic seems genuinely haunted. It is said that on December 17, the anniversary of a female student's death by suicide, her screams can be heard in the attic.

A staff member who worked in the building from 1992 until 1998 reported, "We had heard that when the EMS folks were there testing the fire system in the attic, alarms started sounding and, although all the windows were closed, a big gust of wind came through and the lights started swaying back and forth. The firefighters left the building, they were so scared."

She says the story was verified later when the building had a fire drill. "One of the EMS people that came out for that drill mentioned he was there when it happened and that it was true." He told them he had worked in a lot of campus buildings late at night, but had never experienced anything like that before.[1]

A HAUNT AT HAWTHORN HILL

I have searched without success for ghostly tales of the Wright Brothers. The brothers were not disposed to flights of supernatural fancy. But there may be a ghost at Hawthorn Hill, the Wright's Dayton home where Orville Wright lived with his father Milton and sister Katharine. The classically beautiful Hawthorn Hill stands at 901 Harman Avenue in Oakwood. Owned by NCR, the house is open to the public on rare occasions.

When Katharine Wright's bedroom set was on display at the Old Courthouse in downtown Dayton, there were volunteers who swore that no matter how often you smoothed the bedspread, you would always find the imprint of a body, as if someone had lain there. There were also rumors of Katharine looking wistfully out of a window at the Old Courthouse. Katharine's bedroom set is now at Hawthorn Hill. A young man who went to school with my daughter stayed at the house for several months. He and his mother both told me that they had seen the imprint of a body in the bedspread. They also reported heavy doors opening and closing by themselves.

Orville liked to tell how his "psychic" abilities had saved Wilbur and him from asphyxiation. At the time, the brothers were living on N. Summit St. in Dayton, in a house lit by gas.

Wilbur had come home late one night and Orville, who was already in bed but not yet asleep, had a sudden premonition that when Wilbur went to bed he would blow out the gaslight in his room without turning off the gas.

Afraid to go to sleep, but reluctant to say anything to his brother, Orville stayed awake until all the lights were out. Then he went into Wilbur's room and found that Wilbur had indeed just blown out the light so that the room was slowly being flooded with the toxic and explosive gas.

Orville also had a sense of humor about his "psychic abilities." On a visit to Hawthorn Hill, Griffith Brewer, president of the Aeronautical Society of Great Britain, quoted a line of poetry which took Orville's fancy. Orville asked the author who wrote it. Brewer confessed he didn't know and he

The Old Warehouse Restaurant
Roscoe Village (p. 28)

Mysterious images in Warehouse Restaurant windows?
Roscoe Village (p. 28)

Emmitt House
Waverly (p. 142)

Colonel Taylor Inn
Cambridge (p. 137)

College Hall
Wilmington (p.124)

#1 House
Zoar (p.163)

Fulton Co. Historical Museum
Wauseon
(p.167)

and Orville looked through all Orville's books of quotations without finding it.

The very next day Orville got a letter from a man in Spokane, asking for an autograph and quoting those very lines. He gave the source: Book VI of Milton's *Paradise Lost*. Orville located the lines in his copy of Milton. Then he replaced the book on the shelf and pulled out a book on the shelf directly above it just a fraction of an inch.

After dinner Orville announced to Brewer that he would use psychic power to identify the author of the quotation. Brewer was skeptical. He blindfolded Orville and led him to the library where Orville felt his way along the shelves until he felt the protruding book. He dropped his hand to the copy of Milton on the shelf below. "I feel a strong impulse to pick up this book," he said. Brewer removed Orville's blindfold and Orville riffled through the pages of Book VI until he came to the proper page, then located the quotation.

Fred Kelly, who told the story in *Miracle at Kitty Hawk*, says that Griffith Brewer went to his grave believing that Orville was psychic.[2]

"OH, WHINNY, AND I'LL COME TO YOU"

The whole of Wittenberg University was originally contained in one building: Myers Hall, a four-square, five-story brick building as sober and upright as the Lutherans who built this mighty fortress. Although there is no documentation that the building was ever used as a Civil War hospital, for decades, this is the legend that has been told.

It was the early 1860s. The Republic lay in ruins. The General lay on an iron bedstead in Myers Hall, dying. Not for him the resigned, faraway stare, the quiet sinking into death. No, he roared for reinforcements, cursed the artillery, and whistled for his horse. It began to get on the nerves of the other patients and to keep the peace he was carried up to the fifth floor. It did no good. They could hear him countermanding orders through the floorboards.

Then some bright aide-de-camp got the idea that it might cheer the General if his favorite horse came to visit. Naturally it had to be done at night. Grooms tied flour sacks over the horse's hooves and muffled the bridle. A wakeful soldier standing with the dipper at the water bucket caught a glimpse of the ghostly white animal plodding up the narrow stairs. He was never quite right afterwards.

The General was dazed, but delighted. He raised himself in bed and whispered to the faithful beast. Then, peacefully, he fell asleep, dreaming of swinging himself into the saddle and riding across the river to that distant green land.

Nobody noticed. They were too busy trying to lead the General's horse down the stairs again. The horse scented death. He shied and plunged and refused to move. When he kicked one groom across the room, the aide ordered him shot.

The grooms looked at each other, but right or wrong, it was an order. The aide would have sworn the horse knew what was coming because he lowered his head and stood quietly while the gun was put to his head. When the shot was fired into his skull, he dropped to his knees and groaned like a man.

It took five men to drag the beast down the stairs, causing an unholy racket as the corpse skidded into each landing. The aide was sweating profusely by the time the battered carcass was heaved out the door. He was to sweat even more when the disciplinary board demoted him to supervising the ladies who rolled bandages.

Somewhere, perhaps, the General and his horse ride through the green fields of Heaven. But on the top floor of Myers Hall, Wittenberg students say you can still hear the hoof beats of that faithful animal cantering from one end of the building and back. It is also said that you can hear the horse's carcass smashing as heavily as cannon shot into each landing—four skull-hammering thuds, then silence.[3]

WAPATOMICA

Wapatomica, the Shawnee capitol, was the site of the Council House of the seven historic Ohio Tribes: Shawnee,

Wyandotte, Miami, Delaware, Ottawa, Mingo, and Seneca. The bark-covered council house was an astonishing 150 by 75 feet and stood 16 feet high. It was also the seat of justice for the Shawnee in the 1780s, the burning ground.

Death at the stake was not the death of Joan of Arc. The victim was not tied to a stake piled with wood, but stripped naked and tethered by a rope that let the captive walk in a circle around the stake—a rope just long enough to falsely suggest hope and freedom. There are stories of Indian warriors singing their mocking death songs as their roasted flesh fell from their bones. Such men were admired for their courage.

The execution pole was in the center of the house. It was here that Simon Kenton was brought to be burned, but was saved by Simon Girty. In June-July 1782, one of the greatest Indian councils in American history was held here for 15 days. Logan destroyed the town in 1786.[4]

I visited the site of Wapatomica on October 6th, 1997 with a group including Barbara Lehmann, President of the Simon Kenton Historic Corridor organization and John Switzer of the *Columbus Dispatch*. I found it a very quiet spot. The dance ring was still visible after over two centuries. It was a lovely, sunny day, but there were eyes watching us from the woods, waiting for us to go away.

I have very little sense of smell and so when I do smell something, it seems to be a scent from another dimension. That day, I smelled charred wood. I thought perhaps someone had a picnic there, although it seems in questionable taste to have a cookout at such a spot. I looked around for the remains of a fire. I found none. I was the only one who smelled it.[5]

Barbara later pointed out that General Logan burned Chief Moluntha's village on Mac-o-chee Creek on October 6, 1786. "They burned this town *before* they burned Wapatomica— could this be your smoke smell?"

NOTE: The site is on private property and is not open to the public.

ADENA

"I wish there were!" the guide said wistfully when I asked about ghost stories. Appropriately, Adena means "paradise." It is a deeply satisfying house, a house of balance and thoughtful proportions. Originally it was the home of Ohio Governor Thomas Worthington, his wife Eleanor, and their 10 children. It was a staggeringly sophisticated dwelling for the Ohio wilderness and one of three surviving houses designed by Washington architect Benjamin Henry Latrobe, who designed the Capitol building. Nails, glass, hardware, wallpaper, and marble fireplaces were all hauled over the mountains from the east.

The latest technology has brought the building back to life. Conservation specialists spent hours slicing flecks of paint off woodwork and analyzing it under microscopes to determine the original colors. Floors have been covered with straw matting and painted floor canvases in brilliant colors. Wallpapers have been exactly reproduced.

At the Museum and Education Center, exhibits profile the Worthingtons, their 10 children, and their indentured servants in sometimes poignant stories. I especially enjoyed the TV news, featuring real ONN anchors reporting news from the time when Thomas Worthington was living at Adena: a burglary, an assault, the death of a local child. There were even commercials for a general store and its exciting range of goods ("glass window panes!!!!") and a "public service announcement" where a man denounced his adulterous wife and repudiated her debts.

In the kitchen of Adena I caught a brief glimpse of a little girl pattering up to the window on her tiny flat-heeled slippers to press her face up against the glass.

There was a strong female presence in the workroom at the corner of the house. Another ghostly woman stirred beyond the door to the drawing room, looking around the frame at me and my friend Alexis*. It was easy to envision family evenings or glittering parties in the high-ceilinged drawing room with its game table and piano. In the formal dining room, family portraits gazed down upon the table which hosted famous guests including Tecumseh, President Monroe, Henry Clay, and DeWitt Clinton.

Upstairs were three guest bedrooms, a trunk room, and the children's rooms. The first guest room, with the bright blue chintz hangings, mysteriously felt of death. I wondered if Albert Worthington, second son of the family, had returned to this room to die. He fled New Orleans after killing a man he had no quarrel with in a duel. His friend had been challenged and, as his friend had a family, Albert offered to take his place, believing that the challenger would settle for an apology. He was wrong and ended by killing the man. The authorities chose to enforce the anti-dueling laws, forcing him to flee.

Just off a room with a baby crib and four-poster bed, was a tiny windowless room. I walked in, felt faint, and nearly fell into the end wall. I caught myself with both hands just before I smashed my nose, felt my eyes fluttering back up into their sockets, and tottered into the hall.

Alexis was studying a primitive picture of Vesuvius in the next room.

"Hey, Alexis," I said, up to my old tricks[**], "walk in here...."

"Why?" she said suspiciously. But she went in anyway. She came out frowning. "I felt dizzy," she said, "What's *in* there?"

The office/library holds many family treasures: Worthington's long rifles, writing desk, surveying equipment, and his chair, which made me take a step backwards, the feeling was so strong that someone was sitting in it. "That *can't* be his actual chair," I thought, feeling a little sheepish. But the guide assured us that it was.

The ghosts of the past seem very close at this warm-spirited home. Who can say if Thomas or Eleanor Worthington or the children linger? It is a house anyone would be reluctant to leave.

[**] I had sent Alexis up to a haunted room in my vintage clothing store in Columbus. See *Haunted Ohio*, p. 6.

THE PHANTOM HORSES OF COLLEGE HALL

In an eerie echo of the ghost-horse of Myers Hall at Wittenberg, College Hall of Wilmington also claims a phantom horse. Like Myers Hall, College Hall was the original building, housing classrooms, administrative offices, an auditorium, the library, and a small dormitory.

Shortly after the College opened in 1871, students began to report the sounds of horses hooves and neighing from the top floor. When nothing was found, a legend arose that the nocturnal neighs came from the ghost of Ole Bill, a horse rumored to be entombed between the second and third floors of College Hall. Ole Bill was the horse of Civil War Colonel Azariah Doan. He was a Quaker. Unarmed with so much as a sword, he successfully led his men into battle again and again. The original campus structure began life as Franklin College, which closed in 1868. In 1870, Col. Doan, representing a group of local Quakers, purchased the land and the unfinished Franklin College building.

It was said that Ole Bill died before College Hall was completed and that Col. Doan asked to have his horse interred in the building. During renovation to install an elevator, the horse's remains were allegedly discovered. A horse's skull was displayed at the Class of '07's reunion in 1957. After World War II, students returning to school on the GI Bill heard the unmistakable sounds of a horse on the top floor of College Hall. The legend of Ole Bill had died down by then, so a new legend was invented to account for the manifestations.

At many schools, it's traditional to involve animals in pranks. At Wilmington, went the legend, mischievous students led farm animals to the top floor of College Hall to be discovered by some hapless faculty member. A horse left on the top floor panicked and bolted down the stairwell. It crashed to the landing between the second and third floors. Discovered badly hurt the next day, it had to be put down. It is the vengeful spirit of this horse that is said to whinny on the top floor.

In 1964 three football players climbed to the tower of College Hall to ring the bell after a homecoming victory. Since

the bell ropes had been removed, the students hit the bell with a
tire iron. After the last chime, the men heard the unmistakable
clip-clop of horses' hooves in the hallway below. Panicked,
they raced outside, sure that the ghost-horse was on their tail.

College Hall and horses seemed fated to be linked. The
campus is built on a former county fairgrounds and racetrack.
The Civil War horse Ole Bill is supposedly entombed in
College Hall. And there's that skull.... Wilmington College
instituted an Equine Studies program in 2002. Will it revive the
old stories, or spirits? Perhaps some horses are not ready to be
put out to pasture.[6]

THE THIN WOMAN

My grandfather was guardian to a hapless third-cousin-
twice-removed with obsessive compulsive disorder. Back then
they called it "crazy clean." I can remember sitting in the car at
the Athens State Hospital gazing at the rolling green lawns, the
tall white classical pillars of some gate or pergola, badgering
my grandmother for stories of volcanoes, floods and earth-
quakes while my grandfather visited with his charge. It was the
last time I enjoyed visiting Athens.

In my 20s, I would sometimes ride my motorcycle or drive
my old Suburban down to Athens with a friend or two. We'd
sit in a noisy bar, stay at some bare-plaster walled farmhouse,
or camp at Lake Hope. The entire district made me edgy. I
don't know whether it was the vibes from heavy-drinking
students or if I was sensing the earth energies that make Athens
such a mystical place for so many people.

I have never been able to locate or confirm the often-
repeated comments allegedly made by "The British Society for
Psychical Research" that Athens is "the most haunted place on
earth." Much of Athens's supernatural lore is about black
magic, witchcraft, and strange cults in cemeteries, plus the
usual campus legends of student suicides and sealed rooms.
Athens may be a node point on a ley line—a place of intersec-
tion, where "dragon-paths" collide, explode, or mingle. It is a
place of power, tapped unknowingly by some, deliberately,

perhaps maliciously, by others. I understand little of earth mysteries, but I know what I like. And I don't like Athens. It's nothing personal. When I visit I feel the synapses exploding in my head. Best to stay away.

Although The Ridges' architecture smacks of the Bates mansion of *Psycho*, it was designed by Herman Haerlin, a student of Frederick Law Olmstead, who designed Central Park. There were originally over a hundred landscaped acres of parkland including ponds, falls, trees, and plants, open to the public. It was considered an elegant and pleasant place.

The hospital opened in 1874 as The Athens Lunatic Asylum, to the delight of the Athens business community who prospered selling local products to the facility. Madness is a growth industry. From its second patient who believed himself to be a "Second Christ," The Ridges held thousands of patients—the violently insane to the mildly depressed, the menopausal housewife to the demented alcoholic—until it was closed around 1991. Today part of the main building is Linn Hall and houses the Kennedy Museum of American Art.

By the 1970s the philosophy of imprisoning the mentally ill had changed. Ohio University acquired the property and, as patients were gradually moved out to life in the community or on the streets, wings of the sprawling complex were bricked up to keep break-ins to a minimum.

In January of 1979 a patient I'll call Natalie* signed herself out of The Ridges for the afternoon. When she didn't sign herself back in, a search was made of the buildings and grounds. The Ridges was a maze of halls, staircases, and rooms. No trace of Natalie was found. An article in the *Athens Post* appealed for information. Subsequent searches revealed nothing.

Some say that Natalie was deaf and dumb. Some say that she heard the searchers and hid so cleverly that they never found her. Some say that the searchers fatally locked the door behind them on their way out of the ward where she had taken cover.

It is hard to say what happened next. Did she try to tap at the windows and make the people down below hear her and understand? Or was she so far gone in her mad world that she simply wandered until she lay down for the last time. She had removed all of her clothing, folded it neatly, and composed herself on the floor. To Natalie it may have seemed like the logical thing to do. Various reports state that she died of heart failure or of starvation.

A dead human body begins to liquefy as it decays, the brain first, then other internal organs. The intestinal bacteria and other micro-organisms swarm throughout the body causing bloating. The skin darkens. The woman's body lay in a pool of sunlight, bubbling and fermenting. I once heard an appallingly vivid phrase from a man who owns a company that cleans up after badly decomposed bodies. "Have you ever seen a body melt into a vinyl sofa?" he asked.

Natalie's body melted into the floor. In a grotesque parody of a contact print, the sun and the liquids of decomposition etched the marble floor beneath her like the work of some heartless photographer.

About six weeks later, a maintenance man, alerted by the stench, found her unrecognizable body in the room that had already been searched. When her body, a deflated mass of crumpled skin, had been scraped from the floor, they found her portrait: the shadow of the thin woman. It is a devastatingly detailed image, the folds of her skin, a wasp-waist above fleshy hips, even her hair, flipped up at the ends.

The stain on the asylum floor remains to this day. Scrubbing only seems to darken it. Even acids will not burn it away. The stain is off limits, resealed behind locked doors. There are rumors, only rumors, that Natalie can still be seen at the windows, knocking tentatively at first, then frantically pounding at the glass to try to make the living see her, hear her, and deliver her. She is only a shadow of her former self.

TRADING IN TERROR:
Haunted businesses

You can't take it with you.
-Frederick Marryat-

THE SPIRITS SPEAK AT SNOW HILL

The brick clubhouse at Snow Hill Country Club near New
Vienna gleams under a coat of snowy whitewash, fresh as a
new-sheeted ghost. The older portion of the clubhouse was
opened as an inn and tavern in 1820 by Charles B. and
Catherine Harris from Snow Hill, Maryland. It operated as a
hostelry until 1896 then was sold at auction in 1898 when Lucy
Harris, granddaughter of Catherine Harris died. For 26 years it
was farmland. Then the fourth generation of Harrises came
back into Snow Hill's life with Lucy Harris's niece, Nancy
Norma Crabbs.

Nancy grew up at Snow Hill with her maiden aunt Lucy
Harris after her mother's death. She inherited a substantial
portion of the Philip Carey Company in Cincinnati. She had
been a stenographer to Mr. Carey and it was whispered that her
employer had died for love of her. Carey's accountant, George
Crabbs, inherited an equally substantial portion of the company
and the couple soon married. They became one of the most
prominent couples in Cincinnati. Mrs. Crabbs was interested in
the arts and became an expert on antiques. In the early 1920s,
Mrs. Crabbs bought back the old family home, which had
fallen into disrepair. She restored it and opened it as an
outstanding golf course in 1924, just as golf was becoming a

popular sport. Henry Ford stopped by, both to play golf and to admire Mrs. Crabbs' extraordinary collection of antiques. Mrs. Crabbs died in 1947 with no children. Her niece, who also had no children, inherited the property and sold it to the members of Snow Hill Country Club.

Snow Hill hosts the popular "Dinner and a Ghost" event, an elegant dinner in the dining room followed by a tour of the rooms that formed the original inn. There seems to be plenty to experience at Snow Hill.

Strange things happen "almost daily," said David Stanton, the Club Pro and General Manager. "Nobody's been hurt or pinched or anything. It's just fun stuff. Typically the lights turn on and off. The cabinet in the dining room opens by itself. People report being touched, always three times and always on the arm, in the pink room upstairs and the hall just outside."

The strange events used to be confined to the original part of the Clubhouse, but as time went on, lots of things have begun to take place outside the older section. It's almost as if whatever exists at the site is being fed by the enthusiastic energies of those seeking its mysteries. Or perhaps the energies only enhance what was already there.

Kathleen Madison, Snow Hill history buff, is intrigued by how often former employees return for Dinner and a Ghost, only to say, *Now* I understand what went on!" or "It all makes sense now!" Thirty and forty years ago strange things happened also but nobody talked about them. For example, an employee was staying overnight upstairs when the bed slats all fell out of the bed at once and the bed dropped to the floor.

Several elderly relatives of the Harris family came to visit one day with a local lady who had been showing them family sites. David's wife, Becky, took them through the building. They looked at the then-decrepit front porch.

"Ooh, it's in such bad shape," said the ladies. "It has to come off. Should it be repaired? Should you build a new one? Or just tear it off and landscape in front of the building?"

The lady who had brought the Harris relatives to Snow Hill walked around the area for some 10 minutes. Then, in a low voice she said to Becky, "They don't want you to tear it off."

"Who?" asked Becky, puzzled. Then she realized that the woman was *not* talking about the two elderly relatives but about long-departed Harrises.

Photographs have also captured strange things at Snow Hill. Becky was standing in the parlor on the night of October 19, 2002, with a tour. She felt a cold spot as she stood by the central table. "It's really cold in here!" she exclaimed. In the photo of the scene snapped at that moment, you can see a mushroom of luminous blue haze.

Kathleen showed me a photo taken by an employee in the upstairs hall. It was marked by a lightning-bolt-like stab of light. One photographer pooh-poohed it as nothing more than dust or the camera strap. But another photographer said that he'd been developing film for 25 years and had never seen anything like it.

Upstairs there is an unused bathroom. About five years ago, David was up in the room and found that the bathtub had 18 inches of water in it. "The plumbing hasn't worked in years," he said ruefully. "And this was clear water, not like the roof had leaked a little bit. Even weirder, when the water drained out, there was sand in the bottom of the tub finer than sugar."

The ghosts at Snow Hill seem to be primarily felt and heard. Only rarely have they been seen. On one of those unusual occasions, a deputy sheriff saw a woman in a long white dress in the family room. Another staff member saw her walk by the bar door and smelled the scent of roses. In December of 2002, a Harris relative in her 80s came for the ghost tour. She saw a woman in white walking down the hall toward the front door.

One tour regular is Shelly Suittor, who tape-records what she believes are spirit voices on a hand-held tape recorder. David has put some of these on a CD, which he played for me.

I have never made up my mind about Electronic Voice Phenomena (EVP). Some people believe that the voices, recorded on tape, but not audible at the time of taping, represent the voices of the dead. Others believe that they are radio interference caught on tape or that they are somehow mentally projected onto the tape by the machine operator as a form of poltergeist activity. Some think that the ferrous oxide in the rusty nails of old houses acts like a recording medium and captures the sounds of the past.

In my experience EVP have some common aspects: one is a strange rhythmic cadence, very different from how people actually speak. Sometimes the voices have a metallic quality. Sometimes they react to something that is said or accurately call someone by name. Other times, what they say is completely baffling.

The CD David played for me demonstrates some of the characteristics, limitations, and frustrations of EVP. I could clearly hear some of the voices; others became audible only after I was told what to listen for. Some of them were difficult to hear over the hissing of the tape. Skeptics might add that the human mind, wanting to make sense of stimuli, shapes phrases out of static. A skeptic also might wonder if Shelly is a ventriloquist, but the "ghost voices" overlap those of the living.

• A man's metallic voice says, "Help me, Martha."

• An eerie voice says, "Hush!" after a tour participant complains about her flash not working in the attic.

• Shelly is also heard wondering if the smoke by the bar (photographed as a haze) is just ordinary cigarette smoke. The voice of a young boy or a woman wails, "Noooooo!"

• A little girl says, "Daddy,"

• Part of the basement used to be the men's locker room in 1924. It is now used for storage and when Shelly walked in, she recorded a gravelly voice among the static that seems to say, "This is the men's room. Get out."

• David also told of a time after one of the ghost tours when his wife Becky was relaxing over drinks with Shelly and Kathleen. They were having a good time and Becky used a swear word. On the tape, recorded at the time, she heard someone scold, "Becky!"

"I'll never swear again!" she says.

I spoke to Shelly by phone and then, due to mysterious interference with several different phones, we completed the interview by e-mail. Here are her views on EVP and her techniques for capturing it:

"I've been VERY successful with capturing audio evidence using a plain old magnetic cassette recorder and speaking either directly to whomever wishes to speak and being annoying about it. I say "Hello?" loudly and A LOT. It's a word that demands a reply in the living world, and seems to work fairly well. I refuse to set up a recorder and walk away. Leaving a tape recorder alone in a room hoping some dead guy will go, 'Oh cool, let's do Karaoke while no one's looking!' is pointless. I get better results keeping the mike in my hand, and my attention on someone answering me.

"I listen to the tape at home after the fact. I use headphones, turn it up loud and listen. When I think I've got something, I'll listen for phonetic sounds of human speech as opposed to a conspiracy of sounds *mimicking* human speech. Most of the time though, there's no question of the source or the message."

I asked about the metallic quality of many EVP recordings.

"I personally have only captured one recording that sounds metallic. The men's room guy at Snow Hill. I think he sounded that way because that's all the energy he could muster at the time. Kind of like a low-battery problem. It's my opinion that, just like the living, the dead have different abilities as far as energy goes." She also suggests that software used to load recordings on the web distorts the quality.

Does she think that EVP represents the voices of spirits? "I think EVPs are an electromagnetic impression of the voices of the dead, and sometimes the residual repeat of voices and sounds embedded in the surroundings or the structure itself."

Shelly believes anyone can get EVP results, even using low-tech equipment. She listed the conditions that seem to produce better results:

"Small groups for one thing, one person talking at a time IN NORMAL TONES, no whispering. People tend to want to whisper during a recording session, but a great deal of disembodied voices record as a whisper. Being aware and making note of all the living present, and making sure that when they speak, it's in normal tones, is a key component to an EVP session for me. It's actually *easier* to differentiate an EVP from a living person present, and makes an EVP stick out like a sore thumb when one is captured.

"I couldn't say what makes a place more active than another other than the obvious. I think it's a combination of how badly they want to talk, how strong they are to do it, or how many residual layers there may be at any given location."

Snow Hill's spirits *do* seem to like to communicate. David remembered a strange incident with the phones.

"There's a phone on the 9th hole. Players used to use it to order dinner so they could pick it up when they got back to the Clubhouse. The phone hasn't worked in 4 or 5 years. We figured the line had been cut when the groundskeeper was digging. Last summer I was in the kitchen when the phone rang. We have an internal caller ID and this showed "9 tee" calling, which is the phone on the 9th hole. I picked it up. Nobody. This went off and on all summer. Then fall came—the end of golf season—and it stopped. But when spring came, the calls began again—to the bar."

I like the idea of a ghostly golfer going to Florida at the end of golf season and coming back in the spring, meeting and greeting the lady in white, the man in the locker room, and all the others.

Kathleen showed me a framed poem that seems to sum up the Snow Hill experience. It ends:

"But time has changed with the passing years,
Old friends are gone who gathered here,
But we who are left bless the One who willed
That we meet again at Old Snow Hill."

EXIT STAGE RIGHT

Often when a hotel is "restored," it means bringing in lots of fake antique furniture. At the Renaissance Cleveland Hotel, it meant repainting period murals from old photographs, shining up the original chandeliers, re-gilding the cast-iron balustrades, restoring the lobby's marble fountain, and hanging antique mirrors and art. The Renaissance glows with the vitality of its recent $40 million restoration.

The Renaissance is built on layer upon layer of history. In 1815, Cleveland's first hotel, Mowery's Tavern, stood here. The site was also home to Cleveland House, which burned in 1845, the Forest City House in 1852, Hotel Cleveland, and Dunham House. The white brick, neoclassical 1,000-room hotel we see today was built in 1918 by the Van Swearingen brothers as part of a master plan for the original Terminal Tower Complex. The hotel hosted James A. Garfield's nomination tour and visits from Presidents Bush and Clinton. It also boasted one of Ohio's first indoor hotel pools.

My daughter and I were met in the Renaissance offices by Cara*, a slender, ultra-fashionable woman with shining red hair. We toured the Renaissance upstairs and down for about an hour. It wasn't until we got to the Gold Room, dimly lit by exquisite chandeliers reflected in the mirrored walls, that we encountered anything unusual.

All three of us walked up on the stage. I was drawn to a door at the far right. While Cara waited by the piano, I crossed to the door. My daughter was about 10 feet behind me. I could hear the sound of her flip-flops slapping, as well as the footsteps behind her.

"Stop," I said to her. Being the well-trained teenager she is, she immediately froze. The footsteps went on for a few steps, then silence fell. I immediately replayed the scene. If the floor was popping up, I figured we should be able to duplicate the effect. We walked back and forth and jumped up and down. Nothing made the sound of the footsteps I had heard.

I shrugged and went into the darkened room behind the door. It was a dreadful mistake. I was bombarded with—I couldn't say *what*—from all directions. No presence, no vision, just horrifying pinpricks of energy. I rushed out of the room, shaking my arms and hands, as if to shake off dirty, oily drops of water.

As I talked to Cara, my daughter ventured into the closet by herself. She too came out shivering. Later she told me. "It wasn't happy. It wasn't nice. It was almost threatening, as if it might actually be able to do harm. My stomach was twisting around. I got really *bad* butterflies in my stomach, man-eating butterflies!"

"My God, what is it?" I said to Cara reproachfully. "Is it unshielded wiring or *what*?"

She shook her head knowingly. "We've had it checked. It's not the electricity. I get very upset in there. I even cry. It's very prickly and uncomfortable. I've been at the Renaissance for two years and had no reason to go in there until the last six months or so, when somebody needed an easel out of there. I've never heard, never seen anything."

I was getting the vaguest picture of a groom flinging himself across stage and a gunshot. It was ridiculously melodramatic and completely unprovable. Cara commented that deaths in hotels are notoriously difficult to document.

I took a deep breath and went back into the room, trying to ignore the atmosphere as I shot pictures in the dark. Knowing what to expect made it slightly easier, but I was happier when I was back at the piano. I quickly jotted down some notes.

"Let's get out of here," Cara said abruptly. Her eyes were brimming with tears. It's very upsetting."

After that, the rest of the hotel was a piece of cake. Cara took us up the service elevators and staff staircases. It was a behind-the-scenes look at the inner workings of a fine hotel. A little *too* inner, perhaps. We went to the upper floors with their beautifully appointed meeting rooms, named for famous Clevelanders. Elegant artwork hung in the maze of halls. In the Carnegie Board Room, beyond the immensely long Danish Modern table, there was something hovering in the corner. Again, nothing definite, just a little patch of dark.

"When I had my experience," Cara said, gesturing behind me. "It was over *there*. Maybe it moves around. I had set up the room for a meeting. It had been a *very* stressful day. I took a moment and stood looking out of the window. Behind me, in the empty room, I heard a cough with a smile behind it, almost like somebody was saying, 'Hey, you're doing a good job!'

"I thought, 'Has someone from banquets come into the room?' I felt a cold breeze and turned around but nobody was there."

In a small anteroom at the end of the Stouffer Room, my daughter sensed and I saw a man sitting at a small desk. He was smoking a cigar and the smoke began to make me choke. I fled into the hall.

Most of the manifestations are relatively mundane: non-automatic toilets flushing, sinks turning on by themselves in both public and private bathrooms. On the fourth floor, lights turn on and off by themselves. It is rumored that staff have heard heavy breathing from someone invisible and a general feeling of "someone there." After midnight, it is said that none of the cleaners will willingly go to the fourth floor.

Cara admitted that she has had little success in collecting ghost stories from the staff. It is as if they are afraid that by talking about it they will somehow stir up the spirits. I can't blame them. I wouldn't want to be working alone at night in an upper floor conference room. There are too many doors for things to pop out of, too many hallway angles where things can hide, and too many staircases where ghosts can walk.

It is odd to think of hauntings in such a beautiful and busy building. Cara and I agreed that it feels like the bustle and motion of the living overlay the energies of the dead, at least during the daylight hours. The less traveled parts of the hotel are more apt to retain traces of the past, which is why that negative, crazy atmosphere hides in an obscure closet where the public never goes, just waiting to pounce....

THE COLONEL AND HIS LADIES

The house known today as The Colonel Taylor Inn was an astonishingly elaborate structure even for the 1870s, with multiple porches rich with spindles and turnings, gingerbread-laced gables, a porte-cochere, oriels, and a massive cupola. The lawn once held a strawberry tower, croquet lawn, gazebo and fountain. Once known as "the House on the Hill," it is a splendid sight in its original colors duplicated today: yellow, black, oxblood red.

This is a happy house, a lively, masculine kind of house—like the man who built it, Colonel Joseph D. Taylor. Col. Taylor was a man of substance. He was a teacher, lawyer, and prosecutor. He owned a newspaper in Cambridge, and a bank. He fought in the Civil War, served as a four-term U.S. Congressman, and was close friends with several U.S. Presidents.

As befitted a man in his position, he wanted a house that would reflect his status. The Victorians entertained a great deal and one's visitors needed to be properly impressed by the magnificent décor and lavish entertainment. A gentleman's home reflected his wealth and taste, boasting indirectly (for directly would have been vulgar) of his education, his cleverness in business, and his accomplishments.

Innkeeper Patricia Irvin met me at the door dandling the infant son of one of the housekeepers. In her navy jumper and sensible flats she has a refined English complexion and gracious warmth.

Patricia and her husband Jim moved into the Inn in 1999 after it had stood empty for two years. There was no heat in the front part of the house. Everything was frozen.

"We put in all new heating and air conditioning. We did wiring and plumbing—and wiring and plumbing—and wiring and plumbing." They are just now landscaping the exterior after taking down 18 dead trees.

"When we first moved here, I was by myself. I had always moved a lot so I was used to it, but I *knew* I had a ghost. The hairs just stood up on the back of my neck. It took me some time to get used to the idea."

The house's details are stunning: the original glass-shaded lamps on the newel posts, tall pocket doors, Eastlake brass hinges and hardware, some with original keys, stained glass roundels painted with dainty birds over the doors. Patricia is fortunate in having original photos of the rooms as they were decorated and furnished. She also has a portrait of Col. Taylor hanging in the hall. He has the beard and the look of President Garfield, who, along with Presidents Hayes and McKinley were known to have visited the house.

I started up the stairs lined with family photos. The first room I saw at the top of the stairs was a king-sized bathroom with its own fireplace. Something whizzed along the floor. I blinked. The same something whizzed *through* the wall and into the next room, an immense bedroom with a four-poster bed. The movement was so skittery and unexpected, I stared, then began to laugh. It was a ghostly cat.

Patricia smiled when I told her. She knew just who it was. Samantha was a grey and white tabby, one of a litter of wild cats that Patricia's husband and son found and fed with an eyedropper. "The cat bonded with us. It never went far away. You could go to the door, whistle, and she'd come."

Samantha was the only animal Jim and Patricia let sleep on the foot of their bed. She is now gone, but since her death they have both felt what feels like a cat walking across the foot of the bed. "And there are times when we're lying in bed when it will shake gently in kind of a rocking motion." Perhaps it is Samantha.

Across the landing in a small room with a nautical motif, I saw a little boy, perhaps 7-8 years old. I think he was wearing a sailor suit (although that might have been suggested by the room décor) but I was chiefly focusing on his face, which was distorted in a grimace as he blew me a raspberry and waggled his fingers over his ears. Altogether a rude little boy!

The plain blue-painted boards of the servants' staircase contrasted with the exquisite carvings on the main stair. The stair was in shadow and I flinched as I looked down the dizzyingly narrow stairwell. I caught a glimpse of a servant in a long skirt and apron, carrying a tray, catching her foot on her skirt and falling. It didn't seem to be a fatal fall, but a painful one, now captured for eternity like a recording played over and over.

The top floor had been used as the servants' quarters and for storage. Other than a pair of new French doors, Patricia says, the arrangement of the floor is all original. In the central sitting area I saw a heavy-set woman in an apron. She was very disapproving that things were not as they used to be. I got the impression that she was a housekeeper, but it is possible that she was Elizabeth, the Colonel's first wife. Elizabeth was used to hard work and didn't put on airs. A housekeeper might have complained that the servants' quarters had been taken over by a big-screen TV, a four-poster bed, exercise equipment, and a laundry. Elizabeth might have complained that the house wasn't being lived in by her children or their children because "that woman," the second Mrs. Taylor, had disinherited them.

Elizabeth A. Hill was a Quaker. Her two brothers were conscientious objectors during the Civil War, yet she chose to defy her heritage to marry a soldier. By all accounts it was a happy marriage. During their long-distance courtship, she wrote him witty letters, embroidered slippers for him, and worried. Colonel Taylor, as Judge Advocate of the Department of Indiana was often in danger from those he prosecuted and she feared for his safety. She reveled in her husband's political career and said later in life that she was happy to have escaped the "self-satisfied" smugness of her New England home. When she was dying she told her daughter, "God has given me an easy life to live and an easy death to die."[1]

Elizabeth had a fortune of her own and willed everything to her husband, expecting that he would take care of their children. Instead, in time-honored fashion, Taylor married a much younger school teacher who had grand social aspirations. He and his new wife spent very little time in Ohio, preferring to live in Washington DC or Cambridge, Massachusetts.

Taylor's daughter Gertrude is harsh in her criticism of her stepmother. In her memoirs, she praises her mother's dedication to her father's interests, lauding her as a true helpmeet. She has nothing but quiet scorn for her stepmother who expected to be waited on and reaped the financial rewards of Elizabeth's labors. According to Gertrude she "spoon fed" her delicate son through college. I wondered if the rude little boy was the fruit of the Colonel's second marriage.

Gertrude married in 1894. Her father, who was living in Washington, opened the house especially for the wedding. She wrote, "I thought of my mother constantly in the gaiety of that week. The whole place was hers, every inch of it spoke of her—she was the spirit of our 'new house' which had meant so much to me. And now another woman owned it all, and she took possession with a kind of ostentation that was galling."[2]

When Colonel Taylor lay on his deathbed in 1899, he asked his new wife to call the lawyer so he could put his affairs in order. She fobbed him off with something like, "Oh, don't worry, there will be time for that when you are better." He died shortly afterwards. She and her son got everything. She died in Cambridge, Massachusetts after selling off the Ohio property.

The Colonel would have certainly been justified in haunting his acquisitive second wife. But it is said that he returns to this house where he lived so happily with his beloved wife Elizabeth and their children.

In the 1970s the building was home to a family with eight children. Recently one of the boys came back to tour the house. On the stairs Patricia heard him say, "And Colonel Taylor walks these stairs…"

"We heard footsteps very distinctly when we first moved in," Patricia said quietly.

Even though smoking is not allowed in the Inn, the smell of the Colonel's pipe smoke has been smelled throughout the house, both by Patricia and by guests.

Patricia also explained, "I have a niece who saw him." The young woman is in her 20s, but is developmentally disabled. She was frightened when she woke up and saw the dark figure of a man coming in the door.

"I saw Colonel Taylor!" she said, rushing to her aunt. Patricia reassured her by telling her that "he's just watching over us, like an angel."

"She still won't come back," Patricia said ruefully.

Both guests and family have noticed the extra residents at the Inn. One guest was going up the stairs, stopped and said, "You have a presence here." Another guest felt "presences" in several of the rooms. Still another, standing in the foyer said, "I saw someone go through here—do you have a ghost?"

Patricia and Jim often have their grandchildren to visit. The youngest, a 5-year old granddaughter remarked, "Something funny's going on in your house, Grandma!" She and some other grandchildren have heard footsteps on the back stair although there is never anyone there.

As Patricia and I chatted in the immense paneled foyer, I looked back up the stairs. There I saw a ghostly woman on the landing. She wore a creamy satin brocade gown with huge leg-o-mutton sleeves, long kid gloves and a misty aigrette of white feathers fastened with a jewel in her hair. She stood poised on the landing as if waiting to be admired.

Patricia suggested that it might be Elizabeth, or possibly Gertrude on her wedding day, but the woman on the landing was taller and more slender than Elizabeth. She was also dressed in the fashion of a decade after Elizabeth's death. At the local library genealogy room I looked up the newspaper account of Gertrude Taylor's wedding. Her wedding dress was quite different. But perhaps I was seeing the second Mrs. Taylor dressed for the wedding or for some soiree.

Although the moveable furniture is not the same, Colonel Taylor would still recognize his old home. His glass-fronted bookcases still hold volumes in the library; the fireplaces still have their carved mantles and intaglio tile surrounds; the lamps on the newel posts still glow softly, as they did on the creamy brocade of his second wife's gown.

I sometimes wonder at the sheer *ordinariness* of some of my visions. Why see a falling housemaid? Why not see Gertrude's wedding day? And where was Colonel Taylor? I didn't catch so much as a hint of his tobacco. Perhaps he's off in Washington.

Patricia has many plans for the house. They will be hosting weddings. She's ready to handle buffet parties for up to 150 people and teas for bus tours and charity benefits. She also hosts fundraisers for community and historical organizations.

While Patricia mentions that the building is a work in progress, that it takes time to build a business of this sort, she is too modest to mention that The Colonel Taylor was voted by inn-goers as being the Best in the USA for 2002. The house is 9,000 square feet with 21 rooms, 11 fireplaces, 6 baths and 3 porches. I can't imagine trying to run it without a small army of servants. But Patricia is the kind of hostess who, you sense, makes it all look effortless.

"The servants lived on the third floor," she said with a twinkle in her eye. "They still do..."

THE HON. HAUNTS

The story of the Hon. James E. Emmitt, 1806-1893, in many ways parallels the rise of Ohio from rough-and-tumble pioneer territory to Gilded Age prosperity. Born just three years after Ohio's statehood, into an impoverished Pennsylvania family, Emmitt was a genuine Character.

Much of what we read in his *Reminiscences*, a ghost-written autobiography "as revised by himself," has more than a touch of tall tale about it. He was proud of his humble beginnings and singularly unhampered by false modesty. His *Reminiscences* begins with the statement, "The life story of a remarkable man who has largely aided in transforming Ohio from a deer park and bear garden into one of the greatest states in the nation."

Pike County's first millionaire, Emmitt had an intermittent Midas touch, alternately making and losing several fortunes in his long lifetime. He speaks candidly about his financial reversals and his noble way of rising above them and revels in his successes. When he angers a business rival, his distillery mysteriously goes up in flames. When a mule kicks a can of coal oil into a vat of whiskey, he sells the resulting abomination as "Emmitt's Discovery," an elixir he claimed would cure corns, deafness, consumption, and all other ills.

Emmitt had the route of the Ohio and Erie Canal diverted from Piketon to Waverly. He then spent several decades profiting from the canal traffic, from his mills, and from his whiskey distillery. It was said that he employed half the men in Waverly. In the 1850s, he realized that his business prospects would always be limited as long as the county seat was in Piketon. Almost exclusively for his own personal gain, Emmitt organized Waverly businessmen to lobby the Ohio General Assembly and the citizens of Pike County to move the county seat. He boasted that he'd spent about $40,000 of his own money and had made a profit as business flowed to Waverly.

Emmitt lived ostentatiously. When he made the Grand Tour of Europe, he bargained with artists, buying paintings for his Waverly mansion by the dozen at wholesale rates. He served two terms in the U.S. Senate. He died in his Waverly mansion in 1893 but it is not certain if he rests quietly. Somehow I doubt it.

One of his pet projects was The Emmitt House, built in 1861. Emmitt employed a master carpenter named Madison Hemmings, who had come to Pike County in the early 1830s, to work on the hotel. It was rumored, and never denied by the carpenter, that he was an illegitimate son of Thomas Jefferson by Sally Hemmings, Jefferson's slave.

The canal-side hotel quickly acquired a reputation as one of the Scioto Valley's finest hostelries. It was a mecca for traveling salesmen, or drummers, who would set up their sample cases in the "Drummer's Room" so that Waverly merchants could place their orders.

I drove down to Emmitt House on an overcast summer's day and parked across the street. In most of the windows, I could see crude dummies with masks, which clashed with the careful restoration of the rest of the building.

"I hope they take their ghosts more seriously than that," I thought, wondering if there would be fun house-type effects or booby traps.

Pam, the manager, was over at the pub when I arrived so I went to the ladies room. As I was washing my hands, I saw a ghostly woman, a stoutish, bosomy woman dressed in the style of about 1900. Her arms were crossed in an aggressive and most unladylike posture for a woman of that era. She had coarseness about her, despite her neat shirtwaist and smooth hair. I could see that this cruel woman had pretensions of respectability, an obsession with keeping up appearances. Perhaps she was trying to overcome some unsavory past. I continued to feel her presence as I walked through the dining areas on the main floor, the Drummers Room, the Canal Room, and the Lobby.

Pam arrived and after some pleasantries I followed her up to her office on the second floor where I left her so I could go explore. The first thing a visitor to the second floor sees is an oil portrait, done from a photograph, of a very formidable old bird who looks rather like the former Surgeon General, C. Everett Koop. The brass plate read, "Hon. James E. Emmitt." To the right was a chair holding a wrapped cigar and a package of Swisher Sweets™ in a glass ashtray. "Obviously for the ghost," I thought.

There were footsteps on the floor above. I immediately went in search of Pam. She hadn't walked by me on the stairs, but I didn't know if there was another way up. She was still in her office and assured me that she hadn't stirred and had asked the rest of the staff to stay downstairs in the bar and the kitchen.

I caught only a whiff of Mr. James R. Emmitt. Despite his patriarchal appearance in the portrait, and that straight-laced, "Hon.", I got the feeling he was really just one of the boys.

"Why are you here?" I asked him mentally.

He said something to the effect of, "This is where I'm comfortable." Or "This is where I belong."

When I later mentioned this to Pam, she raised her eyebrows. "But he was a millionaire! He collected art! He traveled to Europe!"

However, reading his autobiography, which gives an excellent, if biased, view of this self-made egotist, it was clear that Emmitt reveled in his rough-and-ready character, his bootstraps approach to life

Visually, much of the upper floors of the Emmitt House reminded me of *The Shining*: a maze of halls, lined with many doors. I walked into as many rooms as I could. Some were being used for storage, others for restoration materials. Still others were empty except for dust or fallen plaster, or the mannequins, which made me jump at every turn. I was certainly prejudiced, but I also got a feeling that whatever spirits were there were not pleased with the dummies.

In room 29, I leaned against the wall and closed my eyes. I felt, rather than saw, a young teenaged boy walk up to me. He reached out a hand to touch my cheek. I opened my eyes and he drew back.

In a dark, empty room to the right of the stairs on the third floor I felt someone stifling, smothering with lung trouble. I saw them beating on the wall with the flat of their hand for help. As I stood there, someone touched the top of my head.

A screen door led to a hall to the attic stairs. Several bird skeletons lay in a dusty nest of feathers in a corner. For the first time, I started to panic. "Do I *have* to go up there?" I thought. I got to the bottom of the stairs and froze. The attic ceiling papers were hanging in jagged shreds. A dark door loomed at the top of the stairs. I took a deep breath and climbed upwards, staring at the steps. If I don't make eye contact, I thought, maybe it won't be so bad. Head down, I turned to the end rooms first. In the light of the single window, I could see traces of silvered slime trails, all that was left of the wallpaper pattern, meandering on the walls. In the opposite room, the exposed plaster was corpse-grey gouged with holes and covered in penciled graffiti.

The under-eave room was dark. I didn't have a flashlight but I could see that there were few floorboards and decided to stay in the hall. I leaned into the room. I could see light coming through a hole in the chimney. Those bird skeletons probably meant that whatever was stirring in the dark was probably a lost pigeon. Probably. But there was a definite threat in the attic. A young man hiding in the dark. I backed away, as close to panic as I could get without running. Clinging to the hand rail, I slid down the stairs and felt the pressure ease off as soon as I got to the landing. To my relief, it disappeared altogether once I was beyond the screen door. I realized that the further up you go, the further away from the living, the stronger the dead become....

A door at the end of the second-floor hall led me into a large banquet room with a bar. I stared at the tin ceiling and at the rows of tables, perplexed. I couldn't visualize what this room had been. Later Pam showed me the markings on the floor and explained that a whole set of tiny guest rooms had been ripped out to make the bigger hall. You could see the outline of halls, doorways, and the cell-like rooms. Several psychics had visited when this area was still guest rooms. They had seen a woman in one room and a little boy in another. The woman was sent on into the light. When the psychic tried to do the same for the little boy, Pam, who was standing in the doorway, felt herself being pushed. She stopped the proceedings and walked into the room. The psychic began again. Again, Pam found herself pushed. That time she stopped the psychic for good.

Pam has worked at Emmitt House for around 12 years.

"The last two to three years, things have gotten more uncomfortable. I've smelled his cigar smoke some four or five times—which is enough!" she laughed. "But the most uncanny part was smelling it at home. I don't smoke and since I was in a negative relationship at the time, I felt like he was trying to protect me."

Pam gets a heavy feeling, a feeling of pressure whenever the spirits seem to be at their busiest. "Whenever that happens—day or night—I just say, 'Goodbye, guys! You can have it!' and go home." She and several other staff members also recognized the pressure I felt up in the attic.

I saw a woman in an old-fashioned "granny apron," the kind that goes over the head, busily cleaning something in a set of rooms over what is now the Pub. The cleaning woman seems to be a recurring motif at Emmitt House. Pam told me about a man who used to deliver soft drinks. "He was here very early one morning, before I came in. 'Where is everybody?' he said. 'I'm the first one here,' I told him. 'No, you're not. I just saw a lady upstairs cleaning.' 'What did she look like?' I asked. 'She was wearing a maid's uniform,' he said. 'Think about it,' I told him. 'Does anybody still wear a maid's uniform these days?' After that he just sort of stopped coming in...I think he got a different route."

A bank drive-through faces the back of the building. Several of the tellers asked Pam about a woman they saw cleaning in a back room when Pam was the only person in the building.

Ghostly customers, including children, have also been seen. Two children of an employee told their mother, "We're going to play with that little girl over there," pointing to an unseen child. Christy, a hostess, saw a little blonde boy standing in the hall. "Hi, honey!" she said. "Are you lost?" He just looked at her. "Follow me and we'll find your mommy," she said. She turned and reached back down to take the little boy's hand. There was no one there.

Hotel ghosts are notoriously difficult to prove. Thousands of people have stayed at Emmitt House. Identifying the individuals who have stayed on past check-out time is usually impossible. But in his *Reminiscences*, Emmitt wrote about the Harper family, nearly wiped out by smallpox when staying at the hotel. Could the Harper children still be roaming around Emmitt House?

Sometimes people get touched. Pam's daughter, Angie, was sitting on the last stool at the end of the bar by the juke box. Angie said, "I picked up my pop and felt a nudge like someone had brushed against my back. I looked at Mom and said, 'Did you just bump me?' She said, no, she was talking to someone else. I jumped off the stool. 'What was *that* then!?' I yelled at her. 'Probably just one of the ghosts got you,' said my Mom. She was right because everyone else was either on a stool at the bar or behind it."

Pam unlocked the basement and turned the light on for me. The basement was a maze of rooms, bricked-up openings and doors. In one room where the ductwork was routed through the door, I couldn't bring myself to walk into the darkness. I caught a glimpse of a terror-stricken black man hiding in this room. "This couldn't have been a stop on the Underground Railroad, could it?" I thought. Pam told me that there have always been rumors about tunnels and the Underground Railroad, but no proof.

I wonder if the frightened black man might have been hiding, not from slave catchers, but from a more local threat. In the late 1820s, there was a community of African Americans farming outside Waverly. Some citizens were jealous of the prosperity of these free blacks. They went so far as to attack one of the more prominent black farmers, trying to drive him off of his property. He fought back and the war was on. His son was shot dead in cold blood. Next, one of the farmers, attacked by a gang, split an attacker's head open with an axe. He was acquitted on the grounds of self-defense, but even the more tolerant whites in the area decided that the blacks must go. In 1830 nearly all African Americans were driven out of the Waverly area. Forced to abandon everything they had worked for, many fled to Michigan.

The staff does not like to spend time in the basement. Ghostly figures have been seen there and the sounds of "little kid noises" and whispering have been heard. Keisha, who does food deliveries, took Kevin, another employee, with her when she went down to the basement to change the pop. Soft drink syrup comes in plastic-lined boxes that snap onto lines going up to the soft drink stations. Kevin pulled the empty box off the machine and they walked into the next room to get a full one. It only took minutes to carry it back to the original machine where they found a full box already in place, hooked up and ready to go.

"*Nobody* could pass through that area of the basement without being seen!" Keisha said. Nobody living, of course.

Keisha was working across the hall from the serving station by the Canal Room when she heard and felt a "BOOM!" She found coffee grounds scattered all over the room. The coffee machine filter holder was lying on a counter opposite the coffee machine.

"Look what you did!" Keisha started to laugh. But the three servers who had been at the other end of the room weren't laughing. They were white with fear. Unable to speak, they shook their heads, no, they hadn't done it.

"That filter holder shot across the room like somebody had slung it!" Keisha said.

The Canal Pub is a cozy wood-lined bar tucked behind Emmitt House. Randalph, who works in the pub, told me about a scare he had last Halloween. The staff always dresses up and Randalph was dressed as The Crow, the graphic novel antihero.

"I was in the bathroom on the second floor, just down the hall from Pam's office. Suddenly there were three nurses in old-style uniforms with the hats and everything. I sensed that they were saying, 'I like what you're wearing...' I would *not* look at them. I just saw them out of the corner of my eye and they kept getting closer and closer..."

Randalph tried to imagine that they weren't there, but they refused to leave. He was hoping that they would go away. They didn't, but he did, bolting back downstairs.

Randalph also has seen ghostly children. One of them was a chubby blonde boy.

"I saw him in one of the rooms out of the corner of my eye. He was playfully picking up pieces of plaster and throwing it against the wall. I started to walk into the room and he gave me this look like, 'DON'T. *Stay out*! Let me play!'"

The Emmitt House has a bit of everything on the menu, from wings at the Canal Pub to, as Pam says, "the best steaks anywhere" in the Drummer Room. They have a full spectrum of spooks here, too, from the playful energy of the child ghosts and the hard-working maids to the lower-key energy of old James Emmitt himself. Could it be that he has mellowed in the afterlife? Or is he running down at last like an unwound watch? Even the most relentless businessmen have to take a vacation. Perhaps it's time for the Hon. James Emmitt to put his feet up and unwrap that cigar....

GHOST FOR THE MILL

Bear's Mill is a very tall building. It stands four stories high just beyond a bend in the road, its weathered wooden clapboard in a grove of lush green by the river. It is a timeless place.

Built in 1849, Bear's Mill is an authentic example of a stone grinding flour mill. Placed on the National Register of Historic Places in 1977, it is still in use today, grinding cornmeal, whole-wheat flour, and rye flour. The mill and buhr stones are powered by water.

Stepping over the threshold, I expected to see chickens scratching at grain on the floor. But there was no grain and the milling machinery stood silent. I wandered idly by the packets of strawberry-flavored popcorn, pancake mix, and cornmeal— the latter still ground on the premises. There were shelves of elegantly minimalist pottery, mossy carved stone basins for a Zen garden, gardenia-white aromatherapy lotions, and rose chintz oven mitts, all a little out of place, a little frivolous in this essentially primitive, working grist mill.

Footsteps creaked overhead. I assumed that the clerk was upstairs—until the tall blonde with the ice-blue eyes came in the side door. She had been enjoying the sunshine outside when my van drove up and only now had come in.

"Hmmm," I thought.

I climbed the stairs to the second floor. A sign cautioned visitors about the uneven floors and I chuckled at the precipitous slant, like the wildly tilting floor of a funhouse. The mill is a museum of rural agricultural life. Looking around, I saw the huge wells holding the buhr stones, a flour sack hung like a horse's nosebag on a wooden chute, colorful Darke County Fair posters printed with winsome, marcel-waved beauties, and handbills advertising livestock sales. I was particularly taken with a calendar from Sprout, Waldron and Co., Milling Engineers, which asked helpfully, "Have you a mill problem?" There were hoppers and milling machines like silent printing presses, a huge electrical panel with a Frankenstein's-lab switch, enormous drive belts stitched together with metal staples.

The third floor was almost completely filled with machinery: The room was an Escher maze of elevator legs, chutes, bins, pulleys, and hoppers. Some of the hoppers were mounted on legs so that I could see to the back of the room, but only beneath shoulder-height. I saw a man walking away from me, apparently tending the machines. He wore blue pants, rolled up at the bottom so I could see his worn, lace-up work shoes. He was not a large man and he moved slowly, as if he was tired. Then he walked around a corner of the machinery and was gone.

On the top floor, I sat down on a bench in a corner and looked to the end of the room. The opposite corner was in darkness. Something throbbed in the distance, like the dim echo of machinery and something stirred in the dark corner—a formless something, like smoke boiling up from the floor. It was as if something were trying to materialize. And yet, I felt peaceful, sleepy even, with the sun pouring in through the windows.

Downstairs a welcome mat of sunlight lay just inside the door. I bought some honey and "the world's best biscotti." The tall blonde's eyes widened as I asked if they had a ghost. "It gets pretty spooky here in the winter," she admitted. "There are always strange sounds."

A chorus of birds chirped outside. As I drove away I glanced up at the dusty windows, but he was probably still busy with his machinery. The shifting green of the trees and the sparkle of the river called to me to stay.

I could think of worse places to spend eternity.

HAUNTS FROM HISTORY:
Historical homes and museum ghosts

*All museums are haunted. The smell of blood on the
suit of armor, the fingerprints of a dead man on the
clay pot, the ghost of a lost love in a portrait...*
-Alexis-

I'm intrigued by survivals: the stump from a tree planted
by Johnny Appleseed, the top hat of George Washington's
valet, or a ghostly mica hand excavated from a Hopewell
mound. And what better place to find survivals of a more
unearthly kind than in those storehouses of the past: historical
homes and museums?

THE CAT CAME BACK

While I am completely at sea with nautical terms and
technicalities, I admire the curve of a hull, the wing of a sail,
and the blazing brilliance of a Fresnel lens. So I happily spent
some time prowling through the Fairport Harbor Marine
Museum.

As I was getting ready to leave the Museum to climb the
Lighthouse, I came in on the tail end of a conversation between
two volunteers about post mortem photographs, the Victorian
practice of photographing the dead. One of the volunteers said
something to the other volunteer about, "They didn't have
embalming in those days." My ears perked up. Any mortuary
topic is dear to my heart.

"Ah, but they did *wonders* with ice!" I said brightly,
leaving the two staring after me.

This exchange on preservation techniques was gruesomely appropriate. The Lighthouse in Fairport Harbor was the site of a grisly discovery: the remains of a mummified cat, found in a sealed crawl space.

The Fairport Harbor Light was designed and built by a Connecticut native named Jonathan Goldsmith. He submitted a bid of $2,900 for the lighthouse and the adjoining keeper's house, but neglected to build a cellar under the keeper's house. He claimed that the cellar hadn't been on the original specifications and soaked the Collector of Customs at Cleveland for another $2,132.

Although Goldsmith had a good reputation, he seems to have cut corners on the lighthouse. The tower's foundation settled so much that it had to be replaced at great expense.

The Collector of Customs had the last laugh. Six years later Goldsmith applied for the position of light keeper. His application crossed the desk of the same Collector of Customs who had handled the cellar addition and the faulty foundations. The position of light keeper was given instead to Samuel Butler, the first of a line of seventeen keepers to serve at the Fairport Light.

The port overseen by the light was busy and prosperous. Goods from all over the world flowed through the harbor. The light keeper kept the records of marine traffic and collected wharf fees. He also handled a different sort of goods from the southern states which began to flow through the port in the 1840s: fugitive slaves on their way to Canada. It is believed that some slaves hid in the cellar of the keeper's house.

Lake Erie winters and the shoddy construction which had dogged the light from the beginning made a new light imperative. This time the foundation was laid 12 feet deep in concrete. On August 11, 1871, the new light threw its beams 18 miles across the lake.[1]

Captain Joseph Babcock was the first keeper of this new Fairport Light. Two of his children, Robbie and Hattie, were born in the keeper's house. Robbie died there at the age of five, of smallpox. The boy is said to haunt the first floor of the museum. The staff have described the ghost as "a presence of dread." The spirit also manifests as a cold breeze and a foul smell either of decay or the distinctive stench of smallpox.

A far more pleasant lighthouse spirit is a ghostly cat. A former curator, Pamela Brent, lived upstairs in the museum for several years. The phantom feline looked like a puff of gray smoke. "It would skitter across the floor near the kitchen, like it was playing, but without feet...I would catch glimpses of it from time to time...one evening I felt its presence when it jumped on the bed. I felt its weight pressing on me. At first it kind of freaked me out. But ghosts don't bother me. They are part of the world."

Other staff members were skeptical of the idea of a cat ghost. That was before workers installing air conditioning vents under the lighthouse found the mummified cat.

I've seen a photo of the mummy. Its skin is leathery. Its empty eye sockets are cobwebbed. It is not a cuddly cat. It is emphatically not a thing to come upon in the twilight in an empty keeper's house at the bottom of the basement stairs.

In addition to doing publicity for the museum, Carol Bertone is also on the building and grounds committee. She went over one spring evening to change the timer on the lights in the Keeper's House basement.

"I was there by myself. It was getting dark and going down into the basement was always kind of creepy. I got to the bottom of the steps and I saw this *thing*. There was a mummi-fied cat kind of standing on all fours, its face turned towards me. I screamed and ran back upstairs. Of course, I'd always heard the stories about the ghost...

"Then I got to the top of the steps and said to myself, 'This can't be. I have to go back down.' So I actually got up enough courage to go back down the stairs and I saw that it was a mummy. It had its whiskers, its eyelashes, its feet so perfectly formed, its claws.... Of course, I had no idea how it had gotten there."

It was discovered when workmen installing air conditioning were working in the basement. One of the men climbed into a tight crawl space with his flashlight.

"He was looking at something and laid his head down on something which just happened to be a mummified cat," Carol said.

The workmen who discovered the cat didn't know what to do with their desiccated discovery. They left it at the foot of the basement stairs to snarl out of the twilight at Carol.

For a time the mummy cat was kept in a cardboard box at the Museum, much to the delighted terror of schoolchildren. Some people thought keeping the cat distracted from the mission of the Museum. Others thought it unhygienic or unsuitable for the faint of heart. The trustees decided to have it taken away.

Where did the cat come from? Captain Babcock's wife was bedridden for a number of years during her husband's tenure as keeper. She kept many cats, both for company and to keep down vermin. It has been suggested that the unfortunate cat was accidentally trapped beneath the house and starved to death, mummifying naturally in the dark, cool space.

I think there are two other possibilities. In the United Kingdom, and in some places in the U.S., it is not at all unusual for mummified cats to be found inside walls, in crawl spaces, and above rafters. Sometimes they are found posed in aggressive positions, sometimes even with a rat or mouse skeleton in their mouths. It's a kind of folk magic: live cats keep away mice and rats; a dead cat will keep away evil spirits and witches. If a witch came prowling around with her "familiar," which was often a cat, your watch-cat in the walls would know how to deal with her.

The second reason a mummified cat might be sealed up in a crawl space has to do with the very ancient belief in foundation sacrifices. This Celtic tradition states that if one wants to ensure that a building will stand firm and to bring good luck to the building, a living creature must be buried alive in the foundation. Humans were preferred, but a cat would do.

Goldsmith's original light and keeper's house were a nightmare of shoddy construction, cracked foundations, and cost overruns. Is it outlandish to suggest that some English or Irish workman privately decided a quiet foundation sacrifice might help save the new Fairport Light from the same fate? After all, who would miss a cat?

In 1925 the light in the tower was extinguished, replaced by an unromantic foghorn station. Scheduled for demolition, the lighthouse was saved by the citizens of Fairport, who raised funds to establish a marine museum and preserve the lighthouse.

Today the light keeper's house is the Fairport Harbor Marine Museum. Displays tell the story of Lake Erie's maritime past and lore through relics like the old Fairport Light Fresnel lens, set like a multifaceted diamond in its polished brass setting, and the pilothouse of the Great Lakes carrier *Frontenac*. There are ships' models, and pieces of tackle, stories of shipwrecks, lake tragedies, and heroic rescues. The 70-foot tower can be climbed by a lace-like spiral iron staircase. Don't look down as you climb, but if you brave the stairs, you will be rewarded with a spectacular view of the lake.

No one lives in the keeper's house anymore so the ghostly cat, who is still heard skittering overhead, perhaps plays with the ghostly little boy Robbie. Carol Bertone assures me that the mummy cat is "still in the village."

There is an old song called "The Cat Came Back" by Harry Miller (1893). To a thumpy jumpy tune the cat comes to the end of its nine lives and falls dead, inspiring the last chorus eminently appropriate to this story:

But its ghost came back the very next day,
Yes, its ghost came back, maybe you will doubt it,
But its ghost came back; it just couldn't stay away.

THE BISHOP'S HOUSE

I have written about Brownella Cottage in Galion several times before. (*Haunted Ohio*, p. 128 and *Ghost Hunter's Guide*, p. 90) It was my ideal of a haunted house in childhood.

It still ranks pretty highly. Here are two new tales from the home of that intriguing character Bishop William Montgomery Brown, "Bad Bishop Brown" or "The Bolshevik Bishop."

AN ALARMING APPARITION

This first-hand story was shared by Doug Osborne of Galion.

It was about 2:30 one morning and I was awakened by the telephone. The phone call was from the police department dispatcher asking me to meet two patrolmen who were responding to a security alarm at Brownella Cottage. It was a dark and stormy night! It really was!

I arrived at the cottage and was greeted by the patrolmen who told me they had checked all of the outside entrances, and found everything in order, but we needed to check out the interior. I entered the house and told the officers that the alarm system indicated that the sensor for the north door of the museum had been activated. The officers searched the house and found no one so we went to the museum to check the north door. It was closed and locked. We came back in the house to try to reset the alarm system but it wouldn't reset.

I told the officers to go ahead and leave and I would call the security company and work out the resetting. I went to the kitchen telephone and found that it was dead.

I returned to the museum to check the door again. I unlocked the door, opened it, closed and locked it again, and returned to the house to check the alarm message board. The board now said the alarm could be reset.

I went back to the kitchen where our master light control panel is located. I was going to turn off the master lights, go to the back hall to the alarm controls, reset them, and leave.

As I turned the lights off I heard someone running up the hall towards the kitchen where I was standing in the dark. He stopped in the hall just before the doorway into the kitchen. I stood silent and he stood silent.

"What do I do now?" I thought. The police missed this person. They were gone and it was just me and him...

I slowly and quietly moved back across the kitchen and turned on all of the lights. As the lights came on, someone ran back up the hall toward the front of the house.

I looked around the corner into the hallway and could not see him. My heart was pounding. I decided to turn off the lights, run to the alarm control panel, set the alarm, lock the door and go outside to wait for the motion detector to be set off by whoever was still in the cottage. Then the police would come and apprehend the intruder.

I waited in my car in the driveway. "As soon as the person moves to leave," I thought. "the alarm will go off and we will have him…."

Twenty minutes passed. No alarm. I decided to go home, have a cup of coffee and wait for the dispatcher to call again. I went home. The motion detectors picked up nothing. The call never came.

The running sounds were loud and clear and reacted to my turning the lights on and moving about the cottage. So who or what ran down the hall in the house? I don't know.

THE WHITE-HAIRED BISHOP

This story was sent to me by Susan, who used to live in Galion.

I used to get up early on Sunday morning and go to the laundromat. One snowy February morning I got to the laundromat a little too early, it hadn't opened yet. So I thought I'd drive through town. It had just gotten light. It had snowed and on a Sunday morning the downtown was deserted.

I turned down this street and found Brownella Cottage. It was my first glimpse of it and I was intrigued. I kept expecting to see someone at the windows. I kept going around the block looking at the house. On the second trip around in the glass walkway right outside the study there was someone sitting there with his back to me. He was dressed in black and had shoulder-length snowy white hair. It sat so still, I thought it was a dummy. I went around the block two or three times and it was still there.

To sit that still for so long in that cold, it *had* to be a dummy. For some reason, I had to see who or what that figure was. I stopped the car and honked a few times and still the figure didn't move a muscle. Thinking by now it was certainly a dummy and I was being silly, I turned the car around and gave one last look before I headed for the Laundromat. The walkway was empty! The "dummy" was gone.

About a month after that, I met a woman who worked for the Historical Society. I asked her about a dummy. There were none. I asked her about the man with long, white hair. There would not have been anyone there at that hour of the morning. She made me feel foolish, yet that man was a real and solid as anything.

NOTE: In his later years Bishop William Montgomery Brown had shoulder-length, snowy white hair. He was a tall and massively-built man, quite a striking figure.

LUCRETIA AT LAWNFIELD

President Garfield's house, Lawnfield, is at its best on a golden summer afternoon.

Before I went into the visitor's center, I stopped by the ladies room, which is in a building outside the center. As I was drying my hands I was suddenly struck by a strong female presence in the room.

"Mrs. Garfield?" I thought. And I saw "Crete" as Lucretia Garfield was known, holding a chicken.

"What in the world would she be doing *here*?" I thought, bewildered. And *what* would she be doing with a chicken?

Completely befuddled, I went in and bought a ticket for the tour of the house. I looked at the exhibits, admired Garfield's smoldering good looks as a young man, marveled at the small size of his feet (his boots were on display) and sympathized with Crete as I read that, early in their marriage, Garfield bluntly told her that their marriage was the biggest mistake he'd ever made. Also on display in a glass case was Garfield's hauntingly realistic death mask.

Having seen all there was to see in the Carriage House, and, finding that there were still 20 minutes until the tour began, I went outside to enjoy the sun. There I found a map of the grounds as they had originally been laid out. Garfield had intended Lawnfield to be a working farm. The map revealed that the parking lot by the restrooms had been the poultry yard.

Lawnfield started life as a nine-room farmhouse. Garfield added eleven rooms to accommodate his family of five children. He also built a campaign office behind the house and added the famous "front porch" where he ran the campaign that won him the presidency. Thousands of citizens flocked to Lawnfield to visit with Mr. Garfield on his front porch.

Garfield only served as president for 200 days before he was shot by a disgruntled office-seeker. After his death, Mrs. Garfield lived much of the rest of her life at Lawnfield.

The home was restored to the period of 1880-1904 by an $11.8 million renovation effort by the Western Reserve Historical Society and the National Park Service. The result is a living house, a house you can actually imagine filled with this extraordinary family. Garfield descendants lived in the house up until 1936 so the majority of the furniture and artifacts are family pieces. I admired tiles painted by the very talented Mrs. Garfield, some stunning stained glass, the glowing golden woodwork, and a Turkish cozy corner in the room of Mollie Garfield.

Using financial gifts from the American people, Mrs. Garfield built the library room onto the house four years after her husband's assassination. She meant to preserve President Garfield's books, private papers and documents and created the first presidential library. The library included a steel-lined vault to hold all of her husband's papers and mementos.

One of the larger rooms in the house, the library felt wonderful: light, vibrant, alive, filled with joy and good memories. It houses Mr. Garfield's desk from his nine terms as a U.S. Congressman. A startlingly realistic bust of Garfield in ghostly white marble stands before a black drape in one corner. We peeped into the vault. There were shelves at the end, with bundles to illustrate how papers were originally stored, although all papers have been removed to the Library of Congress. A tiny table and a chair stood at the far end of the vault.

Tour members went into the vault one or two at a time. I snapped a photo of a framed funeral wreath of waxed flowers, the one sent to his funeral by Queen Victoria, then slid out, noting the tiny painted landscape on the vault door.

I took a few more photos. Then I glanced back into the vault. There was Mrs. Garfield sitting at the table, reading something white, a letter perhaps. She was completely absorbed in her reading and did not look up. I shrugged and continued my circuit of the library.

Perhaps two minutes later, the guide said, "Mrs. Garfield used to go into the vault and sit there, reading old letters and documents. She called it her 'Vault of Memory.'"

Was the vision really a ghost? Or was it just an image, etched on the spot by the widow's grief? Around the corner from the library is Garfield's study. In the hall leading to the study was a bookcase with blue curtains keeping dust and light from the books. There I saw Garfield bending over, rummaging through the books.

It wasn't until I was working on these notes later that I realized the contradiction: that his spirit putters through his books while his wife sits in the vault built after his death. I don't know how to explain it. They both linger—but separately. Perhaps their beliefs during their lives offers a clue. Whether in the poultry yard or in the vault, is she merely a memory, a reflection of grief frozen in time by her loss? In Spiritualist doctrine, death is seen as going from one room into another. Did Garfield's Spiritualist beliefs allow him to continue to exist on another plane, in another room—perhaps his study, filled with books?

It is a paradox, but not one to be solved in my lifetime.

Lawnfield isn't the only Garfield memorial to be haunted. The Garfield Monument at Lakeview Cemetery in Cleveland is a massive mausoleum in a mixture of Byzantine, Romanesque, and Gothic style. Some of the money sent to Mrs. Garfield was given to the Garfield National Monument Association. The monument was completed in 1890. Today it is said that the ghost of President Garfield haunts the striking stone tower. People have reported seeing strange lights inside the monument. Garfield's was a life that was snuffed out far too soon. Perhaps his vitality goes on, even in the tomb.

THE DEVIL DOG OF COSI

My grandfather was a member of the American Legion band. With him I used to spend some time at Veteran's Hall on East Broad Street in Columbus and I always found the building to be very creepy. I'm not the only one to think so.

Tonee, a volunteer at the Center of Science and Industry museum, now called COSI Columbus, told me this story:

"Recently, COSI Columbus moved from 280 East Broad St. to 333 West Broad St. The old 280 location was Veterans Hall before COSI took over in the early 1960s. The ghost of the building wasn't the most pleasant of ghosts to experience, nor the most common. It was a dog, a Scottish terrier that would randomly appear in hallways, on the stairs, and often on the second floor, just staring at people.

"Many people who worked in the 280 location have told me that they saw or heard the dog running around and barking as if at an intruder. I had only one personal experience with the dog. This occurred just a few months before the old COSI was to shut down for the move to the new West Broad location. It was a relatively dead Thursday afternoon. I was walking up the stairs from the second to the third floor when something slammed into my legs, knocking me over. I figured I was just clumsy and fell over by myself. But about five steps later, it happened again, and then once more just as I reached the top. Something kept crashing into my shins like a dog who wants to play. Needless to say, I was freaked! Another volunteer who saw me falling over very simply said, 'He got you too, huh?' Apparently this was something the dog did quite often to volunteers and paid team members alike, but they had never seen it happen to a guest. Later that same day while I was walking back down the stairs, I felt compelled to stop and turn around. I saw what seemed to be a dog watching me from the top of the steps. Like most people who see something, I figured I was crazy and just kept walking.

"That was in August; the following February I started working as a volunteer at the new West Broad location. While I have strong reason to believe that it has its own ghosts (that's another story!) it seems that our "devil dog" who tries to trip people has followed us. It is now playing tricks on team members in their third floor office spaces. The dog is heard barking and people have seen just a glimpse of something going around corners that really didn't seem like it belonged there."

The official nickname of the Scottish Terrier is "The Diehard." The Devil Dog of COSI is living up to that name.

THE GHOSTS OF ZOAR

The Ohio community of Zoar began literally with a dream. The Separatists of Zoar were a sect of Christian pacifists from Germany. One of the original Separatists, Barbara Gruberman, went into trances that lasted for hours and saw uncannily accurate visions. She advised the Separatists to go to America and told them how they might recognize their next leader. If they banded together, she said, they would prosper, but only for "as long as a man lives." If they disbanded, she warned, there would be no end of trouble and if they fell away from their religion, "no two stones they had laid would remain one on top of the other" and strangers would take over their property.[2]

A group of Separatists set sail for American in 1817. Sympathetic Quakers loaned them money to purchase 5,500 acres in the Tuscarawas River. They called their settlement "Zoar" after the town to which Lot fled seeking refuge from Sodom. Harsh winters and poor crops forced the settlers to pool resources, establishing "The Society of Separatists of Zoar." Joseph Bimeler was their Agent-General, or manager, as well as their spiritual leader.

The community was on the verge of starvation. Every available hand was needed to work the fields and produce goods to sell. Pregnant or nursing mothers could not pull their own economic weight. A rule of celibacy was introduced: no one was to marry and married couples were to separate. To retire their debt to the Quakers, the Society contracted to dig seven miles of the Ohio-Erie Canal which passed through their land. By the time the Society paid off the loan, the ban on marriage was lifted. It is said that some Society members introduced Bimeler to a comely young maiden to induce him to revoke the celibacy rule.

The Separatists shared houses which were identified by number. Each house had its own kitchen where meals were prepared and a communal dining area. Every Friday, a representative of the house would take her basket and collect the week's supplies of coffee, sugar, tea, butter, and yarn from the Magazine, or storehouse. All the bread for the village was baked in the bakery building. In the afternoon, the children would bring their bread cloths, numbered with their house number, and the appropriate number of loaves would be distributed to each house. The community was noted for its cleanliness and order. Zoar products like coverlets, tinware, stoves, beer, and harness were much in demand. The Society also established the Zoar Hotel which became a popular resort for the rich of Cleveland, who came to the country for fresh air and wholesome country food. [3]

The canal brought prosperity, and paradoxically worldliness, that would later destroy the Society by opening the area to commercial traffic. By the mid-1800s, the Society had assets of over one million dollars, but with the death of the charismatic Bimeler in 1853, the Society began to decline. In 1898, they divided their assets and disbanded. Each Society member received a share of land, houses, and possessions.

Today many of Zoar's structures have been restored. You can tour the bakery, the hothouse, the gardens, and many of the numbered houses.

On a recent visit, I stayed in a local inn. The room was charming, with its exposed brick and beam construction and its cheerful embroidered patchwork quilt on the high spool bed. Charming, except for the dark curved wood rocking chair with a cranky elderly lady ghost in a white cap sitting in it.

The TV refused to work, my cell phone was swallowed by a black hole, then <u>both</u> the clocks in the room ran backwards. It was freezingly cold, although it was in the humid 90s outside, and there were unexpected little currents of air that played about my face as I sat in bed. And that elderly lady.... I moved carefully around the chair, making every excuse not to get close.

I went out for a stroll in the evening quiet. There was a sliver of a moon in a pink and blue sky. The birds swooped and glided in the air. A mosquito bite reminded me that this was malaria country when the Separatists were digging the Erie Canal. The homes I passed seemed curiously empty. Even private homes were unlit, giving them an abandoned air. Across the main road was the sadly empty Zoar Hotel, resurrected from decay, but a body without a soul. It is said to be haunted by the fun-loving spirit of Alexander Gunn, a non-Separatist, who moved to Zoar and made his life there one long party. The ghost of Mary Ruof who ran the Hotel until her death in 1919, supposedly rocks an empty cradle in the Hotel.

I had expected a large-scale, Williamsburg-style extravaganza. Instead, I found a sleepy little town built around the communal gardens with its central Norwegian Cedar representing Christ, surrounded by twelve arbor vitae bushes known as The Twelve Apostles. These symbolic evergreens are circled by a path representing Heaven, and diagonal paths to show the many ways to walk to Heaven. Girdled by a white picket fence with Zoar blue fence posts, the garden is a living sermon.

The garden is overlooked by the Garden House, the first greenhouse in the state of Ohio. Its tall wall of windows shelters a hothouse, heated by under-floor charcoal furnaces, where exotic tropical fruits and plants could be grown year-round. The Separatists became known all over the world for their seeds, bulbs, and cuttings.

The austerely magnificent Number One House broods over the main street. It was originally built as a home for the aged, but those who lived here complained of ill-treatment and asked to be moved in with other families. Next it was offered to Joseph Bimeler, who declined, thinking it was more of a "king's palace." He did not want it thought that he was seeking special treatment. He finally moved into the house, but only on the condition that several other families join him. The building also served as the administrative offices for the Society.

I asked a costumed guide if he knew of any ghost stories. I had walked past the house in the twilight the night before and peered in at the windows. At dusk it is easy to imagine a figure gliding by a window or through a darkened room.

The guide stressed that he could not vouch for the truth of this story because he was not there when it happened. Guests can wander at will through the large house and through the walkway to the kitchen. Edith*, another guide, found a man sitting on the walkway, "as pale as a ghost," said Edith. At first he seemed unable to talk. She wondered if he was sick or had an accident.

After repeated questioning, he spoke. "Are there any other guides dressed like you in the building?" he asked.

"No, just me," Edith told him.

"That's what I thought," he said, and clammed up again.

After more persuasion, he told her that he had been on the second floor, walking by the staircase, when he caught a glimpse of someone on the stairs to the third floor. He turned and saw an older woman, dressed in the plain dress, fichu, and cap of the Society women. She wasn't doing anything particular, just walking on the stairs in an unhurried way, going about her business. Her face was lined and careworn. He turned his head for a second or two and when he turned back, she was gone. There was nowhere she could have gone in that short time.

Some of the other haunted sites of Zoar:

One of the oldest buildings in the village is a tiny doll house of a log cabin currently known as Cowger House. It was House #9 of the Separatist numbered houses. The ghost is "P.J.", an elderly gentleman in a purple jacket who does little more than just materialize.

The Cider Mills Bed & Breakfast was originally the Zoar cabinet shop. The Separatist who worked here claimed that the ghost of an "Old Indian" came to him with strange but accurate prophecies about both the Battle of Gettysburg where the Zoarites fought with the 107th Ohio Infantry and about the assassination of President Lincoln.

A short way from Zoar is The Inn on the River, haunted by "George," believed to be a man who died while passing through Zoar on the canal boat and who was buried in the Separatist cemetery. He mostly haunts the second floor and tends to throw things when people make fun of him.[4]

The Ghost Field was located just east of Route 212, south of the Peter Bimeler home. A mysterious light has been seen here on certain moonlit nights. It could have been swamp gas or the "Will-o-the-Wisp," seen before the swamps along Route 212 between Zoar and Bolivar were drained. These are spheres of light, up to three feet in diameter, the color of fluorescent lights. They would soar to several hundred feet or hover just above the tree tops, or, worse, follow you if you got too close.[5]

Even today Zoar seems isolated in space and time. You may still hear the ghostly sound of the Zoar Village band, the lapping of the water in the canal, a sermon fervently preached by Joseph Bimeler, or the creak of a not so empty rocking chair.

THE PHANTOMS AT FULTON

The Fulton County Historical Society Museum isn't an enormous building, but it seems to have an unusually high number of ghosts on exhibit for those who can see them. It was built in 1868 as the first high school in Wauseon. By 1897 it was crumbling. The new owner replaced the third floor with an attic and turned the building into a boarding house. Several physicians from Archbold later bought the building and turned it into the area's first hospital in 1903. Now it is the Fulton County Historical Society Museum.

I visited on an overcast day in March. To my disappointment, the Museum was closed. I walked around the building, peering in windows. Finally I boldly put my hands to the glass of the right front window, trying to see through the curtain. It was a mistake.

I recoiled as if burnt. A very irritable woman was standing behind the curtain glaring at me.

"That would be a nondescript, older woman," Museum Director Barbara Berry says, matter-of-factly. "She's been seen in the parlor, the front window or sitting in the window just above it. Other people have described her as annoyed and fidgety. She doesn't mean any harm, but it upsets her when people come into the parlor. She just doesn't like you being there."

That was just the beginning. Barb has a whole roster of ghosts who haunt the building.

There's a gentleman who smokes in the dining room/parlor area. "When you hit where he is, it's like a hot pocket! It's an overwhelming smell, pipe or cigar smoke, very masculine."

There's also a little boy who has introduced himself either as Joe or Johnny. He likes to grab handfuls of tablecloth in the dining room, bunching it up. "He took a young boy on a guided tour of the museum one day. His grandma could hear this one-sided conversation going on, only things that he could have heard from somebody who'd been to the museum. 'I'm talking to Joe,' he told his grandma." The little boy ghost is chatty. Other sensitive people have said that he's said, "Tell Barb that I like her. I like how she decorates for Christmas."

"He seems to like Christmas. He'll take the balls off the tree and line them up in front of the tree. One trustee who was taking down the Christmas decorations got pelted by flying acorns!" Some children have seen him sitting on the stairs and one photo showed a little boy's head looking out the front door.

"Then there's the famous Abigail. Children playing in the park would not come up to the building because she stared at them. She's the most famous ghost. She's seen from the window, shade up or not, daylight or dark.

"We had a painter come in to take off the old wallpaper in one of the rooms. He was in here by himself. After he came back from lunch, he found the door shut and his ladder and drop cloths pushed up against the door. He went back to work. He didn't want to think about it. Then the door slammed. And there she was, standing there in the room with him, looking very upset. Then she was gone. He left too.

"Four different psychics have given the name of "Abigail." Supposedly she was sent for by her fiancé, but when she got here, he was not to be found. She is still waiting.

"I got a letter from a man now living in Florida. He lived in the museum when it was a boarding house. The room with the door to the attic was his bedroom. He would scream every night. His parents were so upset! He could hear *her* coming down the stairs every night. There would be this woman in white, holding a candle, leaning over him."

Most of the manifestations happen on the second floor at the south end of the building. Things are especially lively in the evenings. "It's *insane,*" said Barbara. "The noises, the foot-steps, the chatter…The curator before me heard an elderly woman singing a hymn. That curator was found on the porch, scared out of the building. I just say, 'Good morning, guys!'"

When the building was a hospital, the nurses lived in the attic. Barb doesn't like to think about that part of the building.

"Many visitors have seen the same thing without me saying a word," Barb said, stopping to take a deep breath.

"There's a young lady hanging from the rafter, asking to be cut down. She's wearing white. I don't know if she's a nurse. One visitor started to weep in the attic, crying, 'She's begging me to cut her down!'"

No local legends explain this horrifying apparition. Barb plans to check the records of the local funeral home director.

Barb thinks there's someone else in the attic, "someone who is part of the reason she is hanging there. I don't go up there alone *ever*. It just takes your breath away."

THE LADY, THE LAUNDRESS, AND THE POSSUM

With his salt-and-pepper hair, purple shirt and mauve suspenders, Chuck Jacobs looks like a trendy SoHo gallery owner. Instead, he is the genial curator of the Wolcott House Museum Complex. In addition to Wolcott House, there's a log home from the banks of the Miami and Erie Canal, an 1840s saltbox-style farmhouse, the Clover Leaf Railroad Depot complete with caboose and boxcar, the Monclova Country Church, and an 1840 Greek Revival-style home housing the Talking Turtle Shop.

The gem of the collection, Wolcott House, was built for Mary Wells Wolcott, a granddaughter of Chief Little Turtle. She was the child of Little Turtle's daughter, Sweet Breeze, and Indian agent William Wells.

William Wells was born on the Pennsylvania frontier. When he was about 14, he was captured by Indians and adopted by an elderly Miami chief. Wells learned to love his adopted parents and the Indian way of life. Some say that his prowess as a warrior at the massacre of St. Clair's army brought him to the attention of Little Turtle who gave him the hand of his daughter, Sweet Breeze. Their daughter, Mary was born in 1800.

These were complicated times of shifting allegiances. Chief Little Turtle, an honorable and courageous warrior, became convinced after his defeat by General Anthony Wayne at Ft. Recovery that the Indians could not stand against the whites. At the same time Wells made the difficult decision to return to life with the white settlers. Perhaps he realized that he could do more for his family by making this choice.

According to Darius Heald, grandson of Samuel Wells, William and Little Turtle made a family compact to go their separate ways but agreed not to kill each other in battle. They would remain friends and work for the benefit of both cultures.

Wells acted as interpreter for the Miami at the Treaty of Greenville signing in 1795. Little Turtle spoke eloquently and persuasively to obtain the best possible settlement for his people. For the rest of his life, the Chief advocated peaceful coexistence with the Americans.[6]

Sweet Breeze died when Mary was 4 or 5 and the children were sent to live with their uncle Samuel Wells, a planter and horse breeder, near Louisville, Kentucky. Here Mary was trained in the social graces of Southern high society. Her father was killed in the Ft. Dearborn massacre of 1812, his heart torn out and eaten by his Potawatomi adversaries to absorb his courage.

When her uncle moved his family to Missouri, the orphaned Mary went with them. There she met James Wolcott, marrying him in 1821. They arrived in Maumee in 1826. Wolcott had a finger in every financial pie: ship-building, banking, a hotel and general store, mills, shipping, and real estate. In 1827 he built a splendid home on 300 acres overlooking the Maumee River, using local hand-hewn walnut logs, still visible in the basement ceiling. Wolcott created an elegant house with a sweeping staircase, delicately proportioned two-story portico and handsome mantelpieces. It is said to be patterned after Glenview, Samuel Wells's plantation mansion where Mary grew up.

Mary Wolcott must have felt torn between her American Indian heritage and the genteel Southern life of her plantation-owner uncle. Did the southern belles of Louisville taunt her about her black hair and "savage" blood? Did she finally feel settled when she married James Wolcott and moved into this grand house overlooking the Maumee River? We have only fragments of diaries, letters, and documents about Mary Wolcott. Family tradition emphasizes her intelligence, piety and refinement, and her respect for Native American traditions. She bore five sons and one daughter. She supervised the children's education, entertained her husband's guests and business associates, and saw to it that all residents of the property were housed, fed, clothed, scrubbed, and doctored. She died in 1843 at the age of 43. James died in 1873.

Like many 19th century women, Mary is a woman without a voice. We can only speculate about her feelings, hopes, and fears since only her house remains. Unless you count the spirits.

Chuck obligingly waited in the volunteer room while I prowled up stairs, down stairs, through rooms and halls, and started at things seen only out of the corner of my eye.

It is, as I told Chuck later, a *startling* house. In a literal sense, it is a house of many levels. There are multiple stairs and floors, mostly due to sections being added over the years. It feels as if there are multiple periods of time layered one over the other.

Even looking at my notes, I cannot recall my exact path through the house that day. Up halls and down the back stairs, giddied by mirrors and pictures, gazing down the swoop of the front hall stairs—it is all a muddle.

I do know that I was reluctant to cross the landing above the entrance hall. As I stood in the hall below looking up, a woman in a loose, flowing white dress rushed across the landing, crossing from right to left. In a true tape-loop effect she again flew across the passage with an identical motion. She moved like someone fleeing in fear.

The apparition wore a high-waisted gown, full and gauzy. I tried to reconcile the style with the date of the house. Was the woman pregnant? The 1820s was a transitional period in fashion. It wasn't until I consulted a costume history book that I realized that the high-waisted style lingered through the 1820s. With six living children, Mary Wells Wolcott would frequently have been in a family way. But there is nothing to give us the name of the woman on the landing or where she is going over and over and over so anxiously.

Karen, Chuck's wife, told of a curious occurrence on the landing.

"I was downstairs in the basement with a tour. I heard a thump. Both candles from the candlesticks on the landing were on the floor. I put them back in, screwed them down in the sockets, then went down to my tour.

"I heard the thump again. This time one candle was lying on the floor. Now I don't know if that was just because I didn't push it in hard enough or..."

Or did a ghostly woman knock it over?

The room to the right of the entrance hall is labeled "The Judge's Room." Wolcott was Toledo Common Pleas attorney and an associate judge. He used this room as his office and as an unofficial courtroom. His desk, bookcases, and tall-case clock all survive in this highly masculine room. The clock "has a mind of its own," Chuck told me, as Glenna, Coordinator of Volunteer Special Events found out:

"I went in to close up the house one evening. I turned on the light in the volunteer room and walked into the Judge's office. I was startled to find the clock in the corner was ticking. I thought, 'I just stepped on the floor wrong.' But the next day I jumped all over the room, and never made it tick. Ghosts don't talk to me, furniture does!"

Standing in the hall, I kept catching a glimpse of a woman sitting by the fire in the parlor. She glanced at me without interest. She was wearing a darkish dress of the 1840s and a white lace cap with lappets. The room was crammed with chairs, china dogs, lamps, clocks, an embroidered firescreen, and a pianoforte. There were mirrors and pictures with reflective glass everywhere—one of the details that makes Wolcott House so startling.

Off the dark parlor was a charming dining room with its trim and fireplace painted a cheerful blue. Even the glass in the transom over the door of this pleasing room was painted with compotes of fruit.

The upstairs was arranged as a museum, with glass cases containing flints, pottery, an enormous doll house, and a photograph of a strange carved stone head. I was particularly struck by a detail in a memorial picture: a flock of ash-white, skeletal moths made of scraps of fabric and gilt wire.

The master bedroom was crammed with a four-poster bed and family artifacts including a mannequin dressed in a fawn-brown dress with a "V" of fringe. For a long time, it was thought to be an authentic Native American dress from Sweet Breeze, but it is probably much later in date. I seemed to feel the presence of the same woman I'd seen on the landing in this room.

Helpful Chuck reminded me that I hadn't visited the basement. I felt a chill as I descended the stairs and immediately went into a kind of huddled, defensive mode. For once I knew exactly why I felt shivery cold. The door to the outside was open letting in the cold March air. I shut it. Turning, I saw a door to a space under the staircase. I opened it, to find furnace equipment—and a child sobbing in the dark, shut in for some childish crime.

This time the chill had nothing to do with the weather. I sat down on one of the benches set out for tour groups. I noted the stone threshold cemented into the wall. Could it have been open to the outside? The blackened, hand-hewn beams, some still knobbly where the branches had been trimmed, gave an unsettling impression of the bones of some prehistoric creature.

With its two fireplaces, the basement was the heart of Wolcott House, furnishing food, warmth, and shelter. It is said that the outside door was always left unlocked and that Indians and other travelers would shelter here.

The basement should have been light with its whitewashed walls and many windows. Yet it was dark and all I could think was, "drudgery and depression…"

As I sat there I saw a large woman, full-bosomed, with ginger hair and a flat, piggy face. She was swearing and hitting a dark-haired child, possibly the same child I had seen shut under the stairs. I saw the reddish hairs on her bared arms and smelled hot, soapy water. Chuck later told me that census records from the second half of the 19th century listed what appeared to be an Irish servant.

Some of the busy feel of Wolcott house may have come from underground political activities. There was a movement in

1837-8 to encourage the Canadians to revolt against Britain, mirroring the American War of Independence. We have a letter that James Wolcott wrote urging people to attend a public meeting to support the Canadian Patriot cause. However, his name is not listed in a local newspaper article on the meeting. Lori Schillig, who, with Nick Reiter of The Avalon Foundation, investigated Wolcott House, strongly sensed an anxiety in the house over covert activities and saw barrels of gunpowder hidden in the basement.

Two months after Lori's visit, Chuck found an editorial in an historic *Maumee Express* newspaper, chastising local citizens for aiding and abetting illegal activities. The editorial specifically mentions barrels of arms on their way to Canada. Wolcott was a wholesaler and shipper. He may have been running guns to Canada. This was a highly dangerous game, since anyone caught, even an American citizen, would be either executed as a traitor or transported to Australia. Could this be the reason for the anxious lady on the landing?

Wolcott House also has a report of one of the strangest ghosts I've ever heard of: a ghostly opossum.

In December, 2001, Chuck's wife Karen was sitting in the entrance hall of Wolcott House, reading a magazine. She told me, "[Chuck and I] had been talking about ghosts recently. Chuck mentioned that they are often seen out of the corner of the eye and they vanish when you look at them directly.

"I saw this thing over the top of my magazine. What Chuck and I had been talking about clicked in my head and I had the presence of mind to not move my eyes, but looked at it indirectly. It was larger than a rat but not a cat or dog. It came down the stairs and then crept along the wall, kind of waddling, moving its head back and forth like it was sniffing. It moved somewhere between a saunter and a scurry.

"I watched it for what seemed a long time—in reality about 30 seconds or so—then it went around the corner into the parlor. I lifted my eyes from the magazine and didn't see it after that.

"It was kind of white or light-grey—possum colored, but see-through. It was cool, not creepy, although possums don't strike me as the world's greatest pet," Karen finished.

I'm not fond of the little creatures, either, but I wondered if possums had been used, not only as pets, but as vermin-control, the way some people give hedgehogs the run of the house to keep down the black beetles. In the wild they will eat cockroaches, snails, slugs, spiders, beetles, mice and rats, and carrion of all kinds. Nature's little janitors, naturalists call them. Curiously, President Benjamin Harrison (born in 1833, president from 1889 to 1893) kept a possum as a kind of exotic pet in the White House.

There have been other curious stories from Wolcott House.

One day a maintenance man swore that he heard someone walking on the back stairway. He also claimed to have heard sighing or heavy breathing in the docent room.

It was just outside the docent room Glenna had a frightening experience. She was at the house one evening to lock up.

"I came through the door that leads into the memorabilia room [from the docents' room]. Suddenly I had such a sudden pain in my arm that it floored me. It felt like someone pinching me. The pain was so extreme and hit so instantly that I fell, right down on the stairs. My hand clenched in a fist and I couldn't open my hand. I tried to will it to open, but it wouldn't. I thought I was having a stroke!

"Fortunately there was someone else with me and they immediately got me to the doctor. He said, 'No, no stroke, just a freak muscle spasm.' I finally got my hand open and the pain was not so extreme.

"Well, lo and behold, the next morning I had two bruise spots on my arm, like finger marks, as if somebody had pinched me...."

Chuck said, "The anomalous things that happen at Wolcott House are just day-to-day. We, more or less, take noises in stride. There are always noises and drafts which you couldn't connect with anything, not ordinary house-settling noises.

"About two months ago, I could swear that I heard one, maybe two, women's voices downstairs. It was kind of muffled and I just presumed that the volunteers who were leading a school tour that day were in the building. All the windows were closed and they are pretty soundproof.

"I went downstairs, I saw nothing. I went to the back, I saw nothing. I went to the front, I saw nothing. This only took me about 10-15 seconds and I thought, 'Where are you?' I looked out the window and there, a couple of hundred yards away, were the volunteers, standing in front of the church...."

For all its beauty, artifacts, and history, Wolcott House seems unsettled with a feeling of much coming and going. Given the active life of James Wolcott, that is not surprising. Wolcott House is indeed a house of many levels. It represents the marriage, and the clash, of cultures; it witnessed the passing of both local Native American culture and the primitive life of the pioneer.

All have been swept away. All that remains is the house. And its spirits.

THE HORRORS OF HOMICIDE:
Ghostly echoes of murder

Blood, though it sleep a time, yet never dies.
-George Chapman-

HATCHET MAN

It's one of the oldest stories in the book: the madman with the hatchet runs amok, slaughtering his entire family. Thereafter he haunts his former house/the road by his house/the local lovers' lane, ax at the ready for new, teenaged victims....

Obviously just a tall tale told by guys to their nervous dates when they "run out of gas" on an isolated road. The stuff of horror movies at the drive-in. A rural legend.

Or is it?

The aptly named Andrew Hellman was a tailor from Hesse, Germany, adept with needle and razor-sharp scissors. No records survive to tell us what atrocities turned him into a monster. But he hated women from a very young age.

Hellman first came to this country in 1820 and lodged with George M. Abel, a German farmer in Virginia, richly endowed with both worldly goods and marriageable children. Hellman made a good impression and was allowed to court the affectionate and trusting Mary Abel. Within a year, they were married and on August 8, 1822, baby Louisa was born.

Perhaps it was the unfortunate sex of the child that drove Hellman into a jealous rage, tormenting his young wife with unfounded accusations of infidelity. Perhaps there was some former suitor in the neighborhood whom he suspected of desiring his wife. This may have led him to move his family, first to Carroll County and then to a farm in Logan County close to where Township Road 56 runs today.

Although a rich man, he brutalized his family, starving them and denying them everything except the barest necessities. He fathered two boys by the unhappy Mary—Henry in 1824, whom he disowned as illegitimate, and John in 1828. But by the spring of 1839, Hellman's madness had blossomed into a murderous fury. First he tried to poison his wife, then succeeded in poisoning his three children. Louisa and John died. Henry survived only by his mother's desperate efforts.

Beaten and tortured, Mary stayed, perhaps because she had nowhere else to go or because her spirit was as broken as her body. Or it could have been because the laws of the time would have given Henry into the unmerciful hands of his father if she had sought a divorce.

But on September 26, 1839, while young Henry was out of the house, Hellman found his own solution to his domestic difficulties: he hacked his wife to pieces with an ax. Cannily he smeared himself with her blood and groaned to the officers of the law that his wife had been murdered by the same robbers who had beaten him within an inch of his life. Doctors quickly found that he was unhurt and he was taken to jail in Bellefontaine. While awaiting trial, he stole his attorney's horse and escaped to Baltimore, Maryland in 1840.

He changed his name to Adam Horn, opened a tailoring business, and on August 17, 1842, married Malinda Hinkle. Imprudent though this was, he seems to have honed his technique, for without wasting tedious years in a hateful marriage, he butchered his second wife "on or about the 23rd of March, 1843," and distributed her with impartial liberality about his property. Part of her was found in an upstairs room of his house; another portion had been buried in a coffee sack near his orchard. Her head was never found. According to legend, Horn saw supernatural lights hovering above her many graves, panicked, and fled town, exposing his guilt.

On January 12, 1844, Hellman was hung. It is said that he was buried in the Harrod Cemetery in McArthur Township with his young victims Louisa and John and that his tombstone gives off a ghastly glow in the cemetery at night. It is also whispered, at slumber parties, and in cars with steamed-up windows, that the restless ghost of Andrew Hellman stalks Township Road 56, hatchet at the ready, eager to satisfy his blood-lust with another female victim. So beware if you remind him of young Louisa, whose only crime it was to be female.[1]

FATHER JOSEPH RETURNS

On the morning of Sunday, March 10, 1929, Father Joseph A. Riccardi had just finished Mass at St. Anthony's Church on 11th St. SE, Canton. Still in his vestments, he walked to the font at the front of the church to prepare for a baptism.

His photo in the *Canton Repository* shows an earnest, bespectacled young man in a stiff clerical collar. His hair is sleekly brushed and he leans forward, perhaps posed that way by the photographer, perhaps slumping out of diffidence. Mrs. Mamie Guerrieri's photo is paired with his. She has large, hooded eyes, dark hair parted in the middle and a slight smile. The caption does not say if this is a police mug shot.

According to Father Joseph's deathbed testimony, Mrs. Mamie Guerrieri and her 5-year-old daughter Palmena followed him up to the vestibule. He turned and said, "I'm glad you sent your little girl back to school." At that, Mrs. Guerrieri pulled out a concealed gun and fired five times. Two bullets hit the priest. He was taken to Mercy Hospital where he died the next day.

Mrs. Guerrieri freely talked with the police. She had shot Father Joseph, she said, because he had molested her daughter. Father Joseph had denied any improper relations with the little girl in his deathbed statement.

Bishop Joseph Schrembs issued a statement shortly before Father Riccardi died:

"Prosecutor Harter has interviewed several witnesses and has taken Father Riccardi's statement. From these statements it is my opinion that the shooting was the act of a demented woman. The physician to whom the child had been brought for examination declares that there is absolutely no ground for charges. The physician was puzzled to know why the mother wanted the child examined. She may have been stirred up to this deed by some plot."

The Bishop went on to theorize that Father Riccardi was the victim of criminal elements or of parish factions divided on the removal of the church from Liberty Avenue SE to its present site and that Mrs. Guerrieri was "the hysterical instrument of this bitterness."

"Father Riccardi dies, a sacrifice to his efforts to bring about a wholesome, clean atmosphere in which the Italians of Canton might live. He pled with me constantly for the removal of his church and that is why I ordered it.

"Father Riccardi was fighting for the upbuilding of a decent, clean-living Italian colony, free from the influence of gambling resorts, bootlegging joints and infamous houses which infested the neighborhood of the old church site. Father Riccardi was an exceptionally high type of man, and charges such as this woman's are preposterous, entirely unbelievable."[2]

Thousands of mourners paid their respects at Father Riccardi's bier. His inconsolable family came from Cleveland for the pontifical requiem Mass by Bishop Schrembs and afterwards took his body back to Cleveland for burial.

This might have been the end to a tragic story. But in 1948 a séance was held in a small village in Tuscany. About 10 people gathered at the home of Italian parapsychologist Silvio Ravaldini to watch a local trance medium produce "direct voice" manifestations, which spoke from all over the room.

Suddenly there came a strange voice—a "drop-in communicator"—as it is called in the medium trade. The voice said, "I cannot see you but I feel that you exist, just as I once existed. I was a priest, I was happy. I am glad that you finally know the truth. I was killed with a revolver. I bear no grudge. I was a priest in Canton, Ohio, Giuseppe Riccardi. I do not know who you are—I only know that we are brothers—we are not against one another; we are brothers.

"A woman shot me after I had celebrated Mass. The priest doesn't matter; what matters is Brother Giuseppe Riccardi. When shot, I felt very warm. I raised myself up and wanted to ask this woman why she had shot me with a pistol. She was in a sort of hysterical state, and she paid no attention to me. She did not seem aware that I had asked her to lift me up. But that does not matter anymore. We are all brothers, I wish for you light and the beautiful flowers of Ohio."

"Riccardi" spoke twice more, briefly, then was no more.

Ravaldini wrote to America, unsuccessfully trying to trace the priest. It was not until a 1986 visit from Dr. Ian Stevenson, of the University of Virginia, that the facts about Father Riccardi's death were uncovered.

How could a medium in an isolated Italian village know about Father Riccardi's murder nineteen years earlier? Stevenson and Ravaldini looked for links. The Riccardi family was from Sicily and immigrated to America when Joseph was very young. He returned to Rome for his ordination in 1923, but there was no indication he had visited Tuscany.

The medium had an elementary school education, worked as a barber, and had been an amateur trance medium for 15 years. He was 16 when the priest had been murdered. But Stevenson wondered if he could have seen and later forgotten an account published in a newspaper, *Il Telegrafo* that may have been delivered to some house in the village in 1929. That story was headed "A Tragic Event in the Catholic Church in Canton (Canton, Chio) and briefly told of the murder.

Stevenson and Ravaldini conducted a small survey in the village. Everyone assumed that the "Canton, Chio" misprint referred to Canton, China, not Ohio. Did that rule out *Il Telegrafo*'s story as the source of the medium's information?

In the end, the researchers could not discard the theory of "cryptoamnesia," or utterly forgotten knowledge. Stevenson said that other explanations could not be completely ruled out, but that he personally believed that the message came from the spirit of Father Riccardi who had survived death.[3]

It is a strange story. Yet, if the medium had actually known about Father Riccardi, what motive was there in introducing him at a local séance where no one knew the facts?

Mrs. Guerrieri was acquitted. She was the mother of five children at the time of the murder, including a 6-month old baby. She may have been suffering from post-partum depression or psychosis, which could have been exploited by those who wanted the priest out of the way. Was she really the "hysterical instrument" of those who resented Father Riccardi moving the church? An unwitting agent of some organized criminal element? Father Joseph, in a unique position to know the truth, has not returned again to tell us.

PORTRAIT OF LEO

Leo Nadra was often in the wrong place at the wrong time. Leo, his wife Hannah, a seamstress, and their children left family and friends in Lebanon to try farming, first in Madagascar, then in Tasmania. When these attempts failed, Leo was invited by a relative to immigrate to Ashtabula, Ohio, where other Arab families had settled successfully.

America was the right place to be for a hard-working immigrant in 1908. Within a few years Leo, his brothers, and their extended families built thriving farms and businesses in the Ashtabula area. But when Roda, the matriarch of the family, decreed that her sons and their families should sell everything and return to the old country for an extended visit, Leo and his brothers obeyed. It was 1914. As their ship steamed through the Mediterranean, World War I exploded. The brothers and their families were trapped in Beirut by the Allied naval embargo and blockade until peace was declared in 1918.

Leo and Hannah were luckier than many of their relatives. Several cousins, uncles, and children died from typhoid and starvation during the four year "visit." It took Leo and Hannah until 1920 to save enough money for the cheapest passage back to Ashtabula. Sailing into New York harbor past the Statue of Liberty, Leo must have felt his troubles were over. But he was not an American citizen so the entire family had to stay in a caged holding area on Ellis Island for three weeks until letters vouching for his good reputation could be sent from the Ashtabula area. Finally, they were freed. Surely in America, they would finally be safe from the tragedies that had haunted them.

Throughout the 1920s, the Nadras rebuilt their lives. Soon they had a grocery store on Main Street, selling fresh produce they grew on a farm outside of Ashtabula. Leo, the uncomplaining Hannah, and their daughters worked from morning until night to make a life for themselves. Described by her daughters as tiny, fragile, gentle as a saint, and beloved by all, Hannah worked as hard as the men, tending the store, cooking, washing, and sewing the family's clothes.

The family prospered. By the 1930s, Leo was able to take out a $10,000 bank loan to build greenhouses on the farm to grow mushrooms and hot-house produce.

Leo was a tall, heavyset man with a flowing, dark, handlebar mustache and an old-country, patriarchal manner. He was a stern disciplinarian but also a man of deep generosity. During the Great Depression, he loaned money without interest to neighbors in need. He told his family that no one should be turned away hungry from the store, even if they had no money. Leo was also one of the few men in town offering work.

Every day, Leo would get up before dawn and drive his rusty pick-up truck to collect day-laborers to work on his farm. In the early 1930s, one of the day laborers named Kelly showed up for work drunk. Leo cautioned him, "If I catch you drinking again, I'll fire you." But the man was drunk again the next day and Leo fired him on the spot. There was so little local work that this was a major blow. The man went home and brooded and drank a lot more. Then he got a shotgun.

Leo was driving back into town late that afternoon, hot and dusty from a day's work with the other laborers, when he saw Kelly standing in the middle of the road with the shotgun.

Being a powerful, persuasive man, Leo pulled over and got out of the truck to talk to him. The other men tried to stop him saying, "Don't get out! Don't try to reason with him! He's drunk." But Leo had more confidence than wisdom that day.

The two men got into an argument. Leo tried to get the gun away from Kelly. Whether by accident or not, the gun went off, blowing a hole through Leo's stomach. Kelly fled while the men in the truck drove Leo to the hospital. It was obvious he could not survive with such terrible injuries. Yet he lingered long enough for his horrified wife and daughters to say their good-byes. His last words were an admonition to one of his daughters never to turn away the hungry.

Kelly was tried, found guilty, and sent to prison. When Kelly came up for parole, the women testified that he had destroyed their lives and happiness. He died of pneumonia in jail. Leo's daughters never would speak the man's name.

Leo's widow Hannah was left with five daughters, the store, the new greenhouse, and a $10,000 debt, an immense sum in the 1930s. The grieving women went to the bank and begged the bankers not to foreclose. They swore they could keep the business running and pay off the debt. Hannah and her five young daughters, some with growing families of their own, dropped all plans they had for their own lives and worked like dogs to keep the business going throughout the Great Depression. They not only paid off the debt, they kept a prosperous grocery store until the 1960s when a wave of urban renewal swept away all the small businesses on Main Street.

Later in the 1960s, bent double with age and over-work, Hannah laid down her burden and quietly passed away. The house was full of friends, neighbors, and relatives for the funeral. Hannah's granddaughter Julia was upstairs. Julia's son, about six years old at the time, was standing at the bottom of the stairs when a man he vaguely recognized walked past him.

"Who is that man who just walked downstairs?" he asked his mother, who had just come downstairs herself.

"What man?"

"The man who just walked down the stairs from Grandma Hannah's room."

"Nobody walked down the stairs except me." Julia said.

"It was the man in the picture," he insisted.

"Show me," said his mother.

The boy took his mother by the hand and led her to the living room. He pointed up to the ornate, frame containing an old-fashioned, hand-tinted photograph of Leo Nadra. Julia stared at the portrait. The man on the stairs couldn't be Leo. The boy insisted it was.

Too young to have known about Leo's death, the child thought Leo was real. There was nothing uncanny about him, nothing misty or insubstantial. No living person in the house that day had Leo's big frame or that distinctive drooping mustache.

Maybe Leo came back to escort his beloved Hannah to her rest. Or perhaps he had been keeping an eye on things from beyond the grave. A man so conscientious that his last command was to feed the poor, a man with such indomitable energy and determination, would not easily vanish from his family's life without a trace.

Leo Nadra's life embodied the immigrant spirit and the American dream: that hard work would, in the end, pay off. Ironically, after surviving famine, war, and disease at the ends of the earth, Leo met a violent death in the Land of Opportunity. But perhaps by his solid appearance, 30 years after his untimely end, Leo was making the point that he, and everything he had struggled so hard to build, lived on through his descendants. Leo was a man of substance, in death, as in life.

THE BLOOD OF THE INNOCENTS

The wooden frame farmhouse stands isolated in the sparse Black Swamp farmlands of Putnam County. On the plains of Northwestern Ohio the desolation is unbroken by church steeple or grain elevator. Nights are very dark out here.

It was from this two-story farmhouse that Charles Hanson* saw his three children off to school one morning in 1907. He left his other two children, a 3-year-old girl and an 18-month-old boy, with his wife as he went off to help a neighbor with the threshing.

Shortly after 7 o'clock a.m., Mrs. Hanson* gathered up the children and took them to the woods with her to milk the cows. She said later that she enjoyed having the children in the woods with her. When they came back to the house, she picked up a large butcher knife and herded the children upstairs to one of the two bedrooms. There she cut the boy's head off. Then she started to behead the little girl, but only got half-way through before she stopped. She may have knocked them senseless with an axe handle before beginning her grim work, or she may not.

She drew water and washed the small bodies. She dressed them and tucked them in bed, drawing the covers up under their severed chins. Then she went downstairs, wiped the blood off the knife, and walked over to the home of a neighbor, Mrs. Schmitt*. "Come over and see the children," Mrs. Hanson said. Mrs. Schmitt followed her and, after climbing the stairs, found the children lying in bed. Did she wonder that they looked so pale and lay so still? She drew back the covers....

"See," said Mrs. Hanson. "I've made angels!"

Mrs. Hanson, the former Miss Margaret Pederson*, had a history of mental illness. Some years earlier, her mind became unbalanced and she was taken to the asylum at Toledo. She returned about a year and a half before the murders, pronounced perfectly cured. Since that time she seemed rational, but something that morning must have snapped.

"She remembers that after she returned she got a butcher knife, and after that everything is blank to her until she went to a neighbor's home and told the family there to come and see the children. [wrote the paper] Mrs. Hanson talks quietly and rationally on some subjects, but appears unbalanced. She is overwhelmed with grief for her children at times, and at other times does not seem to realize what has happened.

About 18 months ago she seemed not in her right mind, having a tendency to wander away from home, but that she recovered from this. She did not seem inclined to be violent at that time. For a week past he noticed that she seemed to be brooding over something, and would not speak unless spoken to."

When asked by the officers why she took the lives of her children, she replied that they were better off.[4]

Cindy* and her daughter Mindy* bought the house in the early 1990s. Almost immediately they began to hear footsteps upstairs when they were the only people in the house. Whispered voices and faint singing were also heard. At night, small whitish balls of light were seen whizzing through the house. Smoke alarms without batteries would go off. Figures were sometimes seen to walk by windows when Cindy or Mindy were outside. And, of course, there were the usual cold spots and a feeling of being watched.

Mindy seemed to be sensitive to the presence of spirits. She said that sometimes she could see a woman with straight dark hair, a young child, and an older man. The woman's face was hazy or "blanked out." Both she and her mother were both so unnerved by the phenomena in the house that they went to live with Cindy's sister and put the house up for sale.

Cindy had heard rumors about the house's troubled history, but it was only when she tracked down old newspaper articles that she found the full story. She was the first person to live in the house who was not related to the original owners.

Nick Reiter and Lori Schillig of the Avalon Foundation visited the house in 1998. It was a chilly, drizzly October day. Without much prelude, they went upstairs to the two bedrooms. One seemed perfectly normal. The other, as Nick wrote, "was akin to walking into a different world. The first impression, which struck even my own fairly IN-sensitive 'antennae' was that of coldness. It was dank and clammy, and my breath felt sucked from my lungs. Lori's reactions were stronger. She recoiled at the evil feel of the room and near the single closet could hear screaming. She was unable to stay in the room for more than a moment."

Puzzled by the cold, Nick looked for a logical explanation. There were no drafts. The vent arrangements were identical to the other upstairs room. Given the wind direction, the other room should have been colder. Nick's thermometer showed that the room was 4.5 degrees colder than the landing. He also found a magnetic anomaly in the middle of the room.

In addition to her sensations upstairs, Lori sensed someone being thrown down the stairway. Cindy told Nick and Lori of a family tradition that Charles Hanson, who was nine years younger than his wife, was a brutal, unstable man. The story goes that the oldest daughter had accidentally allowed the family horses to escape when she tied them wrong. Charles beat her and threw her down the stairs, crippling her for life. In her madness, perhaps Margaret thought that she was saving her little ones from their cruel father.

Margaret died on June 20, 1907 of "dementia of the brain" and "exhaustion." It was whispered that she hung herself at the asylum. They said it was a blessing that she died, because when she was herself, she couldn't face what she had done.

Charles sent his other children off to live with relatives. He lived in the house alone until his death in 1947. He was always a strange, spooked man and claimed to have seen Margaret after her death.

Nick and Lori feel that one or more spirits still wander the grim little farmhouse. "Along with these," Nick said, "there seems to be an enormously powerful presence in the room where the crime was committed. It is likely that this force and the taint of this horror will remain with the house until it is some day destroyed. Was the house the abode of 'something' which may have provoked an unbalanced farmwife to the ultimate act of slaughter? Does that something still remain?"[5]

Cindy sold the house. It was bought by an expectant young couple. They did not stay there long. Nor did the next owners. Or the next.

The blood of the Innocents cries out from the ground for vengeance.

THE SADDEST PLACE IN OHIO:
Gnadenhutten

God forgive them, for they know not what they do.
-Luke 23:34-

On March 10th, 2003, I visited Gnadenhutten. I had last taken Ohio history in 6th grade and only remembered that a massacre had taken place there. I didn't know any details.

It was about 4:00 in the afternoon. There was that subtle darkening of the sunlight, the depressed feeling that day is dying. I had never been to Gnadenhutten and didn't know where I'd find the site of the massacre. I criss-crossed the town, thinking that a park I had seen from the main road was the memorial site. Finally I saw a sign that read "Museum."

I followed the signs, getting more fretful and agitated by the moment, pounding on the steering wheel to ease the strain. At last a cemetery came in sight, and then a rustic stone building. I pulled into the parking area just beyond the building, the nose of the car almost up against a low conical mound surrounded by a little fence. The mound was capped with snow-dusted groundcover. I thought it was just some decorative feature, like one of those civic flower beds with clocks or the name of the town outlined in flowers.

I got out of the car with my camera, picking my way across the frozen crust, as if I was walking on water. Looking across the park, I could see a billboard painted with a cartoon pioneer and Native American. The faces had been cut out so that tourists could stick their faces through and take a picture as a souvenir. It was blasphemously out of place.

Further on across the glittering snow stood a tall obelisk monument and several log buildings. I started towards the obelisk, only to break, calf-deep, through the crusted snow. I stared at it, trying to read the inscriptions on the base, but it was too far away. My feet were soaked. I turned to go back to the car.

It was then that I saw a small, shield-shaped sign by the little mound. I walked closer, noting child-sized footprints in the snow covering the mound. The shield read, "Burial Site of the Indian Martyrs."

A group of Delaware Indians who had been converted by Moravian Christians settled at Gnadenhutten in Tuscarawas County. They farmed peaceably and lived a life blending the Indian and European ways of life. Excavations have shown that they had houses with glass windows and pewter household utensils. Old inventories record that the settlement had books and even a spinet piano. But the Moravian Indians were not trusted by either the European settlers or the Indians.

A Colonel Williamson and his men arrived at Gnadenhutten in early March, 1782, with orders to move the Moravian Indians to Pennsylvania. Christianized Indians were being clustered in settlements for their safety as they tried to maintain their neutrality between the British and the Americans. But when Williamson's men arrived, they found the bloody dress of Mrs. Robert Wallace, a white woman recently murdered on the Pennsylvania border. It is not clear whether Williamson's men planted the dress or if one of the Indians had innocently bought the garment from the woman's murderers. Williamson and his men became enraged and accused the peaceable Gnadenhutten Indians of the murder. The Indians were told to prepare for death the next morning.

They locked the men in one house and the women and children in another on the night of March 8th. At first overwhelmed by their fate, the Moravian Indians spent the night in prayer asking pardon of each other, and encouraging one another to meet the end faithfully and bravely.

On the morning of March 9th the victims were led into two houses dubbed the "Slaughter Houses," men to one, women and children to the other. Two young boys escaped to give eyewitness testimony of what occurred that terrible day. One boy was knocked to the ground and scalped. He remained still in the piles of the dead until he could escape under cover of darkness. Another hid in the cellar under the house where the women died, watching the blood flow in streams into the cellar.

As the victims entered the houses they were knocked down and butchered. One Pennsylvanian took up a huge cooper's mallet, hefted it and said with relish, "How exactly this will answer for the business!" He smashed his victims' heads one after another until he had killed fourteen with his own hands. At that he handed the mallet over to a fellow murderer saying, "My arm fails me; go on in the same way; I think I have done pretty well."[1]

Not content with murdering the innocent men, women and children, the soldiers disfigured the dead and dying bodies, returning to make sure that everyone was dead. The toll was 28 men, 29 women, and 39 children.

The night after the massacre, the whites set fire to all the houses of Gnadenhutten and to the slaughter houses filled with corpses. The dead bodies were only partially burnt and their bones lay bleaching in the sun until 1797 when John Heckewelder, a missionary and land agent, returned to the site, burned off the brush, then collected all the human bones he could find and buried them in a single grave which has never been disturbed.

Moravian missionary David Zeisberger wrote in his diary in despair, "The world is all too narrow; nowhere is a place to be found to which we can retire with our Indians and be secure. From the white people, or so-called Christians, we can hope for no protection, and among the heathen we have no friends left, such outlaws are we."[2]

In 1843, the Gnadenhuetten Monument and Cemetery Association was formed to erect a suitable monument at the site of the massacre. The Association obtained about 6 acres of the ground on which the village had stood. The two slaughter house sites could still be identified. Today they have been rebuilt on their original sites as the Mission House and the cooper shop and are open to the public.

I had put new batteries in my camera that morning. As I read the sign by the little mound, I gulped and glanced around guiltily. Then I tried to photograph the mound that marks the mass grave of the dead. The camera shut off. I tried many times, aiming away from the mound, aiming at the stone building, at the obelisk monument. The camera simply would not work on the property.

As I struggled with the camera, I began to notice music far in the distance, rhythmic music, a bit distorted, as echoes often are. For a moment I wondered if I was hearing a marching band practicing, but there didn't seem to be a school close by or anyone in the cemetery. I listened more closely and just as I began to identify it as a choir, the furnace blower rumbled to noisy life by the museum building.

I could still hear the music, but not clearly. It was maddening, trying to listen to the music over the racket. All I could tell was that it had a strong rhythm and was being sung by more than a few people. I struggled to make sense of the tune. The singing went on for a few more minutes, then stopped. It had lasted no more than 5 or 6 minutes.

The fan battered on and I walked here and there to see if the harmonics of the fan could account for the singing. They didn't. No matter where I stood, I could not duplicate the sound of the music. I tried again to photograph the mound or the monument or the museum. The lens came out; the lens went in.

"OK," I said, "I'm sorry. I won't try to photograph you." There seemed to be a shift in the atmosphere, a sigh of approval. I went back to my car and drove to Newcomerstown where the camera worked perfectly.

The next day, I was speaking to a class of middle school students at Indian Creek. The Ohio History teacher had been in my two classes on the previous day and I described my visit to Gnadenhutten. He blanched. Then he told me the details of the massacre. As the Christian Indians were killed two by two, they went to their deaths singing Moravian hymns.

Later, in the 1882 account of the massacre I read the following: "At the dawn of the morning, they offered up fervent supplications to God their Saviour, and united in singing praises unto Him, in the joyful hope, that they should soon enter into His glorious presence, in everlasting bliss….The murderers came to them whilst they were engaged in singing, and asked, whether they were ready to die? To which they received the answer, that they had commended themselves to God, who had given them the assurance in their hearts, that he would receive their souls."[3]

The Gnadenhutten memorial is a quiet place in winter, as quiet as death. It is hard to imagine people picnicking here, or children playing. There is a hushed melancholy in the shadows that fall across the bright snow.

Why does the song still echo down the centuries? I don't have any answers. I do know that the site is alive with the spirits of those gentle souls so brutally murdered. God grant them rest.

The names of the Christian Indians of
Gnadenhutten martyred on March 9, 1782 include:

Joseph Schebosh, his wife Christiana, John
Martin, Luke and his wife Lucia, Philip and his
wife, Lovel, their daughter Sarah, Abraham the
Mohican, Paul, Anthony, Christiana, Mary, Hannah,
Rebecca, Rachel, Maria Elizabeth, Gottlieb,
Benjamin, Anthony, John Thomas, Isaac Glikkikan,
his wife Anna Benigna, Jonah, his wife Amelia,
Christian, his wife Augustina, Samuel More, Tobia,
Israel, Mark the Delaware, Adam, his wife
Cornelia, Henry, his wife Joanna, Salome, Paul,
Michael, Peter Gotleib, David, Lewis, his wife
Ruth, John, Hannah, Judith, John, Catharine, Maria
Susanna, Juliana, Elizabeth, Martha, Anna Rosina,
Salome, Christian, Joseph, Mark, Jonathan, Chris-
tian, Gottlieb, Timothy, Jonah, Christiana, Leah,
Benigna, Gertrude, Christina, Anna Christina,
Anna, Salome, Anna Elizabeth, Schappihillen, his
wife Helen, Nicholas, his wife Joanna Sabina, Abel,
Henry, Anna, Bathsheba, four women and thirteen
babes not yet baptized.[4]

APPENDIX 1
FRIGHT BITES
Still more mini-tales of the macabre

Some of these stories may be Internet folklore or simply made up out of whole ectoplasm, but some may be worth investigation. The Internet has changed everything: the slightest rumor or tale can be spread to a jillion sites in a flash. So don't believe everything you read there. I could have written a whole book just on Ohio Cry Baby Bridge legends, but I've skipped them this time around. Remember that when I say, "the ghost walks at midnight" I mean "the ghost is said to walk at midnight." The first set of stories is my own tales.

At Hower House in Akron, I was standing in the doorway of the North bedroom when someone walked right up behind me. I swiveled to see who it was. The room was empty.

At the Reeves Victorian Mansion in Dover the guide stopped at a closed door.

"This was Mr. Reeve's study," she said. "He gave strict instructions that he was never to be disturbed, even by his wife, unless it was an emergency. I always like to knock on the door, just to be polite," she added, knocking briskly on the door before opening it. We entered the book-lined room and the others smiled as a young woman on the tour said, "I guess Mr. Reeves just stepped out."

"Not really," I thought. Because he was still sitting in his chair.

At the top of the stairs I heard women's voices and laughter coming from the rooms to our left. I wondered if another tour was in the building. They certainly were having a good time! The guide took us in a circular route through the upstairs finishing with Mrs. Reeves's sitting room. When I got back to the Carriage House I asked if another tour had been in the house, only to be told "no, you were the only ones."

I guess Mrs. Reeves was having one of her "afternoons" when friends would call for tea, laughter, and gossip in her sitting room. That was the room where I heard the voices.

At a park in Arcanum, I saw a dead person lying on the ground who dissolved as I watched. I was told that the area behind the park is called "Dead Man's Path." At the Arcanum Library, I saw a man in dark clothing on the landing of the stairs. He has also been seen by staff members.

I visited a now-closed antique shop in Arcanum. Upstairs in a room overlooking the street, I saw a woman holding a child, looking out of the window. She wore a long grey print calico dress, what was called a "wrapper" at the time. Her hair was coming down. She sighed as she looked out the window. She was so bored, she wanted to die.

"Old Lady Loftus" murdered her husband and made it look like he'd hung himself from the Railroad trestle in Wintersville. Old Lady Loftus then haunted her tumbledown home and would chase away anyone who dared trespass. Another student told me that her mother remembered seeing the daughter of Old Lady Loftus—also known by that name, who apparently took over the haunting/chasing tradition.

Loretta Furman, the manager of Grant's Birthplace at Point Pleasant, told me that she as well as visitors has seen the late 18th century English spinning wheel in the front room spinning by itself when there is no wind.

At the Sullivan Johnson Museum in Kenton, anomalous footsteps have been heard. A docent also said that a tour of children walked into the sitting room and found a woman who matched the description of Mrs. Sullivan, the artist for whom the house was built. The woman disappeared.

The Red Brick Tavern at Lafayette is haunted by the ghost of a young woman who killed herself when her husband was unfaithful. She used to sit on a sofa looking out the third-floor windows. After her death, the neighbors still saw her looking out.

Wittenberg University's Sigma Kappa House is haunted by the ghost of Vaudeville booking agent and theatre owner Gus Sun and his daughter, who died in a fire.[1]

Morley Music Hall at Lake Erie College is haunted by the ghost of Helen Rockwell. She was unhappy when her son, Charles Rockwell Morley, fell in love with a German-born language instructor at the College and it wasn't until after her death that Charles married his love. Donating money to build a music hall did not placate her spirit; the ghost of Helen still is heard in the halls.[2]

Just after the 1990 flood, neighbors who could stay in their houses on lower Pipe Creek in Belmont County took turns watching for vandals, scavengers and thieves. Their vantage point was one front porch, located on a rise. One night a man sat down in one of the chairs alone in the dark to start his watch. While he sat watching the road, there was a small creak from the porch rocker. He looked over to see the seat sag as if under someone's weight. The chair began to rock

quietly, rocking all through his watch that night. He says he didn't
think of being afraid after that. Whoever it was had come by to help.[3]

In the early 1930s, "Uncle John" LeMasters was hit by a car near
Kelley's Bridge on Ohio 93, about five miles out of Ironton and killed.
For years after travelers along the highway reported seeing a dog
come out of nowhere and disappear into nowhere near the spot
LeMasters was killed.[4]

A man killed in the mines near Vesuvius furnace would return to
the area every night to complete his work. He would come out of the
mines with a wheelbarrow and walk around just like he was hauling
something, and then take it back in.[5]

Caesar's Creek Pioneer Village is a collection of relocated
buildings from the late 1700s to the 1800s. The only house original to
the site, the Levi Lukens house c.1807, is haunted by "Uncle Bob"
who was killed in a car crash in the 1940s.[6]

Waynesville's Angel of the Garden Tea Room reportedly
contains a ghost only glimpsed as a sad face looking out of an upstairs
window. Human bones were found in the attic in the 1950s.[7]

The ghost of a young woman, possibly a schoolteacher boarder,
was seen walking down the stairs of the Waynesville Friends Boarding
Home, now the Waynesville Area Heritage & Cultural Center.

A "lady in gray" haunts the master bedroom of the magnificent
65-room Seiberling mansion, Stan Hywet Hall in Akron. The ghost,
who is said to be an Englishwoman who died in the early 1700s, may
have arrived with the bedroom, which was reassembled from an
English manor room.[8]

The Goldsmith House at Hale Farm and Village is haunted by an
elderly woman who said, "This is my house and I'm staying." The
builder's widow, determined to stay on after his untimely death,
turned it into a boarding house.[9]

The last remaining house in the ghost town of Craneville in
Paulding County is haunted by a man hung in the attic of the house by
his two sons.[10]

A local developer who had a life-long dream to own Cleveland's
Franklin Castle plans to restore the original interior design and turn it
into a private social club that will open in May of 2004. He plans to
recapture the original look of the mansion in 1881. The club will offer
suites, meals, and other amenities. A package including an overnight
stay and dinner will also be available for nonmembers.[11]

Town Hall Theater in Centerville is haunted by a grumpy,
female-hating male ghost who blows out the pilot light on the furnace

if he's unhappy with the production. "It goes to theatrical performances and if there is anything suggestive or any adult language, the entity takes offense. It likes nice moral Victorian-style plays.[12]

A former sub house on North Water Street in Uhrichsville was haunted by a ghost nicknamed "Zachary T. Ghost" by the owners, perhaps the ghost of a man murdered in the restaurant when it was a bar in the 1930s. One evening a dance was held at the pub. The decorative candles were blown out before the owners left. But in the morning when they came in to open up, every single candle was lit.[13]

In a cemetery at the corner of routes 306 and 312 on Ridge Road (off University Drive) is The Warlock's Grave. The sorcerer's grave is encircled by a low stone wall. Supposedly his head was cut off and placed at his feet. When his head moves back to the top of his body, he will rise from the dead. If you lie down on the tomb at midnight with your head where the Warlock's head should be, you will die a year later.[14]

Mt. Unger Cemetery, Blue Creek, Adams Co. is haunted by a wife murderer who hung himself to spend eternity with the wife he killed.

A runaway slave suffocated when he was trapped in a false-back cupboard at an Underground Railroad station in Springboro. An owner of the house reported seeing a black man beckoning at the foot her bed as if pleading for help.[15]

At Oak Grove schoolhouse in Jefferson County unearthly lights were often seen flitting about the windows, carried by grinning skeletons and headless figures clothed in white, where during the day children went to school.[16]

At the Burnison Farmstead near Kenton Mr. Burnison was out plowing one day. He looked across the furrow and saw a mantle clock, his wife's prize possession. He thought, "O my God, someone has ransacked the house!" He grabbed the clock and ran to the farm house, only to find that his wife had just died.

The Portage County Administration Building in Ravenna was formerly the county hospital. Two women employees said that one night they saw a young girl wearing the typical open-back hospital gown of the 1970s, slowly walking the halls. The eerie voices of children have also been reported in the building at night.[17]

KSU police officers have been called to investigate a mysterious light seen in a third-floor window of Moulton Hall. From the outside, it was a strange, bright blue light like a "blue torch" or a "floating spark, about the size of a baseball."[18]

The section of railroad track crossing Industry Road near Giddings Road between Rootstown and Atwater used to pass by a large pond where a boy from the Chapman family drowned. Railroad workers filled in the pond with large boulders, but the area was still dubbed "Ghost Hollow." There were rumors that it was haunted by the ghost of the dead child, wailing in the night. It was considered bad luck if a train broke down or had to stop near Ghost Hollow after dark.[19]

There used to be a clicking tombstone in Old Western Cemetery where City Hospital in Chillicothe now stands. The children from the school opposite refused to go near it because of its peculiar sound.[20]

A ghost named Elizabeth Bradford is said to haunt a Georgian house on Social Row Road in Centerville. In life she lived there from 1838 to 1844 with her Irish husband. To any unusual noise, the owners would say "Here comes Mrs. Bradford." One night, right after she moved in, the owner was awakened by what appeared to be the entire china cabinet, complete with dishes, being hurled down the stairs. The next morning, nothing was out of place or broken.[21]

While the C.C.C. & I. Railway, [then called the Bellefontaine and Indiana Railroad] was being built, one of the workmen was killed in a fight and buried secretly. Many claim to have seen his ghost hovering around the "Big Fill."[22]

Marysville's Lentz Butter Tub Company, which stood in a large brick building on the west side of Chestnut Street, eventually became an auto parts store. It was during the 1970s when an employee of Parts Plus heard footsteps on the stairway when he was there alone at night. He left the room to see who might be coming up the stairs and when he returned, he found an old invoice which had been in a file in the middle of the floor.[23]

A local farmer was plowing one of his fields near Damascus when he suddenly began to plow up tombstones. He scoffed at his neighbors' warnings that plowing and planting a cemetery would bring him bad luck. Shortly afterwards he drove his tractor off a bluff into the Maumee River and was drowned."[24]

In Fallsville, every Christmas Eve a ghostly Indian in full regalia would knock at the Clouser sisters' door and try by signs to tell where treasure buried by the Indians was hidden.[25]

North of Bellville was the "Dutchman's bridge," which spanned Deadman's Run. The Deadman, who has been seen on the bridge, was a local judge's hired man swept away by a flood.[26]

Johnny Mango's in Ohio City has a trio of ghosts. The oldest is named Margaret, a woman who died when a trolley car crashed into the Cuyahoga River in 1895.[27]

Oberlin College's Warner Center is haunted by a ghostly woman with red hair.[28]

Miss Dosha White haunted the two-story frame house at the southwest corner of Niles Street and Creston Avenue in Marion. She was murdered there by her sweetheart, Miller Herman in 1919.[29]

Marion City Prison was haunted by the ghost of a one-legged shoestring peddler who hung himself (on a shoestring) in the jail.[30]

The Gothic mansion, now the Kent Masonic Temple, was once the home of William S. Kent, for whom Kent State University is named. In 1886, Mrs. Kittie Kent was lighting a kerosene stove in the top floor of the house when it exploded, burning her so badly burned that she died the next day. The ballroom was sealed off for many years. Some people say that they have heard creaking noises as if someone is walking around on the top floor. Others say that they've seen the flickering of flames at the upper windows.

It is said that on stormy nights and on the anniversary of the Battle of Fallen Timbers, the ghostly troops and Indian warriors return to re-enact the bloody drama.[31]

APPENDIX 2
HAUNTED PLACES
Sites open to the public

NOTE: Phone numbers are included *only* for calling for hours or directions. Please do not call and ask questions about the ghosts. Go and see for yourself.

ASHTABULA
  Chestnut Grove Cemetery, Grove Dr., Ashtabula 44004
ATHENS
  Ohio University, Athens
CLARK
  Pennsylvania House, 1311 W Main St., Springfield 45504
  (937) 322-7668
  Wittenberg University, Myers Hall, Springfield
CLERMONT
  Grant's Birthplace, in Point Pleasant, just off of U.S. Route 52
  (513) 553-4911

CLINTON

Snow Hill Country Club, 11093 SR 73, New Vienna 45159
(937) 987-2922

Wilmington College, College Hall, Wilmington

COSHOCTON

The Old Warehouse Restaurant, 400 N. Whitewoman St., Coshocton
43812 (740) 622-4001

CRAWFORD

Brownella Cottage, 132 S. Union, Galion 44833 (419) 468-9338
(419) 468-1861

CUYAHOGA

Johnny Mango's, 3120 Bridge Ave., Cleveland

Renaissance Cleveland Hotel 24 Public Square, Cleveland 44113-
2201

DARKE

Arcanum Public Library, 101 North St., Arcanum 45304

Bear's Mill, 6450 Arcanum-Bear's Mill Rd., Greenville 45331
(937) 548-5112

FAIRFIELD

Hawk's Taverne at the Mill, 431 S. Columbus St., Lancaster 43130
(740) 654-6423

FRANKLIN

COSI, 333 W.Broad St, Columbus (614) 228-2674

Ohio State University, Columbus

FULTON

Fulton County Historical Society Museum, 229 Monroe St., Wauseon
(419) 337-7922

GUERNSEY

The Colonel Taylor Inn, 633 Upland Rd., Cambridge 43725
(740) 432-7802

HAMILTON

Habits Café, 3036 Madison Rd., Cincinnati

20th Century Theater, 3021 Madison Rd., Oakley (513) 731-8000

HARDIN

Sullivan Johnson Museum, 223 N. Main St., Kenton (419) 673-7147

LAKE

Fairport Harbor Lighthouse and Maritime Museum, 129 Second St.,
Fairport Harbor (440) 354-4825

James A. Garfield National Historic Site, 8095 Mentor Ave., Mentor
44060 (440) 255-8722

LORAIN

Oberlin College, Warner Center, Oberlin

LUCAS
    Club Bijou, 209 N. Superior St., Toledo 43604 (419) 243-4446
MADISON
    The Red Brick Tavern, 1700 US Hwy 40, Lafayette (740) 852-1474
MARION
    The Harding Home, 380 Mt. Vernon Ave., Marion 43302
    (740) 387-9630
MUSKINGUM
    Prospect Place, 12140-12150 Main St., Trinway 43842
    (740) 754-1054
PICKAWAY
    Roundtown Theater, 165½ E. Main St., Circleville
PIKE
    Emmitt House, 123 N. Market St., Waverly 45690 (740) 947-2181
RICHLAND
    Bellville Opera House, Rt. 97 & Rt. 13, Bellville (419) 522-5058
    Renaissance Theatre, 138 Park Ave. West, Mansfield 44901
    (419) 522-2726
ROSS
    Adena, south end of Adena Rd., off Pleasant Valley Rd., Chillicothe
    1-800-319-7248
SHELBY
    The Monumental Building, 126 N Main Ave, Sidney 45365
    The William A. Ross Jr. Historical Center, 201 North Main Ave.,
    Sidney (937) 498-1653
SUMMIT
    Hale Farm and Village, 2686 Oak Hill Rd., Bath 44210
    (330) 666-3711
    Hower House, 60 Fir Hill, Akron (330) 972-6909
    Stan Hywet Hall, 714 N. Portage Path, Akron 44303 (330) 836-5533
TUSCARAWAS
    Gnadenhutten Memorial, 352 South Cherry St., Gnadenhutten
    J.E. Reeves Home and Museum, 325 East Iron Ave., Dover
    (216) 343-7040
    The Cowger House, 197 Fourth St., Zoar, (330) 874-3542
    The Inn on the River, 8806 Towpath Rd., NE, Zoar (330) 874-3770
    Zoar Village, on Rt. 212
WARREN
    The Chokolate Morel, 101 E. Main St., Mason (513) 754-1146
    Caesar's Creek Pioneer Village, 3999 Pioneer Village Rd.,
    Waynesville 45068 (513) 897-1120
    Waynesville Area Heritage & Cultural Center, 115 Fourth St.,
    Waynesville 45068, (513) 897-1607

WOOD
> *Fort Meigs State Memorial*, 29100 West River Rd. (State Rte. 65),
> Perrysburg 43552 (419) 874-4121
> *Wolcott House Museum Complex*, 1031 River Rd., Maumee 43537
> (419) 893-9602

MORE GHOSTLY TALES

(Also see the bibliographies in previous *Haunted Ohio* books.)

Everett, Lawrence, *Ghosts, Spirits and Legends of Southeastern Ohio*,
2002 Everett is a native-born Southeastern Ohioan and he was able to
get the inside story on the many ghosts of the Athens area. I find
Athens extremely creepy and no wonder—there are some 50
cemeteries that form a pentagram, many of them with their own
legends of spirits. The great thing about this book is these are first-
hand accounts from real people of their experiences in houses,
hollows, and cemeteries.

Igo, Harold, *Haunted Houses: Spooky Tales of Yellow Springs as told by
Harold Igo*, 2001 This is an absolute model of what local history/
ghostlore/folklore should be! Tales collected by local writer Harold
Igo in and around Yellow Springs with annotations on local history,
murders, scandals, folktales, etc. There are photos and maps of some
of the haunted sites and the local characters involved. These are not
predictable urban-legend type folktales, but are a fascinating
reflection of the preoccupations of a small Ohio town in the 19th and
early-20th century.

Reevy, Anthony W., *Ghost Train: American Railroad Ghost Legends*,
1999 Headless brakemen, spook lanterns, ghostly hobos, and
phantom engines ride the haunting rails throughout the US in this
engaging collection.

Smith, Robin, *Columbus Ghosts, Historical Haunts of Ohio's Capital*,
2002 A delightfully well-researched and well-written collection of
historical haunt-spots in Ohio's capital city. Each story has a wealth
of meticulous historical detail and interviews with contemporary
witnesses of the ghost or ghosts.

Thay, Edrick, *Ghost Stories of Ohio*, 2001 A great compendium of haunts
of various sorts all over the state. From legendary tales to interviews
with eyewitnesses.

Troy Main Street, Inc., *Troy Ghost Stories, Authentic, first-hand accounts
of supernatural experiences in historic Troy, Ohio!* 1994. Gentle-
spirited tales told by the witnesses themselves. A ghost who quilted,
badly, Blanche, the little girl ghost.

REFERENCES

Chapter One – Disease and Disaster

[1]Thomas E. Corts, ed., *Bliss and Tragedy: The Ashtabula Railway-Bridge Accident of 1876 and the Loss of P.P. Bliss*, (Birmingham, AL: Sherman Oak Books, 2003)

[2] Walter Blair, ed., *The Sweet Singer of Michigan: Poems by Mrs. Julia A. Moore*, (Chicago: Pascal Covici, 1928)

[3]John Clough, *To Act as a Unit: The Story of the Cleveland Clinic*, (Cleveland: Cleveland Clinic Foundation, 1996)

[4] http://www.cleveland.com/haunted/index.ssf?/halloween/more/ghosts/halfway.html

[5]Joan Grant, *Far Memory*, (NY: Harper Bros., 1956) 46

Chapter Two – Dining with the Dead

[1]"Murder at Mason," *Miami Gazette*, 17 April 1901

"McClung Case Now in Court," *The Western Star*, Lebanon, 27 June 1901

"McClung Case Will Go To The Jury This Morning," *The Western Star*, 11 July 1901

"Secret lies buried in Rose Hill Cemetery," Mike Newton, *Pulse-Journal* 22 April 1987

Chapter Three – Phantoms of the Furniture

[1]"Lethal legacy leaves impression on small town," Mike Harden, *The Columbus Dispatch*, 14 July 2002

[2]Lonnie R. Speer, *Portals to Hell, Military Prisons of the Civil War*, (Mechanicsburg, PA. Stackpole Books), 1997

[3]"Mysterious Picture on a Mirror," *The New York Times*, 12 April 1896

[4]Carl Sferrazza Anthony, *Florence Harding: the first lady, the jazz age and the death of America's most scandalous president*, (NY: Morrow, 1998); Robert K. Murray, *The Harding Era: Warren G. Harding and His Administration*, (Minneapolis, MN: University of Minnesota, 1969)

[5]Harding's Tomb Guards are Annoyed," *Elyria Chronicle Telegram*, 3 Jan. 1924

Chapter Five – Ghosts Along the Maumee

Larry L. Nelson, *"Men of Patriotism, courage & enterprise:" Fort Meigs in the War of 1812*, (Canton: Daring Books, 1985)

[1]Captain Daniel Cushing, *The Diary of Captain Daniel Cushing of the 2nd US Artillery*, June 26, 1813, 129

[2]Alfred M. Lorrain, *The Helm, The Sword, And The Cross. A life narrative by Alfred M. Lorrain.* (Cincinnati, 1862) 129-130.

Chapter Seven – Stage Frights

[1]"Theater Man Shot During Mystery Movie," Marguerite Miller, *Mansfield News Journal*, 11 Jan. 1951

Chapter Eight – Polt-pourri

[1] "Spooky stories surprise many students," *The Lantern*, 22 July 2003

[2] Fred C. Kelly, ed., *Miracle at Kitty Hawk: the letters of Wilbur and Orville Wright*, (New York: De Capo Press, 1996) 463-4

[3] Wittenberg's ghostly population," Laura Stehle, *The Wittenberg Torch*, 30 Nov. 1999

[4] Ray Crain, *The Land Beyond the Mountains*, 1994

[5] "Hunting ghosts at the Shawnee seat of justice," John Switzer, *The Columbus Dispatch*, 12 Oct. 1997

[6] Communication from Randy Sarvis, Director of Public Relations, Wilmington College

Chapter Nine – Trading in Terror

[1] [2] Gertrude Taylor Slaughter, *Only the Past is Ours* (New York: Exposition Press, 1963) 94

[3] M.J. Carrigan, *The Life and Reminiscences of the Hon. James Emmitt, as revised by himself* (Chillicothe, O., Peerless printing & mfg. co., 1888)

Chapter Ten – Haunts from History

[1] http://www.ncweb.com/org/fhlh/

[2] Hilda Dischinger Morhart, *The Zoar Story*, (Dover, OH: Seibert, 1969)

[3] *Zoar, An Ohio Experiment in Communalism,* (Columbus: The Ohio Historical Society, 1960)

[4] "The Thrill of the Haunt," Jenny Pavlasek, *Ohio Magazine,* 1 Oct 2000

[5] Morhart, *Op. cit.*, 129

[6] Charles M. Jacobs, "The Wolcott Family: A Legacy of American Indian Relations," 2003.

Chapter Eleven – The Horrors of Homicide

[1] "A horrific tale for Halloween," Brian J. Evans, *Bellefontaine Examiner* 31 Oct. 2002

"Hatchet man The First Murderer Confined Within the Walls of the Logan County Jail," *Weekly Examiner*, 10 April 1896

[2] *Canton Repository* 11-12 Mar. 1929

[3] Jeffrey Iverson, *In Search of the Dead*, (NY: Harper Collins, 1992) 136

[4] "Crazy Woman Beheads her Children," *Toledo News Bee,* 6 Sept. 1906

[5] Special thanks to Nick Reiter and Lori Schilling of The Avalon Foundation for sharing their report.

Chapter Twelve – The Saddest Place in Ohio

[1] [3] *True History of the Massacre of Ninety-six Christian Indians at Gnadenhuetten, Ohio,* March 8, 1782, Published by the Gnadenhuetten Monument and Cemetery Association, 1882.

[2] Bliss, Eugene F., trans. and ed. *Diary of David Zeisberger, a Moravian Missionary.* (Cincinnati, Ohio: Robert Clarke & Co. for the Historical and Philosophical Society of Ohio, 1885)

[4] "The Moravian Massacre," William M. Farrar, *Ohio History* [Volume 3/ Annual 1891] 276-300

Appendix 1 – Fright Bites

[1]"Wittenberg's ghostly population," Laura Stehle, *The Wittenberg Torch*, 30 Nov. 1999

[2]"In good spirits—and bad", Mark Vossburgh, *Cleveland Plain Dealer*, 31 Oct. 1996

[3] *Still Here So Far: 200 Outrageous Years in Pipe Creek and Dilles Bottom*, Rebecca Steadman Morgan, (Pipe Creek Historical Society, 1993) 47

[4 5] "Tales of the unknown, Stories of ghosts and witches fill the county's hills and hollows," Amanda Stein, *Ironton Tribune*, July 13 1990 IB

[6 7]"Waynesville a popular haunt with ghosts," Randy McNutt, *The Cincinnati Enquirer*, 31 Oct. 1997

[8 9]"In Search of Spooky Sites," Michelle Laliberte, *Medina Gazette,* 30 Oct. 1999

[10]"Legends tell researchers that spirits remain behind," *Defiance Crescent News,* 31 Oct. 1991 15

[11] "New twist for Gothic mansion," Damian Guevara, *The Plain Dealer*, 8 July 2003

[12] "Area Rife with Haunted Houses, Tales of Fright," Martha Hardcastle, *Dayton Daily News*, 26 Oct 2000

[13] "Stories of ghosts threaded through county's history," Jon Baker *New Philadelphia Times-Reporter* 29 Oct. 1990

[14]http://www.tuscazoar.org/ZoarValleyTrail.htm and http://www.ulrc.com.au/html/grimoire.asp?RefNum=SSRT0061&Page=1&View=Legend&

[15]"Ghosts Where We Live," Randy McNutt, *The Cincinnati Enquirer*, 28 Oct. 2001

[16] *Ohio History, The Scholarly Journal of the Ohio Historical Society,* (Volume 6) 281

[17] "Haunting tales of Portage County," Tim Hahn and Robert A. Blunk, [Kent-Ravenna] *Record-Courier*, 31 Oct. 1993

[18] "Haunts, Howls and Horrors," [Kent-Ravenna] *Record Courier*, 27 Oct. 1996

[19] L.L. Miller, editor, *Randolph, Atwater and Rootstown Revisited*, (Brady Lake: Heritage Publications, 2000)

[20] *Ohio Tombstones Magazine*, (Vol. 1 No. 1 Feb. 22, 1935)

[21] *Sense of Community: In Celebration of the Bicentennial of Centerville/Washington Township 1796-1996*, (Centerville: The Centerville Historical Society, 1996) 8-9

[22] *History of Logan County and Ohio* (1880) 451

[23]F.T. Gaumer, *My Two Cents Worth,* (Marysville: *Journal-Tribune*, 1988) 81-82

[24] Richard Helwig, *Ohio Ghost Towns No. 11, Henry County*, (Galena, OH: The Center for Ghost Town Research in Ohio, 1988) 31

[25] Violet Morgan, *Folklore of Highland County*, (Greenfield: Printing and Publishing Company 1946)

[26] "The Bellville Gold Region," A.J. Baughman, *Ohio History*, (Vol. 13) 83-87

[27] "Ghosts, Haunts and Urban Legends Northeast Ohio's Spookiest Spots," John Petkovic, *The Plain Dealer*, 31 Oct. 2000

[28] "Ghost walks halls of OC, Red-headed spirit taunts, haunts Warner Center visitors," Glen Miller, *Elyria Chronicle-Telegram*, 30 Oct.1990

[29] *Marion Star*, 25 Mar.1921 6

[30] *Marion Star*, 31 Mar. 1909 7

[31] "Watervillore……" *Anthony Wayne Standard*, 18 Dec.1969

INDEX

GENERAL INDEX

INDEX OF STORIES
BY LOCATION

NOTE! *PLEASE DO NOT TEAR OUT THIS PAGE. XEROX THIS FORM OR COPY YOUR ORDER ONTO A SHEET OF PAPER.*

HOW TO ORDER
YOUR OWN AUTOGRAPHED COPIES OF
THE *HAUNTED OHIO* SERIES
Visit our web site at www.invink.com

Call **1-800-31-GHOST (1-800-314-4678)** with your VISA or MasterCard order or send this order form to: **Kestrel Publications, 1811 Stonewood Dr., Dayton, OH 45432 • Fax (937) 320-1832**

_____ copies of ***GHOST HUNTER'S GUIDE*** @ $14.95 ea. $_____

_____ copies of ***HAUNTED OHIO*** @ $12.95 each $_____

_____ copies of ***HAUNTED OHIO II*** @ $10.95 each $_____

_____ copies of ***HAUNTED OHIO III*** @ $10.95 each $_____

_____ copies of ***HAUNTED OHIO IV*** @ $12.95 each $_____

_____ copies of ***HAUNTED OHIO V*** @ $12.95 each $_____

_____ *Haunted Ohio* T-shirt @ $14.00 each $_____
Size ___S ___M ___L ___XL ___XXL ___XXXL

_____ *Haunted Ohio V* full color BOO-centennial T-shirt
printed with the Great Seal of the State of Haunted
Ohio @ $15.00 each $_____
Size ___S ___M ___L ___XL ___XXL ___XXXL

+ $2.50 Book Rate shipping, handling and tax for the
first item, $1.00 postage for each additional item. Call
(937) 426-5110 for speedier mail options. $_____
TOTAL $_____

NOTE: We usually ship the same or next day. Please allow three weeks before you panic. If a book *has* to be somewhere by a certain date, let us know so we can try to get it there on time.

MAIL TO (Please print clearly and include your phone number)

_____

_____

_____

FREE AUTOGRAPH!

If you would like your copies autographed, please print the name or names to be inscribed. _____

_____

PAYMENT MADE BY:

☐ Check ☐ MasterCard ☐ VISA
($15 min. order on credit cards)

Card No. _____ Expiration Date:

Signature _____ Mo_____ Yr_____

IF YOU LIKE GHOST STORIES, YOU'LL LOVE INVISIBLE INK:

¬®

OHIO, SO MUCH TO DISINTER...

Just in time for Ohio's BOO-centennial, a collection of all-new, all-chilling tales from the Buckeye State.

Ohio's 200 years of ghosts include:

- The ghostly mummified cat at Fairport Harbor Lighthouse
- The unquiet dead of Massillon's Black Plague Cemetery
- A real-life Hatchet Man, Ohio's first serial killer?
- The ghostly songs of 96 murdered Indians at Gnadenhutten
- The strange aftermath of the Ashtabula Horror
- President Harding and the Finch of Doom

And dozens of ghostly tales from historic sites from Adena to Zoar.

Shelve under
Ohio /Occult/Folklore/Guidebooks

Kestrel Publications

$12.95

ISBN 0-9628472-8-3

51295>

9 780962 847288